SOUTH CAROLINA

GENEALOGICAL RESEARCH

by

George K. Schweitzer, Ph.D., Sc.D.
    7914 Gleason, C-1136
    Knoxville, TN 37919

Typed by
Anne M. Smalley

Copyright: 1985 by Geo. K. Schweitzer
All rights reserved. Except for use in a review,
the reproduction, copying, recording, or
duplication of this work in any form by any means
is forbidden without the written permission
of the author.

ISBN 0-913857-08-4

TABLE OF CONTENTS

Chapter 1. SOUTH CAROLINA BACKGROUND....................5
1. South Carolina geography.............................5
2. The proprietary period, 1670-1729...................9
3. The royal colony period, 1729-69...................12
4. The revolution, 1769-82............................14
5. Early statehood, 1782-1828.........................17
6. The middle period, 1828-61.........................20
7. The Civil War, 1861-5..............................23
8. Reconstruction and after...........................26
9. The 20th Century...................................28
10. The SC counties...................................30
11. County and district origins.......................32
12. Recommended readings..............................43

Chapter 2. TYPES OF RECORDS.............................45
1. Introduction.......................................45
2. Bible records.....................................47
3. Biographies.......................................48
4. Birth records.....................................49
5. Cemetery records..................................50
6. Census records....................................51
7. Church records....................................58
8. City directories..................................64
9. City and county histories.........................64
10. Colonial record compilations.....................65
11. Court records....................................69
12. Death records....................................76
13. Divorce records..................................77
14. Emigration and immigration.......................77
15. Ethnic records...................................80
16. Gazetteers, atlases, and maps....................81
17. Genealogical indexes for SC......................84
18. Genealogical periodicals.........................86
19. Genealogical societies...........................88
20. Historical societies.............................89
21. Land records.....................................90
22. Manuscripts......................................95
23. Marriage records.................................97
24. Military records: colonial.......................98
25. Military records: Revolutionary War.............100
26. Military records: 1812-1860.....................104
27. Military records: Civil War.....................108
28. Mortuary records................................112
29. Naturalization records..........................112

30. Newspaper records..............................114
31. Published genealogies for the US...............119
32. Regional records...............................120
33. Tax, voter, & jury lists.......................121
34. Wills and probate records.....................123
35. WPA & CWA transcripts.........................126

Chapter 3. RECORD LOCATIONS.........................129
   1. Court houses.................................129
   2. The major facilities.........................130
   3. The South Carolina Department of Archives....131
   4. The South Caroliniana Library................137
   5. The South Carolina Historical Society........143
   6. Genealogical Society of UT and its Branches..144
   7. National Archives and its Branches...........148
   8. Regional Libraries...........................148
   9. Local libraries..............................150
  10. Large genealogical libraries.................151

Chapter 4. RESEARCH PROCEDURE & COUNTY LISTINGS.....153
   1. Finding the county/district..................153
   2. Recommended approaches.......................155
   3. State-wide records...........................158
   4. The format of the listings...................159
   5. Abbeville County.............................162
   6. Aiken County.................................162
   7. Allendale County.............................163
   8. Anderson County..............................163
   9. Bamberg County...............................164
  10. Barnwell County..............................165
  11. Bartholomew County...........................165
  12. Beaufort County..............................165
  13. Berkeley County..............................166
  14. Calhoun County...............................166
  15. Camden County................................167
  16. Charleston County............................167
  17. Cheraws District.............................168
  18. Cherokee County..............................168
  19. Chester County...............................168
  20. Chesterfield County..........................169
  21. Claremont County.............................169
  22. Clarendon County.............................170
  23. Colleton County..............................170
  24. Darlington County............................171
  25. Dillon County................................171
  26. Dorchester County............................172

Handwritten annotations (margins):
- also forgive ourselves
- Song = prayer
- Be happy, positive attitude
- Gospel is joy
- hold fast
- Pres. Benson's talk on Pride
- Keep on ...
- See footnote
- thine to guide us in all we are asked to do
- don't be obsessed w/ things of the world
- God's word to all
- Emma told to collect 3 months after Church organized

---

12 For my soul *a*delighteth in the *b*song of the *c*heart; yea, the *d*song of the righteous is a prayer unto me, and it shall be answered with a blessing upon their heads.

13 Wherefore, *a*lift up thy heart and *b*rejoice, and *c*cleave unto the covenants which thou hast made.

14 Continue in the spirit of meekness, and beware of *a*pride. Let thy soul delight in thy *b*husband, and the *c*glory which shall come upon him.

15 Keep my commandments continually, and a *a*crown of *b*righteousness thou shalt receive. And except thou do this, where I am you *c*cannot come.

16 And verily, verily, I say unto you, that this is my *a*voice unto all. Amen.

16a TC Retribution.
18a Matt. 10:9 (9–10); Luke 10:4; D&C 84:78 (78–80, 86).
19a Jacob 5:61 (61–74); D&C 39:17; 71:4; 95:4. TC Millennium, Preparing a People for.
  b TC Priesthood, Ordination.
  TC Sons and Daughters of God.
25 1 John 1:12.

  b TC Kingdom of God, on Earth.
2a Deut. 30:16.
  b TC Virtue; Zion.
  c D&C 52:42 (2, 5, 42); 58:51 (17, 28, 51); 63:48 (29, 31, 48); 64:30; 85:7 (1–3, 7, 9); 99:7; 101:18 (1, 6, 18); 103:14 (11, 14).
3a Matt. 9:2.
  b 1E one chosen or set apart. 2 Jn. 1:1 (1, 13).
  c TC Woman.
  d TC Authority; Called of God.
4a TC Murmuring.
  b TC Knowledge.
  c Luke 24:16 (10–24); Alma 40:3; Ether 3:25. TC God, Wisdom of.
5a TC Comfort; Compassion; Family, Love within.
  b TC Marriage, Wives.
  c TC Affliction.
  d 2 Cor. 10:1.
7a OR set apart.

7b 1 Cor. 12:8. TC God, Spirit of.
8a TC Hands, Laying on of.
9a TC Marriage, Husbands.
  b TC Called of God; Stewardship.
  c TC Prophets, Mission of; Revelation.
10a TC Covetousness.
  b 2 Cor. 6:17; D&C 30:2. TC Treasure; World.
  c Ether 12:4.
  d TC Reward.
11a TC Sacred.
  b Eph. 5:19 (19–20).

of Righteousness.
  b TC Communication.
  c TC Heart.
  d 1 Chr. 16:9; Ps. 33:3; 96:1; D&C 25:11; 136:28. TC Prayer; Singing.
13a Lam. 3:41.
  b TC Joy.
14a TC Meekness; Pride.
  b TC Family, Love within; Marriage, Continuing Courtship in.
  c TC Glory.
15a TC Exaltation.

  b TC Righteousness.
  c John 7:34.
16a Jer. 42:6; D&C 1:38.
26 1a TC Time.
  b TC Scriptures, Study of; Study.
  c D&C 24:3; 37:2.
  d TC Industry.
  e TC Guidance, Divine.
2a 1 Sam. 8:7; Mosiah 29:26; Alma 29:4. TC Common Consent; Sustaining Church Leaders.
  b 1 Chr. 13:4. TC Church; Church

[Margin notes at top: "to encourage and strengthen in a time of persecution"]

SECTION 25

Revelation given through Joseph Smith the Prophet, at Harmony, Pennsylvania, July 1830. See HC 1: 103–104; see also heading to Section 24. This revelation manifests the will of the Lord to Emma Smith, the Prophet's wife.

1–6, Emma Smith, an elect lady, is called to aid and comfort her husband; 7–11, She is also called to write, to expound scriptures, and to select hymns; 12–14, The song of the righteous is a prayer unto the Lord; 15–16, Principles of obedience in this revelation are applicable to all.

HEARKEN unto the voice of the Lord your God, while I speak unto you, Emma Smith, my daughter; for verily I say unto you, all those who ᵃreceive my gospel are sons and daughters in my ᵇkingdom.

2 A revelation I give unto you concerning my will; and if thou art ᵃfaithful and ᵇwalk in the paths of ᶜvirtue before me, I will preserve thy life, and thou shalt receive an ᵈinheritance in Zion.

3 Behold, thy ᵃsins are forgiven thee, and thou art an ᵇelect lady, whom I have ᵈcalled.

4 ᵃMurmur not because of the ᵇthings which thou hast not seen, for they are ᶜwithheld from thee and from the world, which is wisdom in me in a time to come.

5 And the office of thy calling shall be for a ᵃcomfort unto my servant, Joseph Smith, Jun., thy ᵇhusband, in his ᶜafflictions, with ᶜconsoling words, in the spirit of ᵈmeekness.

6 And thou shalt go with him at the time of his going, and be unto him for a scribe, while there is no one to be a scribe for him, that I may send my servant, Oliver Cowdery, whithersoever I will.

7 And thou shalt be ᵃordained under his hand to expound scriptures, and to exhort the church,

[Margin notes:]
Chapter
Conditional — if we want the blessing we must pay the price
to ourselves, gospel, church, Father in Heaven
Don't complain when you don't know
Soft answer
Woman sets tone in home
Set apart
Teacher of righteousness

27. Edgefield County.................................172
28. Fairfield County.................................173
29. Florence County..................................173
30. Georgetown County................................174
31. Granville County.................................174
32. Greenville County................................174
33. Greenwood County.................................175
34. Hampton County...................................175
35. Hilton County....................................176
36. Horry County.....................................176
37. Jasper County....................................176
38. Kershaw County...................................177
39. Kingston County..................................177
40. Lancaster County.................................177
41. Laurens County...................................178
42. Lee County.......................................179
43. Lewisburg County.................................179
44. Lexington County.................................179
45. Liberty County...................................180
46. Lincoln County...................................180
47. Marion County....................................180
48. Marlboro County..................................181
49. McCormick County.................................181
50. Newberry County..................................182
51. Ninety-Six District..............................182
52. Oconee County....................................182
53. Old Berkeley County..............................183
54. Old Marion County................................183
55. Orange County....................................183
56. Orangeburg County................................183
57. Pendleton County.................................184
58. Pickens County...................................184
59. Richland County..................................184
60. Salem County.....................................185
61. Saluda County....................................185
62. Spartanburg County...............................186
63. Sumter County....................................186
64. Union County.....................................187
65. Washington County................................188
66. Williamsburg County..............................188
67. Winton County....................................188
68. Winyah County....................................188
69. York County......................................188

LIST OF ABBREVIATIONS

```
A     = Agricultural census
BLGSU = Branch Library(ies) of the Genealogical Society
        of UT (Utah)
C     = Civil War Union veterans census
CH    = Court house(s)
GSU   = Genealogical Society of UT (Utah)
I     = Industrial census records
LGL   = Large genealogical library(ies)
LL    = Local library(ies)
M     = Mortality census records
NA    = National Archives
P     = Pensioner census, Revolutionary War
R     = Regular census records
RBNA  = Regional Branches of the National Archives
RL    = Regional library(ies)
S     = Slaveholder census records
SC    = South Carolina
SCDA  = SC Department of Archives
SCHS  = SC Historical Society
SCL   = South Caroliniana Library
X     = State census records
*     = When on libraries, indicates good genealogical
        collection
*     = When on records, indicates index
```

Chapter 1

SOUTH CAROLINA BACKGROUND

1. South Carolina geography

The state of South Carolina (hereafter abbreviated SC), one of the thirteen original colonies, is located in the southern region of the eastern seaboard of the US. In shape, it roughly resembles a triangle with its longest side on top and with two downward sloping sides on the left and right (see Figure 1). The state is about 250 miles wide at the top and its greatest height of about 200 miles is shown in the center. The coastline runs an overall distance of almost 190 miles, but if it is traced through all the inlets and bays, its irregular measurement is over 2800 miles. The state is bordered on the east by the Atlantic Ocean, on the north by NC, and on the west and south by GA. The capital of the state is located at Columbia (Co) in the central region, and the state is divided into 46 counties. The principal cities of SC (listed in order of their size and with their approximate populations in thousands) are Columbia (101K), Charleston (70K), Greenville (59K), Spartanburg (44K), Rock Hill (36K), and Florence (31K). Florence (F) is in the northeastern region; Greenville (G), Spartanburg (Sp), and Rock Hill (R) are in the northwestern area. There are also three sizable cities just across the SC border: Charlotte, NC (315K) (Ch) just above the north-central region, Augusta, GA (48K) (A) just below the south-central area, and Savannah, GA (142K) (S) just below the southern tip of the state. In the areas surrounding most of the above cities there are high population densities. The state of SC has an exceptionally large rural population even though most of its people are not farmers.

An understanding of the progressive settlement of the state and genealogies of its earliest families is greatly enhanced by an examination of its major geographic regions and features. These are depicted in Figure 1. Beginning in the east, the first region is the Atlantic Coast. In the north the coastline is relatively even, being interrupted by only a few indentations, the chief ones being Murrells Inlet (MI), Winyah Bay (WB),

Key to Figure 1

A   = Augusta
AR = Ashley River
BD = Broad River
BR = Black River
C   = Charleston
CA = Camden River
Ch = Charlotte
CM = Combahee River
CO = Cooper River
Co = Columbia
Cp = Cowpens
CR = Congaree River
ER = Edisto River
F   = Florence
FH = Four Hole Swamp River
G   = Greenville
GA = Georgia
K   = Kings Mountain

LP = Little Pee Dee River
LR = Lynches River
MI = Murrells Inlet
NC = North Carolina
NF = North Fork Edisto River
PR = Port Royal Sound
R   = Rock Hill
S   = Savannah
SA = Santee River
SF = South Fork Edisto River
Sp = Spartanburg
SR = Saluda River
SV = Savannah River
WA = Wateree River
WB = Winyah Bay
WO = Wando River
WR = Waccamaw River

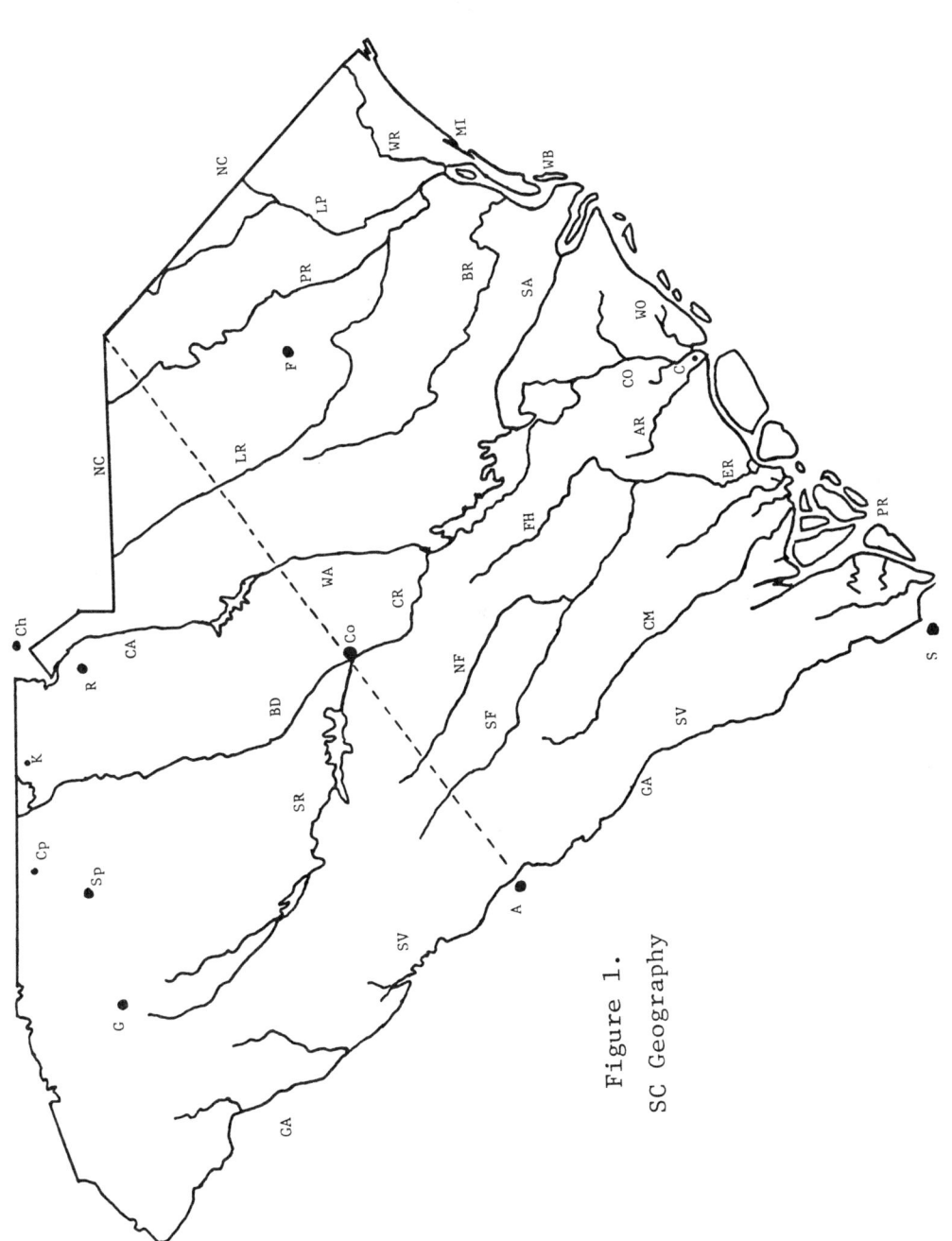

Figure 1.
SC Geography

and the mouths of the Santee River (SA). A few coastal and inlet islands appear at the Santee mouths, and the coastal islands increase considerably as one goes south, as do the number of inlets and bays. Important features which you should note in the southern portion of the coast are the large bay at Charleston (C), the inlet where the Edisto River (ER) enters the Atlantic, Port Royal Sound (PR), and the numerous islands in these areas. Along the coast the land is low, flat, and often quite swampy, there being many salt marshes in the south. The soils are usually sandy and mostly infertile. Somewhat inland from the Atlantic Coast (10-30 miles), the <u>Coastal Plain</u> begins. This region occupies more than half the area of the state. It extends 120 to 150 miles inland to the Fall Line. The Fall Line (dotted line) is a narrow strip of land that drops quickly (from northwest to southeast) so as to produce rapids and falls in the southeasterly flowing rivers. The Fall Line stretches across the state on a line running from Augusta through Columbia then straight northeast to the state line. As you move from the coast toward the west in the Coastal Plain, the land starts out flat, then becomes very gently rolling, then finally gives way to a low hilly section at the Fall Line. Much of the region has abundant fertile soils, especially the lower parts.

Crossing the Fall Line, you enter the region known as the <u>Piedmont</u>. This is a hilly area that rises gradually and becomes steeper as you proceed from the Fall Line toward the northwestern corner of the state. In general, the soils in the Piedmont are poorer than those in the Coastal Plain, although throughout the state, there are fertile soils in the valleys of the larger rivers. Finally, in the northwestern corner of SC, there is the <u>Blue Ridge</u> area. This is an intensely mountainous region occupying only a very small area of approximately 500 square miles. The major feature of the geography of the state is the Fall Line. This line separates the state into the <u>Up Country</u> (northwest of the line) and the <u>Low Country</u> (southeast of the line). The early settlers in the two regions developed widely differing outlooks, attitudes, and values. The interactions of these two groups played a significant role in the history of the state, and quite likely influenced the lives of your SC ancestors.

Figure 1 also depicts the major river systems of SC. As you may have realized from the previous discussion, the state of SC may be viewed as tilted from high in the northwest to low in the southeast. This means that all the rivers flow in this direction. Beginning in the east, notice the Pee Dee River system which empties into Winyah Bay. The Lynches River (LR) joins the Pee Dee River (PR) just south of Florence (F), then the Little Pee Dee River (LP) comes in, then the Waccamaw River (WR), and finally the Black River (BR). Next is the Santee River system, which is made up of the union of the Broad River (BD) and the Saluda River (SR) at Columbia to form the Congaree River (CR), which with the Wateree River (WA) then makes up the Santee River (SA). The northern reaches of the Wateree River are known as the Camden River (CA). A careful look now at the three rivers which flow into Charleston Harbor is in order; notice the Wando River (WO) coming in from the northeast, then Cooper River (CO) from the north, and the Ashley River (AR) from the northwest. The Edisto River system empties into the Atlantic Ocean on down the coast from Charleston. Three rivers come together in the interior to compose this system: the Four Hole Swamp River (FH), the North Fork Edisto River (NF), and the South Fork Edisto River (SF). Now turn your attention to Port Royal Sound (PR) and the Combahee River (CM) which enters it. Then finally glance at the Savannah River (SV) which constitutes the SC-GA border and flows into the Atlantic Ocean just north of Savannah. The reason we have paid such careful attention to the rivers is that they were the major transportation routes in SC until into the 1800s. As such, they figured prominently in the settlement patterns.

2. The proprietary period, 1670-1729

In 1526, the Spanish placed a 500-person settlement on Winyah Bay in what is now SC, but the colony did not last long. Then, in 1562, French Hugenots established Charlesfort on Parris Island (near present-day Beaufort), but it also failed shortly. In 1566, the Spanish established another settlement by building Fort San Felipe on Parris Island. This northernmost outpost of Spain in the New World endured for 21 years, when the Spanish withdrew to their base at St. Augustine. For the next 83 years (1587-1670), no further settlements were attempted. During this time events in Europe made English settlement possible.

Charles I of England granted in 1629 the territory known as Carolana (containing present-day NC, SC and GA and all land west) to Robert Heath, but he failed to colonize the area. Still desiring to plant English settlements in the region, Charles II in 1663 re-granted the territory to eight noblemen, who became the proprietors of the province of Carolina. The proprietors began colonization in 1670 by settling about 150 people at Albemarle Point, a place on the west bank of the Ashley River across from modern-day Charleston. They named the settlement Charles Town, fortified it, and began farming plots of land around it. More settlers began coming so that by 1672 there were about 30 small houses in the town, then the colonists started moving to farm land up the Ashley and Cooper Rivers. Plans began to be made to move to the present site of Charleston, and as the decade progressed, the move was gradually made such that by 1680 Charles Town had been relocated. It contained 100 wooden houses, a church, a town house, a militia ground, and wharves, and was surrounded by plantations. The population of the colony was now almost 1000, and it was about to undergo rapid increases.

In 1680 some French Hugenots came, then English Dissenters began to arrive and form towns south of Charles Town, then a Scottish colony settled at Stuarts town (near present day Beaufort) in 1864, followed by more French Protestants in 1685 who settled on the south side of the Santee River. Three counties were set up in 1682; Berkeley (with towns of Charles Town and Goose Creek, region of Anglicans), Colleton (to the south, area of Dissenters), and Craven (to the north, home of Hugenots), but the centralized government of governor and council in Charles Town granted them no local government. In 1686 a Spanish raid followed by a hurricane destroyed the Scottish colony at Stuarts Town. In 1691, the council was split into an upper appointed house and a lower elected house, the latter having the power to propose laws. Even though some black slaves had been brought in before, the decade of the 1690s saw their numbers increase dramatically. By 1703, the colony had about 8300 persons, of which there were about 4200 whites, about 33 black slaves, and about 800 Indian slaves. The colony was approximately 45% Calvinist (Presbyterian, Hugenot), 42% Anglican (Episcopalian), 10% Baptist, and 3% Quaker. A legislative act of 1706 established the Anglican Church as official and divided the colony into 10 parishes (others were later added).

Reflecting the British-Spanish Queen Anne's War (1702-14), the Carolinians launched raids into FL, including an attack on St. Augustine. In 1706, the Spanish and French attacked Charles Town, but were repulsed and dealt heavy losses. In spite of the wartime threat, a sizable settlement was founded at Beaufort in 1710. Responding to the massacre by Tuscarora Indians of settlers in 1711 around what is now Newbern, NC, campaigns against the Indians in 1712-3 drove them to flee to NY. During the following period 1714-9, the colony was beset with further defense problems. Resentment of corrupt traders and settler encroachments on their land caused the Yemassee Indians in the south of the colony to inaugurate a war in 1715, which ended in 1718 with their removal to FL. Little help was given the colonists by the proprietors, as was the case in Carolina's battles with pirates who marauded off the coast. The defeat of several pirate bands in 1717-8 effectively ended their terrorization of shipping. In 1719, the lower house of the legislature, listing many grievances against the neglect and oppression by the proprietors, declared themselves free of the proprietors, elected their own governor, and thus supported in action appeals to England for a royal government which they had been making since 1709. In 1721, a provisional royal governor arrived, and in 1729 the change over to a royal colony was essentially completed when seven of the eight proprietors sold their interests to the King.

During this proprietary period (1670-1729), the colony had developed into a strong functioning society of traders, slaves, merchants, and planters. The population had moved from about 150 (1670) to about 6000 (1700) to about 10000 (1710) to about 18000 (1720) to about 30000 (1730). Initially, the economic prosperity of the colony was due to Indian trading (deerskins, furs), timber, and naval stores (tar, pitch, rosin, turpentine). But, very quickly rice cultivation on large plantations along the coastal plain and in the tidal swamps of the rivers came to the fore. At first, the major work force was made up of white indentured servants, who paid out their transportation with several years of labor, and afterwards received land. This labor was supplemented by Indian and imported black slaves. Very rapidly the black slaves became the predominant laborers as increasingly large numbers were brought in. By 1719 they outnumbered the whites. Charleston was the center of government, culture, trade, and shipping for the whole southeastern area with its harbor, warehouses, merchants, officials, and public buildings. As the period ended, an aristocracy of wealthy merchants and planters had developed with Charleston as their base and with the surrounding land worked by slaves as their source of riches.

3. The royal colony period, 1729-69

With the switch-over from a proprietorship to a royal colony in 1729, a new era of Carolina history set in. The major events of this period center around the expansion of the colony into the Up Country. These events include immigrations by many groups, almost constant Indian troubles, and the development of strong cultural differences between the low country society and the peoples on the up country frontiers. In 1730, two important land-related actions were taken. The first was the separation of Carolina into NC and SC. The second was the setting up of some townships (large plots of land) on the frontiers (still mostly in the low country) to be settled by immigrants so as to provide a defense line against the Indians and to offset the black majority in SC. The settlement of these townships and the areas around and between them proceeded rapidly with the Swiss coming to Purrysburg on the lower Savannah River in 1732, the Irish to Williamsburg on the Black River in 1732, the Germans to Saxe-Gotha on the Congaree River in 1734, the German-Swiss to Orangeburg on the north Edisto River in 1735, and the Welsh to an area of the Pee Dee River near the present town of Society Hill in 1736. In 1732, the territory which is now the state of GA was split off from SC to form a separate colony. Thus, by about 1740, the middle country had been fairly well settled, and the frontier had been pushed back to the Fall Line.

In 1739, there was a small slave revolt (Stono revolt) which so alarmed the assembly that it adopted in 1740 a very strict slave code. In the early 1740s indigo (a very useful dyestuff) was introduced to SC, and its cultivation expanded very rapidly such that very soon it joined rice and deerskins as an important high-volume SC export. The 1750s represented a time when settlement began in the Up Country (beyond the Fall Line) and increased rapidly. Large groups came down the Great Wagon Road from PA, NC, and VA including Scotch-Irish, Scottish, German, Quaker, and Hugenot peoples. These hard-working, self-sufficient small farmers who were members of dissenter churches (non-Anglican) met the usual dangers of frontiersmen: hostile Cherokees, Indians agitated by the French and Spanish, renegade-Indian groups, marauding white bandits, and disease. In 1755, SC made a treaty with the Cherokees. In exchange for promises of better trade prices, control of corrupt traders, and protection from the French and their Indian allies, the Cherokees ceded all their lands to the King and agreed to become his subjects. Violations of the agreement by groups on both sides caused an erosion of relationships and clashes between settlers and the Cherokees gradually escalated. Then in 1760, the Cherokees set in motion a full-scale war as they attacked settlers and spread terror through the Up Country. Several military expeditions were sent to the Piedmont, the Indian villages were laid waste, their crops were set afire, and their warriors were attacked. In 1761, the Cherokees sued for peace and essentially abandoned most of the country to SC, except for a portion in the northwestern part of the state.

The end of the Cherokee War brought more settlers into the Piedmont with the population rising sharply. In 1765, bands of brigands, marauders, pillagers, and robbers began operating in the area, and as their operations increased, the settlers started organizing vigilante groups to drive them out. Realizing that the Up Country was grossly underrepresented in the Assembly, a coalition of vigilantes, called the Regulators, demanded representation and the benefits of law enforcement, courts, jails, roads, and schools in their territory. A legislative act of 1769 set up courts and jails in seven judicial districts: Beaufort District with the courthouse at Beaufort, Charles Town District with the courthouse at Charles Town, Orangeburg District with the courthouse at Orangeburg, Georgetown District with the courthouse at Georgetown, Cheraw District with the courthouse at Long Bluff, Camden District with the courthouse at Camden, and Ninety-Six District with the court house at Ninety-Six.

At the end of this period, SC was divided into two quite distinct cultures, one in the eastern section of the Low Country, and another in the western section of the Low County and the Up Country. The people in the coastal section had developed a culture based on large plantations manned by slave labor. The focus of the society was the town of Charles Town where the planters, merchants, and shippers lived in a society of wealth, refinement, and cosmopolitanism. Charles Town dominated the entire southern coast as a commercial and cultural center, and was a worthy rival of Philadelphia, New York, and Boston. Those in power had structured the laws and the government to perpetuate their situation and to prevent any other groups from changing things. The settlers in the interior were individualistic small farmers, rough and sturdy in demeanor, belonged to dissenting denominations, were stongly committed to the work ethic, and had little tolerance for anyone who tried to tell them how to run their lives or communities. In their society, there were very few slaves. These people resented their lack of representation in the government and the neglect which the officials in Charles Town practiced toward them.

4. The revolution, 1769-82

In 1763, the French and Indian War ended with Britain getting all of Canada and the French being pushed across the Mississippi River. To pay their large war debt the British began enforcing old tax laws and passing new ones. The colonists resented taxation without representation, and resistance involved boycotts and mob action. In April 1770, all taxes were repealed except on tea. This did not placate the colonies who set up committees to cooperate with each other in continuing protest. On 16 December 1773, fed-up Bostonians threw a cargo of tea into the harbor. This led the British to punish Boston by blockading the port. A province-wide general meeting was held in Charleston, including back country representatives, and delegates to the First Continental Congress were elected. The Congress agreed to cooperate in boycotting British trade, except for export of rice, and adopted a Declaration of Rights, which they accused Parliament of violating. In January 1775, SC organized a Provincial Congress, including back country delegates. Three months later, a Secret Committee seized British arms in Charleston. When a report of the Battles of Lexington and Concord came on 09 May 1775, the Provincial Congress met, took over SC government, called out troops, and began to demand allegiance of all people to the revolutionary war cause. Both persuasion and military action were brought to bear on the many neutrals and British Loyalists in the SC Up Country. The Second Continental Congress in Philadelphia about this time was electing Washington to command the Continental Army. In September 1775 the British governor fled the colony. The first SC bloodshed of the war occurred when Up Country Loyalists attacked a fort at Ninety-Six 19-21 November 1775, the event ending in a stand off. During December 1775, Patriots subdued Loyalist forces around Ninety-Six.

In February 1776, the British launched a campaign against NC, sending ships and land forces to join Loyalists there. The plans were foiled, however, when NC troops defeated the Loyalists on 17 February 1776 at the Battle of Moore's Creek. The forces of Britain then headed for Charleston which they attacked on 18 June 1776, but a series of misjudgements and disasters led to failure and withdrawal. Thus, the southern colonies remained Patriot, even though there were many Loyalists in the Up County. The Continental Congress approved the Declaration of Independence on 04 July 1776, and the SC delegates signed on 02 August. The British would not return to SC until 1779, but this does not mean that all was quiet until then. SC contributed more than 6000 men to the Continental Army, many militia remained British, and other militia were Patriot. In July 1776, a Cherokee War broke out on the frontier. Militia from SC, GA, NC, and VA moved against them, and SC received the land in its NW corner in the treaty of May 1777. Skirmishes and marauding attacks of Patriots and Loyalists on each other continued in the back country. Many Loyalists departed, but many stayed and kept a low profile. During 1776-9, the scene of warfare was chiefly in the north with the capture of Ticonderoga (10 May 1775) and the Battle of Bunker-Breed's Hills (17 June 1775). The invasion of Canada by the Continental forces ended in disaster at the Battle of Quebec (1775-6). This was followed by the loss to the British of New York City (15 September 1777) and then Philadelphia (04 October 1777). The next major event was the astonishing victory of the colonists at Saratoga (17 October 1777), which led to the frustration of the British plan to split NY state, and was followed by France's entry in the war against Britain. The terrible winter spent by the Continental Army at Valley Forge (1777-8) followed. In 1778-9 George Rogers Clark with VA and KY riflemen took the Northwest Territory from British forces.

The British abandoned the northern campaign and turned their efforts to taking the south in full hopes that many Loyalists would join them when they got there. The first move was the capture by the British of Savannah in December 1778, and very soon the up-river crossings also were taken. In May, the British laid seige to Charleston by both land and sea, and on 12 May 1780, the city capitulated. They then began to penetrate the back country and rapidly established a series of outposts. American forces tried to invade SC in August, but were defeated on 16 August 1780 at Camden in a catastrophic rout. The previously suppressed Loyalists now rose up, and some of them began to plunder farms in guerrilla activity, which broke out into local civil war in many areas. Cornwallis, the British general, then set out toward Charlotte, but his left flank was met by courageous mountain men who defeated them at Kings Mountain on 07 October 1780. This forced Cornwallis to withdraw from Charlotte to Winnsboro. The Patriots by this time had marshalled several sizable guerrilla forces under the commands of Marion, Sumter, and Pickens. These forces harried the British outposts, as did the regular Continental Army, and threatened to get between Cornwallis and his supply base at Charleston. On 17 January 1781, Cornwallis again suffered a defeat of his left wing in a rout at Cowpens. Outposts then began to fall to the Patriot guerrillas, and Cornwallis moved into NC, leaving the British troops in the back country no option but to pull back into Charleston. After fighting American troops to a draw at Guilford Court House (15 March 1781), Cornwallis was so weakened that he moved to

Wilmington on the NC coast. Meanwhile, the Patriots in SC and GA were busy laying seige to and driving the British out of the back country. A clash at Camden (10 May 1781), a seige at Ninety Six (22 May-19 June 1781), and a battle at Eutaw Springs (08 September 1781) were major conflicts in this action. The Americans won none of them, but so weakened the British that they had to withdraw. The British forces in SC now were almost all in Charleston, where they were surrounded and watched by Patriots.

From Wilmington, Cornwallis moved north into VA to join forces with other British troops from their base at Portsmouth. On 05 September 1781, Washington's Continentals and Rochambeau's French Army moved south toward VA, just after French Admiral DeGrasse had put his fleet at the entrance to Chesapeake Bay. The British fleet tried to dislodge DeGrasse, but they were repelled. When Washington and Rochambeau arrived north of Yorktown, Cornwallis found himself trapped. After about two weeks of seige, on 17 October 1781 Cornwallis surrendered, effectively ending the hostilities. However, with the British still in Charleston, the newly-elected SC legislature had to meet in Jacksonborough in January 1782, where they started a vengeful crackdown on Tories with a confiscation of their property. It was not until 14 December 1782 that the British finally left Charleston, over 4000 Loyalists going with them. That afternoon the governor entered the city and proclaimed the beginning of an independent SC.

5. Early statehood, 1782-1828

In the few years just after the war (1782-5), considerable vengeance was practiced upon remaining and returning Tories, but this passed fairly soon. The economy was exceptionally poor because of several bad growing seasons and the loss of English crop supports and markets. In the improving economic climate of 1785, the legislature under Up Country urgings established 34 counties out of the seven districts which had been set up in 1769. They also chartered three institutions of higher education at Charleston, near Ninety-Six, and at Winnsboro. Then in 1786, it was voted to move the capital from Charleston to Columbia (not done until 1790-1). In this same year, a company was organized to build a canal between the Santee and Cooper Rivers. The SC members of the Federal Congress, representing the Low Country position, favored a strong central government for the Thirteen States, but the Up Country was fearful of too much centralized power. When SC sent delegates to the 1787 Philadelphia Constitutional Convention, they too were selected by the Low Country favoring Legislature. In 1788, the SC Legislature called for a state convention to consider ratification or rejection of the newly-framed Federal Constitution. Since the delegates to this convention were chosen under the apportionment system which gave the Low Country control, it ratified the document 149 to 73, most of the Up Country voting in opposition. Thus SC became the 8th state to enter the Union.

In 1790, another state convention was called under Up Country pressure to write a new state constitution. The meeting, again controlled by the Low Country, gave the Up Country increased representation, but the balance of power remained with the Low Country. Legislators still had to be owners of much land, most local oficials were still chosen by the legislature, but freedom of religion was introduced, and primogeniture (inheritance by the first-born son) was abolished. Further concessions to the Up Country were made in 1808 and 1810, but the Low Country remained predominant. In the early 1790s two related events occurred which were to determine the economic, social, and political life of SC for the next 80 years. These were the invention of the cotton gin in 1793 and the introduction of a type of cotton which would grow in the soils of the entire southeastern US. Prior to this time cotton was grown in the Low Country, but it was not a major crop. With the coming of the cotton gin and the new cotton type,. cotton cultivation spread very rapidly throughout SC. To illustrate this rapid change, the south exported about 140,000 pounds of cotton in 1792, then 1,600,000 pounds in 1794 (11 times as much), then 18,000,000 pounds in 1800 (over 120 times as much). This exceptionally fast spread continued through the 1810s, as SC became a one-crop state. The plantation system was extended into the Up Country, the plantations increased the demand for slaves, slave-holding was spread to the entire state, and there was produced a new group of cotton aristocrats who joined the old Low Country elite to unify the state and to control its government. The result was that slaves came to outnumber whites by 1820, the small and poorer farmers were squeezed out, trade flourished in the port of Charleston, and an economic boom was experienced throughout SC. Several state projects in transportation were carried out in order to provide for movement of cotton to Charleston: river improvements, canal building, and road construction. The state became the major advocate of slavery and of states' rights in order to protect its economy, and thus supported an issue which ultimately divided the nation.

In the first decade of the 1800s, a very effective series of religious revivals swept the state, making the people of SC largely a churched population. The chief denominations which were active were Methodist, Baptist, Presybterian, and Episcopal, and even though they originally opposed slavery, economic pressure brought them to switch sides. Out of a strange mixture of land greed (for Canada and FL), hope for a short war of conquest (England was occupied in Europe), and resentment of British interference with American sea trade and sailors, the US went to war with Britain in the War of 1812 which lasted over two years. Among the most hawkish of the members of Congress was the SC delegation which strongly supported the conflict, accurately reflecting the attitude of the state. The war was an incredible one in which the US made blunder after blunder, three attempted invasions of Canada failing miserably, Washington being burned, Baltimore barely escaping a like fate, the entire coastline of the US suffering a British blockade, and numerous British raids being made on US coastal cities. The treaty of late 1814 which ended the conflict resulted in not a single one of the US aims; nothing had been gained. Charleston was strongly fortified, but British action in SC was confined to some raids along the coast and on sea islands. SC contributed 5000 troops, considerable financial aid, and several generals to the war effort. The greatest American victory of the War of 1812 was the disastrous defeat of the British at New Orleans, a battle which took place in 1815 after the peace treaty had been signed, but before news of it had arrived. Much of the US populace thought of this victory as the winning of the war, and thus saved face and celebrated an increased nationalism. The war did not damage the cotton prosperity which continued.

As SC approached the 1820s, a great deal of migration from SC to AL, MS, and LA was occurring. This was due to movements of large farmers who went to set up cotton plantations on the rich soils of these new areas, of small poor farmers who had been crowded out, and of farmers who had exhausted the land they were cultivating. In the 1820s, more land lost its fertility, the plantations in AL, MS, and LA brought competition, cotton prices dropped, slave prices rose because of labor shortages, and other ports took the trade of Charleston away (Norfolk, Wilmington, Savannah, Mobile, New Orleans). All of these developments caused a severe economic depression, and SC's economy and population growth stagnated. Canal and road building projects failed to restore Charleston as the main cotton port. The economic problems of the 1820s were destined to be ones that SC had to grapple with for the next 40 years. They had their roots in a state which had become almost completely dependent on a single product which was in turn dependent upon a slave labor system.

6. The middle period, 1828-61

As the previous section stated, SC had become economically dependent upon the institution of slavery. The years 1828-61 were filled with three major fears for SC: (1) the fear that the slaves would revolt, (2) the fear that as the US admitted new states, they would be anti-slave states, thus increasing the anti-slave representation in Congress, and (3) the growing fear that the US would eventually move to outlaw slavery everywhere, including SC. The fear of a slave revolt was fed by the discovery of a slave conspiracy in Charleston in 1822 which was suppressed, another one in Georgetown in 1829 which never materialized, and the Turner slave revolt which occurred in VA in 1831. These were sufficient to cause the passage and tighter enforcement of laws controlling slaves. The fear of new anti-slave states and territories being admitted to the US caused the Congressional representatives of SC to strongly oppose all such moves. A north-south compromise was worked out after a bitter debate in 1820 permitting MO to be admitted as a slave state, but prohibiting slavery in US territory north of latitude $36°30'$. This compromise served for awhile, but the issue would rise again, as SC became more and more defensive about slavery, economically, morally, and politically. Apologies for slavery by the planters as an economic necessity, by about 1825, were turning into assertions that slavery was a positive good, sanctioned by the God of the Bible.

The tensions and fears mentioned above came to a head in what has come to be called the nullification crisis. SC had opposed tariff bills enacted by the US Congress after the War of 1812, because these laws meant higher prices for imported manufactured goods they had to buy. They also feared that Europe, where the state's cotton was sold, would retaliate by levying their own tariffs on cotton. In 1828, the US put into effect a very high protective tariff which caused SC leaders to argue that the tariff violated states' rights. Calhoun, SC's leading national figure, asserted that any state had the right to refuse to obey any federal law that infringed on the constitutional rights of the people. When a revised tariff act of 1832 offered SC little relief, a state convention declared the law null and void (nullification), refused to enforce it in SC, and threatened to secede from the US if federal force was used against them. The counter-threats of President Jackson, US and SC beginning preparations for war, and a compromise bill of 1833 kept SC from seceding. From this time onward, SC never dropped the idea of secession as the slavery issue became more acute. Outside abolitionist's attacks on slavery increased, the question of extension of slavery into newly acquired territories in the West kept cropping up, and SC sensed herself losing influence in the federal government.

During the years 1835-60, several important developments in SC other than the slavery issue need to be mentioned. A number of groups began to recognize the economic unsuitability of a one-crop agricultural policy, and reforms began to be encouraged by local farming societies: diversification of crops, rotation of crops, better agricultural practices, use of fertilizers, and the introduction of textile industry. A number of these were implemented to some extent, but a lack of capital was a severe retardant. In this period (1835-60), canal building was replaced by railroad construction. By 1833, Charleston was connected with Hamburg, by 1842 with Columbia, and in the 1850s with Greenville and Spartanburg. A number of private academies and colleges were established and became strong during these years, but public education at the elementary level continued to be neglected. The state, however, established and supported SC College at Columbia, an institution that had a great influence on the state through its graduates. Much of the state was plagued with a high crime rate, a goodly portion of it being alcohol-related. Most punishments were physical because of the lack or inadequacy of jails, and they were largely carried out by local officials. Blacks were seldom brought to court because the planters judged and punished them. In this era, SC remained under the rule of its upper class, namely, those who held sizable property and many slaves.

Shortly after the annexation of TX to the US, General Taylor occupied Point Isbel at the mouth of the Rio Grande River. Seeing this as aggression, Mexican troops invaded TX and bombarded Fort Taylor, whereupon the US declared war on 12 May 1846. Taylor drove the Mexican troops back across the Rio Grande, Santa Fe was taken by US General Kearny, and CA switched to American rule. In February 1847, Taylor and Mexican President Santa Anna clashed at Buena Vista, the battle ending in a Mexican withdrawal. The final campaign of the war began in March 1847, when US General Scott landed at Vera Cruz and began a drive on Mexico City. US forces entered Mexico City on 14 September 1847, and the treaty of 02 February 1848 provided for Mexico's cession of two-fifths of its land to the US. Northern efforts to keep slavery from spreading to this vast territory incensed SC. In 1854, the MO Compromise of 1820 was replaced by the KS-NE Act which permitted new states to decide for themselves whether they would be free or slave. SC sent settlers and money to KS in an effort to make the state slave, but to no avail. By the middle 1850s, the Northern and Southern states were clearly divided by numerous issues: sectional rivalry, industrial against agricultural interests, economic and trade regulation, state's rights, Congressional control, and slavery. SC occupied an extreme position in this regard, it being the Southern state which differed most from the North. Compromises had worked numerous times, but they had become increasingluy unsatisfactory, and conflict loomed large, especially in SC, where secession had been seriously considered since 1832.

7. The Civil War, 1861-5

When Lincoln was elected president in 1860, the South clearly remembered his campaign statement that a government cannot endure permanently half slave and half free. Before the inauguration, the SC legislature called a state convention, which quickly and unanimously seceded from the Union on 20 December 1860. In the war to come over 63,000 SC men were to serve, about 15,000 being lost. No state sent such a large fraction of its men into the war. In addition, SC provided a more than representative number of trained military officers. Very shortly after seceding, SC took two US forts in Charleston harbor and the Federal Arsenal in Charleston, all on 27 December 1860. Then on 09 January 1861, when a US ship tried to reinforce Ft. Sumter (the remaining Union fort in the harbor), SC artillery fire drove it off. By 01 February 1861, the secession of SC had been joined by AL, FL, GA, LA, MS, and TX. After failed negotiations between SC and the US, bombardment of Ft. Sumter by SC began, and on 14 April 1861 the fort surrendered. When US President Lincoln called for troops from all states to suppress the rebellion, the secessions of NC, VA, AR, and TN followed. Thus the 11-state Confederacy was constituted. The two sides, Union and Confederate, mobilized their men and resources and four years of horrible conflict began. We will now summarize the war, and then we will look at SC's part in a bit of detail.

The intention of the Union came to be defeat of the Confederacy by confinement, invasion, and subdual. Five strategies were to be pursued: (1) the blockading or capture of southern ports to cut off supplies, (2) the taking of the Confederate capital at Richmond by attack from the north, (3) the splitting of the Confederacy by driving down and up the MS River, (4) the further splitting of the Confederacy by driving from the northwest corner of TN down the TN and Cumberland Rivers to Nashville to Chattanooga to Atlanta to Savannah, and then, if necessary (5) driving north from Savannah into SC, then NC, then assaulting Richmond from the south.

Strategy 1, the sea blockade, was accomplished early in the war with most Atlantic and Gulf ports blockaded or captured by the end of 1862. Strategy 2, the drive toward Richmond from the north, failed again and again, the Confederacy even making two counter-invasions to threaten Washington, until success began to be had by Grant in 1864, Richmond falling on 02-03 April 1865. __Strategy 3__, the drives to take the MS River, had been completed with the collapse of Port Hudson 09 July 1863. __Strategy 4__, the drive from northwest TN to Savannah took 34 months, but ended in the capture of Savannah on 22 December 1864. __Strategy 5__, the drive north from Savannah, was accomplished by the taking of Columbia and Charleston in February 1865, then pushing into NC where one of the two remaining major Confederate armies surrendered on 26 April 1865. The other had capitulated after the fall of Richmond at Appomattox on 09 April 1865.

It is obvious from the above account that the major Civil War actions in SC took place under Strategies 2 and 5. From the date of its secession (20 December 1860), SC organized and trained troops, built fortifications (especially around its major harbors), and accumulated supplies, thus turning the state into an armed military camp. The over 63,000 combatants from SC fought on the sea, in SC, in the western states, in practically every major battle, but chiefly in VA and NC. Among the states, SC was 12th in the number of military events during the Civil War, there being 239. As part of __Strategy 2__, the blockade of the south, the Union placed blockading ships along the NC-SC-GA coast early in 1861 and began occupying strategic off-coast islands shortly thereafter. Especially tight blockades of Cape Fear (Wilmington, NC), Charleston Harbor, Port Royal-Hilton Head (Beaufort, SC), and Savannah were put in place. On 07 November 1861, Union naval forces placed landing parties on shore in the Port Royal, Hilton Head, Beaufort, and adjacent area, which was taken and held throughout the war. The fall of Ft. Pulaski, which guarded the harbor at Savannah, on 11 April 1862 made the blockade there very effective. On 03 June 1862, the Federals began operations on James Island (near Charleston), but were driven off by the 28th of the month. Nine months later, on 28 March 1863, US troops occupied several islands near Charleston, and on 07 April both naval bombardment of Charleston Harbor defences and landings on nearby islands began in earnest. Landing on Morris Island (very close to Charleston) was made on 10

July 1863 and all Confederates had been forced off by 07 September. The Union forces used these coastal and coastal-island bases for control of shipping and for excursions into the interior. A number of attempts were made to break through the outer defences of Charleston, but all efforts were repulsed. In spite of the Union blockades, both Charleston and Savannah were effective ports for Confederate blockade runners who brought in tremendous amounts of supplies.

In the Union pursuit of <u>Strategy 5</u>, US General Sherman moved his major forces north from Savannah into SC on 01 February 1865. His troops consisted of several large contingents plus a number of smaller detachments, totalling about 60,000 in all. Over against them, there were about 22,000 Confederate troops in SC. Sherman sent his main forces toward Columbia with smaller detachments heading for Augusta and Charleston. Their orders were to destroy railroads, supplies, and buildings which were militarily related. Sherman's troops moved to Lawtonville, Lopers (02 February), Rivers Bridge, Bufords Bridge (04 February), Combahee River Ferry (05 February), Barnwell (06 February), Blackville (07 February), Williston (08 February), Binnakers Bridge (09 February), Orangeburg, Aiken, Branchville (11 February) and the Congaree River (15 February) just opposite Columbia. On 17 February, Columbia was turned over to the Federals, and that night most of the city burned. The fire was probably started, against orders, by vengeful and drunken Union soldiers. On the next day, 18 February, Charleston was evacuated and surrendered to a Northern contingent. The march of Sherman's soldiers toward NC was resumed and from Columbia they proceeded to Winnsboro (21 February), Camden (24 February), Hanging Rock (26 February), Mount Elon (27 February), Rocky Mount (28 February), Chesterfield, Cheraw (02 March), and Monroe's Cross Roads (08 March). On 06 March 1865, the movement of the Federal troops into NC near Rockingham, NC got underway. The Union forces were successfully opposed by the Confederates on only a few occasions, the Southern forces having to withdraw toward NC continually. The state of SC was left in ruins; burnt, pillaged, destroyed, devastated, crippled.

8. Reconstruction and after

Under the lenient policy of the US after the war and the supervision of about 7000 Federal troops, a SC govenment dominated by former Confederates was set up. Under them, the SC soldiers returned to a desolate state in which about 400,000 slaves had become full-fledged citizens. These blacks showed little tendency to work since they were being fed on rations provided by federal relief agencies, and they were thus not available to work in reestablished rice or cotton growing. SC was also rapidly filled with do-gooders, some with integrity who truly offered welfare assistance to both whites and blacks, and some who came to steal and defraud. Most of the population turned to the farming of small plots where they raised crops to supply themselves with badly-needed food. The situation in SC was so bleak that many former soldiers left SC for areas to the west. In September 1865, a new state contitution was drawn up, but shortly after the legislature voted for a Black Code which was designed to regulate blacks and limit their freedoms. SC shortly thereafter refused to ratify the 14th Amendment (guaranteeing civil and voting rights to all citizens).

The failure of SC to evidence good intentions to enfranchise the blacks and the overzealous attitude of the US Congress led to the establishment of a military government in SC in 1867. The state was not to be readmitted to the Union until it adopted an acceptable constitution. On 14 January 1868 a constitutional convention elected by black and white citizens and made up of 63 blacks and 34 whites met in Charleston. They drew up a document which marked a notable advance in democracy in SC. The new constitution provided for universal male suffrage, elections on a population basis, more elective offices, a free public school, and no educational or property requirements for voting. On this basis SC was readmitted to the US on 25 June 1868. From this time until 1876, the Republican party governed SC, the government consisting of SC blacks, SC whites sympathetic to the new democratic trends, and Northern whites and blacks who came to SC. Unfortunately, their potential to bring in a new era of equality in SC was subverted by a fraction of them who used their offices for corruption, fraud, bribery, favoritism, and theft of public monies. This strange mixture of good and bad was met by an equally strange mixture of good and bad on the part of the Democratic Party who represented the old SC elite class. This opposition party was composed of people who deplored the corruption, people who felt they were being unjustly excluded from the policy-making, people who were greedy for their lost power, people who wanted to deprive the blacks of their newly-granted freedoms, and people who desired to reverse the democratic gains of the state. The Ku Klux Klan with its violence emerged in the Up Country, mob actions occurred elsewhere, two taxpayers' conventions opposing high governmental costs, and other events of this sort kept cropping up in the early 1870s. A reform governor named Chamberlain (1874-6) made many benevolent changes and came close to reconciling the opposing factions, but two corrupt judges and a race riot at Hamburg in July 1876 repolarized the state.

In 1876 there occurred the most violent election campaign in SC history, the Republican (Fusionist) Chamberlain running aginst the Democrat (Straightout) Hampton. A militant political group called the Red Shirts bribed and intimidated the blacks and at the same time Hampton promised them a continued equality. Considerable fraud was practiced by both sides, and both sides claimed victory. However, when Federal troops were withdrawn from SC in April 1877, Hampton became governor. Thus the Democrats and therefore the whites had regained control of the state. Despite the racist attitudes of many of his supporters Hampton pursued a policy of justice and humanity toward both blacks and whites, many blacks being appointed to state offices. During this period (1865-76), SC had gradually recovered economically as cotton growing was expanded beyond the prewar level. Times, however, were especially hard for the ex-slaves who had no property and the small farmers who had lost their land through indebtedness. Both groups had found jobs and had advanced the cotton recovery by becoming sharecroppers or tenant farmers, an arrangement that would last long into the next century. In the 1880s cotton mills began to increase in the Up Country, and many tenant farmers went to work in them. The growth of these mills was fostered by the proximity of cotton, the availability of water power, and an abundance of cheap labor.

In 1890, an Up Country farmer Tillman began to campaign for the governorship on a platform addressed to the white lower and middle classes of SC and based on agrarian reform. He railed out against the wealthy, the government, and the blacks, and set a pattern of demagogic politics which was to be practiced many times after him. Following his election, he brought about the development of an agricultural college Clemson, a female college Winthrop, some agricultural advances and reforms, a work-limiting law for mill laborers, and state-owned liquor stores. Tillman also continued to voice that in a state with a black majority a new state constitution should be drawn up containing safeguards against the possibility of blacks participating to any great degree in the political process. This led to a constitutional convention in 1895 which produced a document with provisions for depriving blacks of their votes, for segregating the schools, and for banning intermarriage. In 1898, SC furnished for the Spanish-American War two regiments, an independent battalion of infantry, and a unit of naval reserves.

9. The 20th Century

The 1st decade of the 1900s were years which were very bad ones for SC blacks. The Ku Klux Klan was very active, there were numerous lynchings, and segregation became complete. Considerable growth in railroads was occurring. In the period 1910-20, the number of textile mills with their associated mill villages continued to increase in the western Up Country. They employed former white tenant farmers, but many blacks moved out of the state as agriculture became less rewarding. A number of major reforms were brought to the state by Governor Manning who introduced programs for the care of the mentally ill, state correction institutions, workmen's compensation, child labor regulation, tax equalization, highway construction, and compulsory school attendance. The coming of World War I (1917-8) brought labor shortages in the north, and more blacks went there to take jobs. The economy of SC was temporarily boosted by the war, which also saw the establishment of major military installations at or near Columbia, Beaufort, Charleston, Greenville, and Spartanburg. SC provided about 62,000 participants in this conflict, about 57,000 serving in the army, about 5000 in the navy, and about

300 in the marines. When the war ended, cotton prices dropped, the boll weevil attacked the plants, and worn-out soil had its impact. The result was that the SC economy became worse than it had been before the war.

The decade of the 1920s was characterized by bitter poverty for the rural population of SC, both for blacks and whites. The emigration of blacks continued so that 1922 was the year in which whites became the majority for the first time since about 1820. Cotton farmers continued to suffer from the boll weevil, worn-out eroded land, and low prices. During this time (1920-30), the textile industry continued to expand, road building was pursued, and the educational system was upgraded.

The great depression of the 1930s hit SC very hard because the state had many poverty-stricken residents before it came. The national New Deal program (beginning in 1933) benefited SC immensely bringing employment, agricultural assistance, minimum crop prices, public works projects, welfare relief, and dams for the generation of electric power. World War II (1941-5), however, was the major factor which brought the state out of the depression. SC became the site of several large army, naval, air force, and marine operations, which brought federal funds in. The war generated a new group of SC people who began to break with many of the previously-held viewpoints, and SC underwent a rapidly-accelerating set of changes in the years following 1945. By 1980, the state had established civil rights for blacks, had become much less rural, had seen cotton superseded by tobacco, meat animals, and soybeans, had developed much forest industry, had developed greatly industrially, and had gained a prosperity which had not been seen since before the Civil War. The development of tourism has been remarkable over the recent past as historic sites have been preserved and restored, resorts have increased, state parks have been placed around the major lakes, and the beaches have become major attractions.

One of the major ways to see the development of SC, and a way of particular interest to genealogists, is to follow the increasing population of the state (given in parentheses in thousands [K] followed by the % black): 1670 (0.15K, 3%), 1720 (18K, 64%), 1734 (37K, 59%), 1749

(64K, 61%), 1760 (84K, 62%), 1773 (175K, 63%), 1790
(249K, 43%), 1800 (346K, 43%), 1810 (415K, 48%), 1820
(503K, 53%), 1830 (581K, 56%), 1840 (594K, 56%), 1850
(669K, 59%), 1860 (704K, 59%), 1870 (706K, 59%), 1880
(996K, 61%), 1890 (1151K, 60%), 1900 (1340K, 58%), 1910
(1515K, 55%), 1920 (1648K, 51%), 1930 (1739K, 46%), 1940
(1890K, 43%), 1950 (2117K, 39%), 1960 (2383K, 35%), 1970
(2591K, 31%).

Among the SC historic sites of genealogical interest are Beaufort Historic District, Charleston's Old Town, Charles Towne Landing Tricentennial Park, Cheraw, Cowpens National Battlefield Site (near Chesnee), Fort Moultrie (Charleston harbor), Fort Sumter (Charleston harbor), Georgetown Historic District, Historic Camden, Kings Mountain National Military Park (near York), Old Columbia, Old Dorchester Historical State Park (near Summerville), Rivers Bridge Confederate Memorial (near Allendale), Rose Hill Historical State Park (near Union), and Sesqui-Centennial State Park (memorial to Columbia's 150th anniversary). Museums well worth a visit include: Beaufort County Museum, Charleston Museum, Confederate Museum (Charleston), Lexington County Museum (Edgefield), Fairfield County Museum (Winnsboro), Pickens County Historical Museum (Pickens), and Spartanburg County Regional Museum (Spartanburg).

10. The SC counties

The present-day state of SC is divided into 46 counties. The locations of these counties are depicted in Figure 2. Accompanying the large map in Figure 2 is a small outline map which divides SC into 5 regions: one in the northwest NW, one in the northeast NE, one in the middle west MW, one in the middle east ME, and one in the south S. To locate a county, look its name up in the following alphabetical listing, then take note of the region indicated and the county abbreviation, then glance in that area on the large map of Figure 2. The numbers following the county abbreviations refer to charts showing county origins which appear in the next section. The 46 counties are: Abbeville [MW: Abb,7], Aiken [MW: Aik,4], Allendale [S: All,2,4], Anderson [NW: And,7], Bamberg [MW: Bam,4], Barnwell [MW: Bar,4], Beaufort [S: Bea,2], Berkeley [ME: Ber,1], Calhoun [ME: Cal,4], Charleston [ME: Cha,1], Cherokee [NW: Chero,5,7],

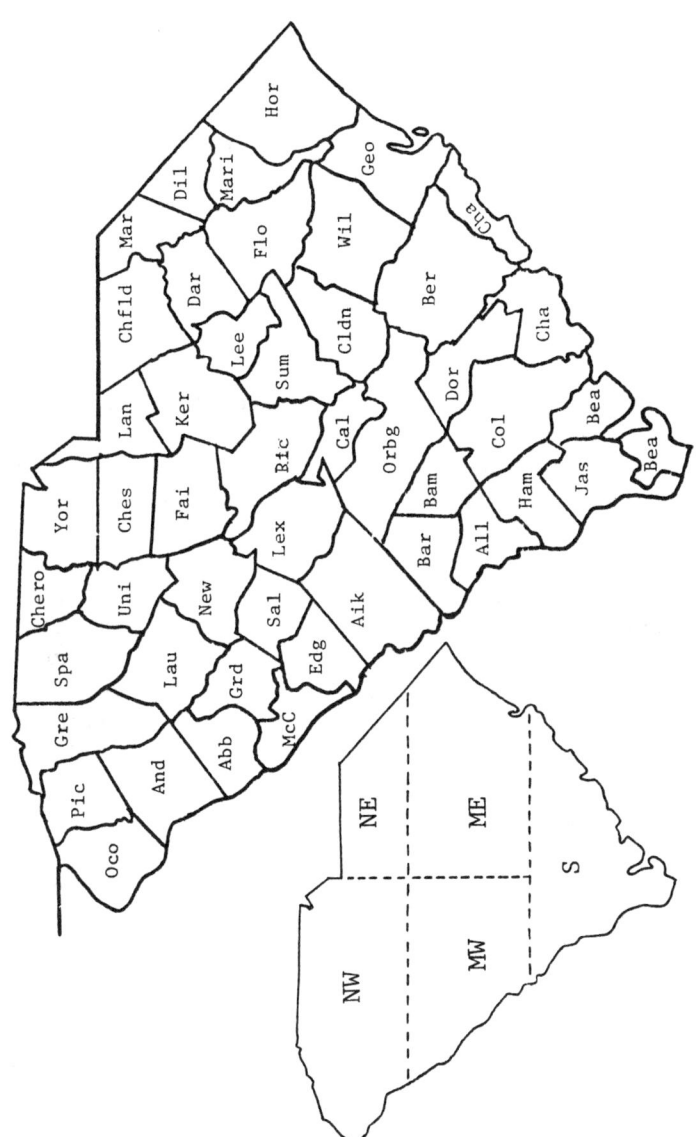

Figure 2. SC Counties

Chester [NW: Ches,5], Chesterfield [NE: Chfld,6], Clarendon [ME: Cldn,5], Colleton [S: Col,1], Darlington [NE: Dar,6], Dillon [NE: Dil,3], Dorchester [ME: Dor,1], Edgefield [MW: Edg,7], Fairfield [NW: Fai,5], Florence [ME: Flo,3,6], Georgetown [ME: Geo,3], Greenville [NW: Gre,7], Greenwood [MW: Grd,7], Hampton [S: Ham,2], Horry [ME: Hor,3], Jasper [S: Jas,2], Kershaw [NE: Ker,5], Lancaster [NE: Lan,5], Laurens [NW: Lau,7], Lee [ME: Lee, 5,6], Lexington [MW: Lex,4], Marion [NE: Mari,3], Marlboro [NE: Mar,6], McCormick [MW: McC,7], Newberry [MW: New,7], Oconee [NW: Oco,7], Orangeburg [ME: Orgb,4], Pickens [NW: Pic,7], Richland [ME: Ric,5], Saluda [MW: Sal,7], Spartanburg [NW: Spa,7], Sumter [ME: Sum,5], Union [NW: Uni,7], Williamsburg [ME: Wil,3], York [NW: Yor,5].

11. County and district origins

Up until 1785, all the governmental records of SC were kept for the entire colony (state) in Charleston at the county courthouse or in the various state offices. Essentially no county, district, or regional records were kept during this time (1670-1785) because of the strong centralized governmental structure. However, during this period (1676-1785), there were set up some non-record-keeping regions which it is important for genealogists to know about. This is because these regions are often mentioned on the records and a knowledge of them assists in locating where your ancestor lived. There are three of these regional sub-divisions that you need to be acquainted with: (1) the 4 early colony counties, (2) the 25 parishes of the Church of England, and (3) the 12 settlement townships. Remember that no governmental records were kept by these early geographical subdivisions, even though some non-governmental church records were kept by the parishes, which were also used as tax districts.

In 1862, SC was roughly divided into three vaguely defined counties: Berkeley, Colleton, and Craven. Berkeley County centered around Charleston and included the land northwest of the town between the Stono and Avendaw Rivers. Colleton County was to the south of Berkeley and was the area between the Stono and Combahee Rivers. Craven County was all the territory north of Berkeley. In 1685, the land between the Combahee and

Savannah Rivers (south of Colleton) was called Carteret County. Its name was changed to Granville County about 1708/10. These four counties kept no records; they only provided for locating the general regions in which land was granted. Figure 3 depicts these subdivisions of SC which were to be kept until 1785.

During the period 1706-78, twenty-five Church of England parishes were established in SC. They kept christening, marriage, and burial records, as well as other church records, and the areas assigned to each parish provided a way of locating land. In 1706, ten parishes were established: (1) St. Philip's, (2) Christ Church, (3) St. Thomas', (4) St. John's, (5) St. James' Goose Creek, (6) St. Andrew's, (7) St. Denis', (8) St. Paul's, (9) St. Bartholomew's, and (10) St. James' Santee. Then, in 1712 (11) St. Helena's, in 1717 (12) St. George's Dorchester, in 1721 (13) Prince George's Winyah, in 1734 (14) St. John's Colleton and (15) Prince Frederick's, in 1745 (16) Prince William, in 1746 (17) St. Peter's, in 1751 (18) St. Michael's, in 1754 (19) St. Stephen's, in 1757 (20) St. Mark's, in 1767 (21) St. Luke's and (22) All Saints', in 1768 (23) St. Matthew's and (24) St. David's, and in 1778 (25) Orange. The approximate parish areas for these are shown in Figure 4, with the numbers on the map corresponding to the numbers given above.

A proposal made in 1730 led to the establishment of twelve townships in the frontier regions of the colony. These were settled largely by immigrants and people who came down from the northern colonies. In 1732, (W) Williamsburg was established on the Black River, in 1733 (Q) Queensboro on the Pee Dee River, (A) Amelia on the Congaree-Santee River, (O) Orangeburg on the North Fork of the Edisto River, and (S) Saxe Gotha on the Congaree River, in 1734 (F) Fredericksburg on the Wateree River, (P) Purrysburg on the Savannah River, and (N) New Windsor on the Savannah River, in 1735 (K) Kingston on the Waccamaw River, in 1761 (L) Londonborough on Hard Labor Creek and (B) Boonesborough on Long Cane Creek, and in 1764 (H) Hillsborough on the New River. These township settlements are shown in Figure 5, with the capital letters on the map corresponding to those given in this paragraph.

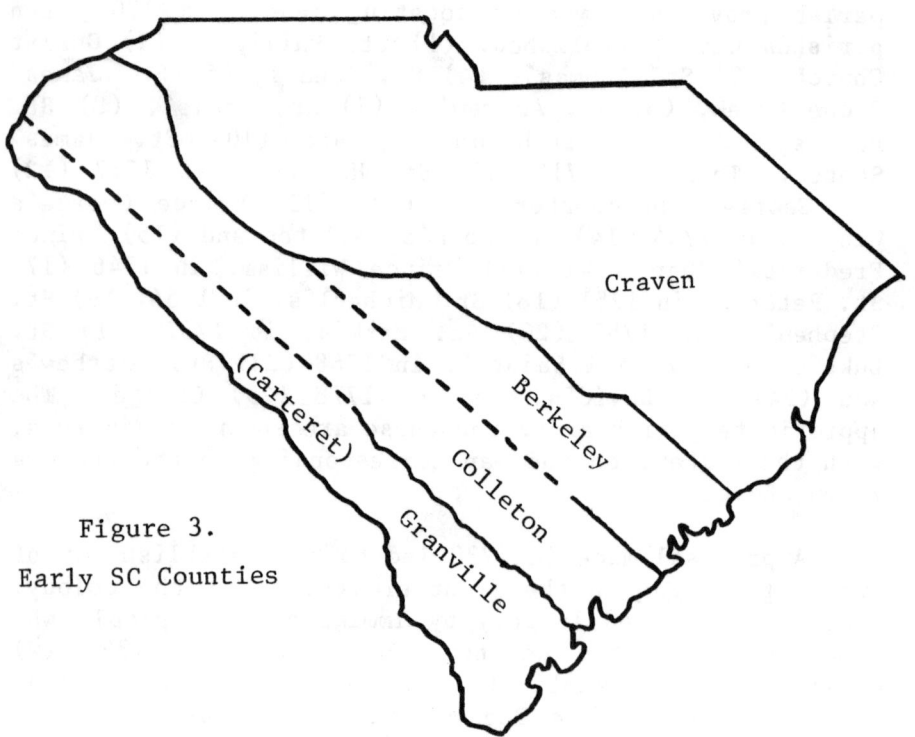

Figure 3. Early SC Counties

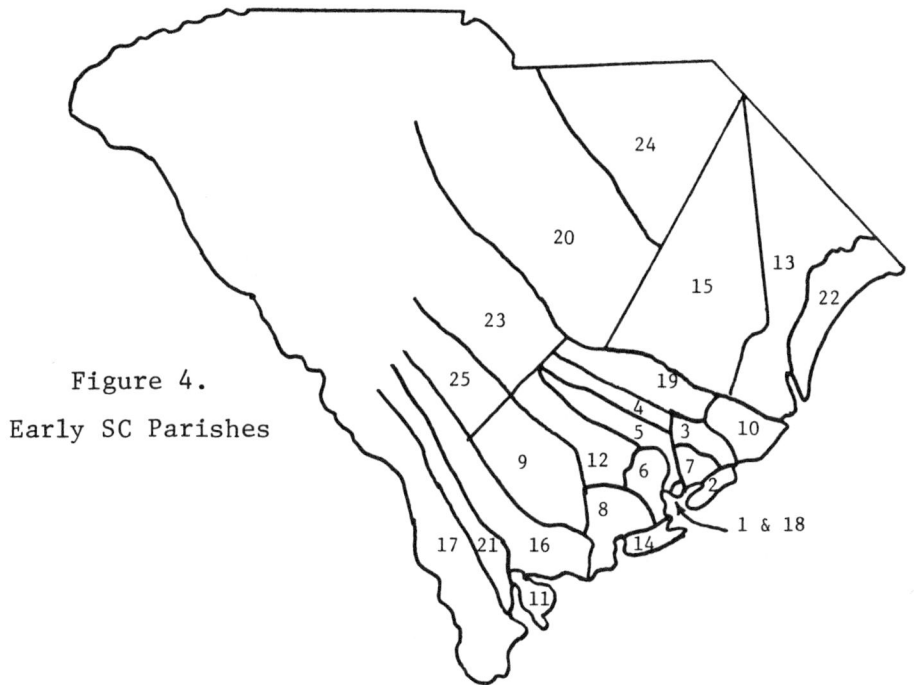

Figure 4. Early SC Parishes

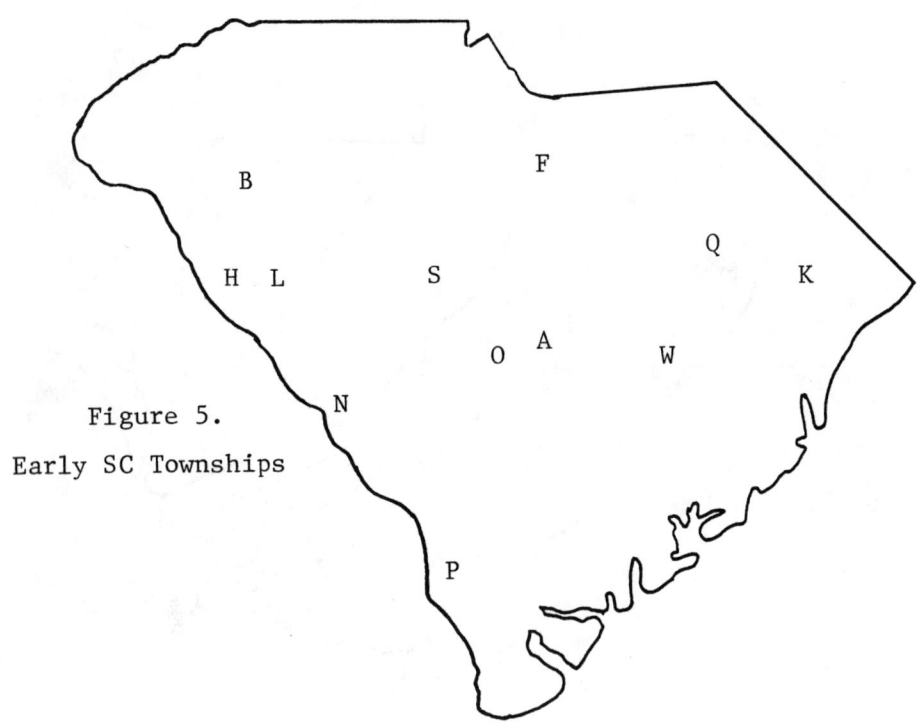

Figure 5. Early SC Townships

In 1769, the colony had expanded into the Up Country such that there was a severe need for courts in these areas. The single court at Charleston was simply too far away to take care of the expanding population in the frontier regions. To meet this need, seven circuit court districts were formed and courthouses were set up in each. In 1772, the courts in these places began to function. The seven districts and the courthouse towns in each were: (1) Charleston District, Charleston, (2) Beaufort District, Beaufort, (3) Georgetown District, Georgetown, (4) Orangeburg District, Orangeburg, (5) Camden District, Camden, (6) Cheraws District, Long Bluff, and (7) Ninety-Six District, Ninety-Six. These districts are depicted in Figure 6, but please note that they were not broken up into subdivisions at this time (1769).

In 1785, the state of SC laid out counties in each of the districts and authorized them to keep many of the records which only Charleston had done up to this date. The counties in each of the districts were: Charleston District (Bartholomew, Berkeley, Colleton, Marion, and Washington Counties), Beaufort District (Granville, Hilton, Lincoln, and Shrewsbury Counties), Georgetown District (Kingston, Liberty, Williamsburg, and Winyah Counties), Orangeburg District (Lewisburg, Lexington, Orange, and Winton Counties), Camden District (Chester, Claremont, Clarendon, Fairfield, Lancaster, Richland, and York Counties), Cheraws District (Chesterfield, Darlington, and Marlboro Counties), and Ninety-Six District (Abbeville, Edgefield, Laurens, Newberry, Spartanburg, and Union Counties). The counties in Charleston, Beaufort, and Georgetown Districts declined to keep records, and therefore the record-keeping was done at the district courthouses: Charleston, Beaufort, and Georgetown. The counties in Orangeburg District kept records for about 6 years (until about 1791) but then turned the record-keeping back to the district with its courthouse at Orangeburg. In the other districts (Camden, Cheraws, Ninety-Six), the counties did much of the record-keeping for their areas, but the districts also kept some records. The exact date when record-keeping was transferred from the District to the various counties was not always 1785, sometimes being a year or two or three or four later. Sometimes both kept records for a few years, and sometimes record-keeping of

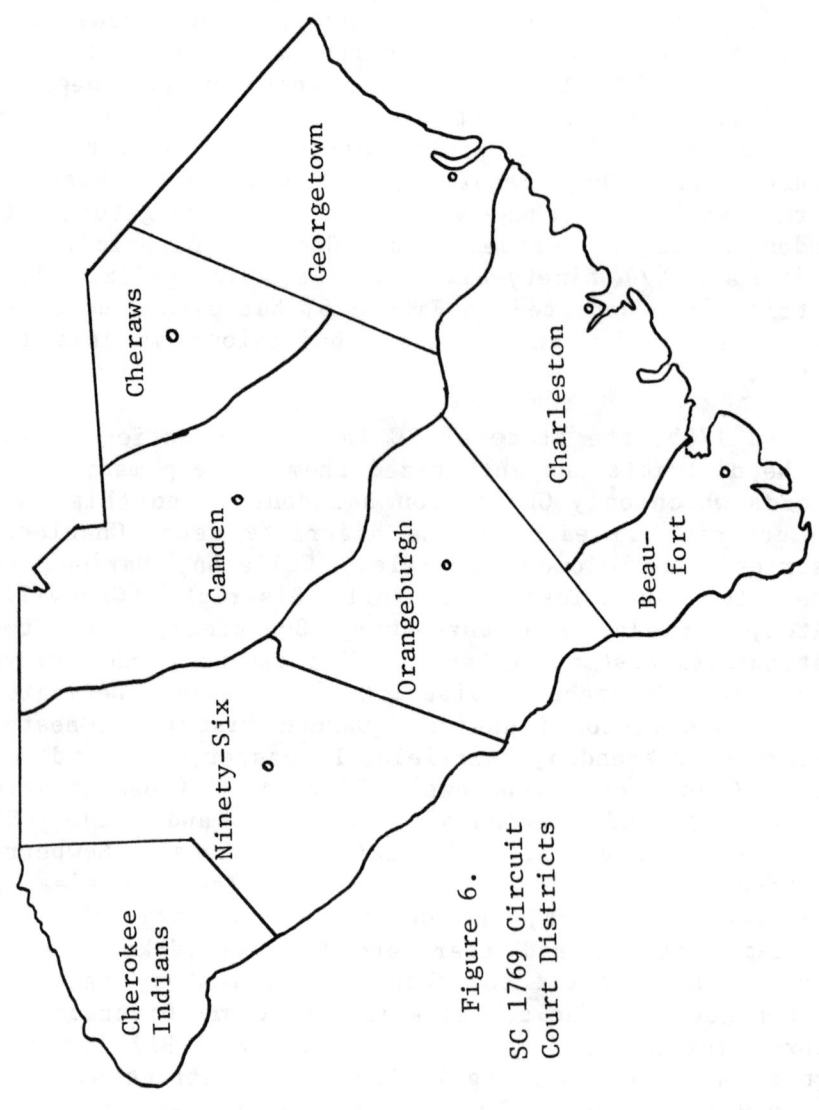

Figure 6.
SC 1769 Circuit Court Districts

different records was transferred at different times. The district courts continued to meet at the district towns and to keep their own records.

In 1786, Greenville County was formed and taken into Ninety-Six District, in 1789 Pendleton County was set up and added to Ninety-Six District, in 1791 Kershaw County was formed from parts of Claremont and Lancaster Counties, and in 1792 Salem County was established from portions of Claremont and Clarendon Counties. In 1791, two new districts were formed, Washington District (taking Greenville and Pendleton Counties), and Pinckney District (taking Chester, Spartanburg, Union, and York Counties).

In 1800, the 37 existing counties were changed into 25 districts. Most of the counties were simply changed into districts, some of the counties were combined to form districts, and a few counties were made into districts with changed names. All of these districts became record-keeping ones. Details of these changes can be seen in Charts 1, 2, 3, 4, 5, 6, and 7 which are presented a few pages after this page. In these charts a superscript[a] means the county or district was abolished, a superscript[n] means the name was changed, a superscript[r] means the county or district kept records, and a dotted line connects counties and/or districts which occupied about the same area. When no superscript[r] appears, this means that the county or district did not keep its records; they will be in those marked with a superscript[r]. From 1800 to 1868, the 25 districts expanded into 30 districts, as new districts were formed out of parts of older ones. Again, details may be seen in Charts 1, 2, 3, 4, 5, 6, and 7. Then in 1868, the new state constitution decreed that all districts would now be designated counties, and so the 30 districts became 30 counties, all keeping their same names. In the period 1868-1919, the 30 counties divided into 46. Details are given in Charts 1, 2, 3, 4, 5, 6, and 7.

Charts 1, 2, 3, 4, 5, 6, and 7, which have been referred to several times in the previous paragraph, present the somewhat complicated history of the districts and counties of SC. The charts also contain information relating to the precise places to seek records, these being indicated by a superscript[r]. The history of a

-40-

1. (1769)Charleston D^r
   - (1785)Bartholomew C^a ─── (1800)Colleton D^{rn}
     - in Charleston D^r
   - (1785)Colleton C^a
     - in Charleston D^r
       - (1868)Colleton C^r ─── (1897)Dorchester C^r
       - (1882)Berkeley C^r
   - (1785)Old Berkeley C^a
     - in Charleston D^r
   - (1785)Old Marion C^a
     - in Charleston D^r ─── (1868)Charleston C^r
   - (1785)Washington C^r ─── (1800)Charleston D^{rn}
     - in Charleston D^r

   a = abolished
   n = name changed
   r = records kept
   --- = same area

2. (1769)Beaufort D
   - (1785)Granville C^a ─── (1800)Beaufort D^{rn}
     - in Beaufort D^r
   - (1785)Hilton C^a
     - in Beaufort D^r
       - (1868)Beaufort C^r ─── (1912)Jasper C^r
       - (1878)Hampton C^r
   - (1785)Lincoln C^a
     - in Beaufort D^r
   - (1785)Shrewsbury C^a ─── (1919)Allendale C^{r*}
     - in Beaufort D^r

   a = abolished
   n = name changed
   r = records kept
   --- = same area

   *Allendale also from Barnwell

3. (1769)Georgetown D
   - (1785)Kingston C^n ─── (1801)Horry D^{rn} ─── (1868)Horry C^r ─── (1910)Dillon C^r
     - in Georgetown D^r
   - (1785)Winyah C^a ─── (1800)Georgetown D^{rn} ─── (1868)Georgetown C^r
     - in Georgetown D^r
   - (1785)Williamsburg D^n ─── (1804)Williamsburg D^{rn} ─── (1868)Williamsburg C^r
     - in Georgetown D^r
   - (1785)Liberty C^n ─── (1800)Marion D^r ─── (1868)Marion C^r ─── (1888)Florence C^{r*}
     - in Georgetown D^r

   *Also from Darlington & Clarendon

   a = abolished
   n = name changed
   r = records kept
   --- = same area

-41-

4. (1769)Orangeburg D
   ├─(1785)Lewisburg C^r──(1791)Lewisburg C^a──(1800)Orangeburg D^{rn}──(1868)Orangeburg C^r
   │   in Orangeburg D^r
   ├─(1785)Lexington C^r──(1791)Lexington C^{an}───(1804)Lexington D^{rn} (1871)Aiken C^r*
   │   in Orangeburg D^r
   │   (1868)Lexington C^r (1908)Calhoun C^r
   ├─(1785)Orange C^a──(1791)Orange C^a
   │   in Orangeburg D^r
   └─(1785)Winton C^r──(1791)Winton C^n──(1800)Barnwell D^{rn} (1919)Allendale C^r*
        in Orangeburg D^r
                                              (1868)Barnwell C^r──(1897)Bamberg C^r

   *Aiken also from Edgefield & Barnwell   a = abolished
   Allendale also from Hampton   n = name changed
                                                 r = records kept
                                                 ─── = same area

5. (1769)Camden D
   ┌─(1785)Clarendon C^{rn}─────(1855)Clarendon D^{rn}──(1868)Clarendon C^r
   │   in Camden D^r ╲
   ├─(1785)Claremont C^{ra} (1792)Salem C^{ra}──(1800)Sumter D^{rn}──(1868)Sumter C^r
   │   in Camden D^r
   ├─(1785)Fairfield C^{rn}──────(1800)Fairfield D^{rn}──(1868)Fairfield C^r (1902)Lee C^r*
   │   in Camden D^r
   ├─(1785)Lancaster C^{rn}──(1791)Kershaw C^{rn}*──(1800)Kershaw D^{rn}──(1868)Kershaw C^r
   │   in Camden D^r
   ├─(1785)Richland C^{rn}───(1800)Lancaster D^{rn}──(1868)Lancaster C^r
   │   in Camden D^r
   ├─(1785)York C^{rn}──(1791)York C^{rn}──(1800)Richland D^{rn}──(1868)Richland C^r
   │   in Camden D^r in Pinckney D^r
   │   (1800)York D^{rn}──(1868)York C^r──(1897)Cherokee C^r
   └─(1785)Chester C^{rn}──(1791)Chester C^{rn}──(1800)Chester D^{rn}──(1868)Chester C^r
        in Camden D^r in Pinckney D^r

   *Cherokee also from Union & Spartanburg   a = abolished
   Kershaw also from Richland   n = name changed
   Lee also from Darlington   r = records kept
                                                 ─── = same area

6. (1769)Cheraws D
   ├─(1785)Chesterfield C^{rn}──(1800)Chesterfield D^{rn}──(1868)Chesterfield C^r──(1888)Florence C^{r*}
   │ in Cheraws D^r
   ├─(1785)Darlington C^{rn}──(1800)Darlington D^{rn}──(1868)Darlington C^r──(1902)Lee C^{r*}
   │ in Cheraws D^r
   └─(1785)Marlboro C^{rn}──(1800)Marlboro D^{rn}──(1868)Marlboro C^r
      in Cheraws D^r

a = abolished
n = name changed
r = records kept
--- = same area

*Florence also from Marion, Williamsburg, & Clarendon
 Lee also from Kershaw & Sumter

7. (1769)Ninety-Six D
   ├─(1785)Abbeville C^{rn}──(1800)Abbeville D^{rn}──(1868)Abbeville C^r
   │ in Ninety-Six D^r ├─(1897)Greenwood C^r──(1916)McCormick C^r
   ├─(1785)Edgefield C^{rn}──(1800)Edgefield D^{rn}──(1868)Edgefield C^r
   │ in Ninety-Six D^r └─(1897)Saluda C^r
   ├─(1785)Laurens C^{rn}──(1800)Laurens D^{rn}──(1868)Laurens C^r
   │ in Ninety-Six D^r
   ├─(1785)Newberry C^{rn}──(1800)Newberry D^{rn}──(1868)Newberry C^r
   │ in Ninety-Six D^r
   ├─(1785)Spartanburg C^{rn}──(1791)Spartanburg C^{rn}──(1800)Spartanburg D^{rn}──(1868)Spartanburg C^r
   │ in Ninety-Six D^r in Pinckney D^r ├─(1897)Cherokee C^{r*}
   ├─(1785)Union C^{rn}──(1791)Union C^{rn}──(1800)Union D^{rn}──(1868)Union C^r
   │ in Ninety-Six D^r in Pinckney D^r
   ├─(1786)Greenville C^{rn}──(1795)Greenville C^{rn}──(1800)Greenville D^{rn}──(1868)Greenville C^r
   │ in Ninety-Six D^r in Washington D^r
   └─(1789)Pendleton C^{rn}──(1795)Pendleton C^{rn}──(1800)Pendleton D^{ra}──(1826)Anderson D^r──(1868)Anderson C^r
      in Ninety-Six D^r in Washington D^r
                                                              └─(1826)Pickens D^r──(1868)Pickens C^r──(1868)Oconee C^r

a = abolished
n = name changed
r = records kept
--- = same area

*Cherokee also from York

given county may be traced by following the lines backwards on the proper chart. For example, suppose we wish to trace the derivation of Calhoun County. First, look the county up in the alphabetical list given at the end of section 10 of this chapter. There you will find that Calhoun County appears in Chart 4. Second, go to Chart 4, locate Calhoun County^r, and notice that it was formed in 1908 from Orangeburg County^r and Lexington County^r. Third, now trace Orangeburg County back. Orangeburg County^r came from Orangeburg District^r in 1868. Orangeburg District^r came from a combination in 1800 of three counties in the pre-1800 Orangeburg District^r, but notice that the three counties (Lewisburg, Lexington, Orange) did not keep records from 1791-1800. Instead the records were in Orangeburg District^r. However, records during 1785-91 were kept in the three counties (Lewisburg^r, Lexington C^r, Orange C^r), and in the Orangeburg District^r. Before 1785, all records were kept in Charleston^r. Fourth, now trace Lexington County. Lexington County^r came from Lexington District^r in 1868. Lexington District^r came from Orangeburg District^r in 1804. And from then on back has been traced in the third step. Now, fifth, summarize the places you need to look in order to trace a piece of land now in Calhoun County back. The records may be found in Calhoun County^r (1908-present), Orangeburg County^r (1868-1908), Lexington County^r (1868-1908), Orangeburg District^r (1800-68), Lexington District^r (1804-68), Orangeburg District^r (1785-1800), Lewisburg County^r (1785-91), Lexington County^r (1785-91), Orange County^r (1785-91), and Charleston^r (1670-1785). All these places should be checked since they were the record-keeping locations, but you should also check a few years before and after each period, since the changeover of record jurisictions seldom occurred instantaneously.

12. Recommended readings

A knowledge of the history of SC and of its local regions is of extreme importance for the tracing of the genealogies of its former inhabitants. This chapter has been a brief treatment of that history. Your next step should be the detailed reading and study of an exceptionally good one-volumed work. These are recommended:
__L. P. Jones, SC, Sandlapper Store, Lexington, SC, 1971.

__L. B. Wright, SC, Norton & Co., New York, NY, 1976.
After reading one of these, it is recommended that you purchase and make good use of the best detailed one-volumed history of the state and its peoples:
__D. D. Wallace, SC, University of SC Press, Columbia, SC, 1969.
If you care to go further, you may wish to employ one of the very-detailed multi-volumed histories of SC:
__D. D. Wallace, SC, American Historical Society, New York, NY, 1934, 4 volumes.
__Y. Snowden, HISTORY OF SC, Lewis Publ. Co., New York, NY, 1920, 5 volumes.
In order to locate books and articles on specific time periods or specific areas of SC, consult:
__R. N. Cote, LOCAL AND FAMILY HISTORY IN SC: BIBLIOGRAPHY, Southern Historical Press, Easley, SC, 1981.
__J. H. Easterly and W. Polk, GUIDE TO STUDY AND READING OF SC HISTORY, Reprint Co., Spartanburg, SC, 1975.
__L. P. Jones, BOOKS AND ARTICLES ON SC HISTORY, Tricentennial Commission, Columbia, SC, 1970.
__R. J. Turnbull, BIBLIOGRAPHY OF SC, University of VA Press, Charlottesville, VA, 1956-60, 5 volumes.
Individual county/district histories will be listed in Chapter 4 of this book, and these and other historical works dealing with regions, districts, counties, divisions, cities, and towns of SC are listed in:
__M. J. Kaminkow, US LOCAL HISTORIES IN THE LIBRARY OF CONGRESS, Magna Carta Book Co., Baltimore, MD, 1975, volume 2.

Chapter 2

TYPES OF RECORDS

1. Introduction

The state of South Carolina (SC) is relatively rich in genealogical source materials, even though there are notable gaps in the early years, and there are problems with the loss of records in court house (CH) fires, which were fairly common in the 18th and 19th centuries. A great deal of work has been done in accumulating, preserving, photocopying, transcribing, abstracting, printing, and indexing records. The best overall collections in existence are in two buildings within a few blocks of each other in downtown Columbia, SC, the capital city of the state. These buildings house the South Carolina Department of Archives and History (SCDA) and the South Caroliniana Library (SCL) of The University of South Carolina. The SCDA has extensive holdings of original records and microfilms of original records (city, county, district, regional, colonial, state, federal, British, Revolutionary, Confederate), numerous indexes and finding aids to these records, original and microfilmed copies of manuscripts, and a well-stocked reference collection (transcribed records, reference works, bibliographies, guides, monographs, periodicals). The SCL has large holdings of books (transcribed records, abstracted records, histories, biographical works, city directories, record compilations, published genealogies, bibliographies, indexes), periodicals and periodical indexes, pamphlets, microfilms, maps, documents, newspapers, pictures, and manuscripts (Bible, church, cemetery, family, political, personal, institutional, corporate, business, military, legal, plantation), and indexes, catalogs, and other finding aids.

Another genealogically-related collection in SC is very important. This is the South Carolina Historical Society Library (SCHS) in the downtown area of Charleston, SC. This library has a wide-ranging collection of books (biography, society rosters, histories, family genealogies, census indexes, church records and histories, atlases, military lists and histories), periodicals, maps, manuscripts (many types), and indexes, alphabetical card files, and other finding aids.

The Genealogical Society of UT (GSU) in Salt Lake City, the largest genealogical library in the world, holds a large number of books and microfilm copies of books and original records relating to SC. The microfilms are available to you through the numerous Branch Libraries of the Genealogical Society of UT (BLGSU) which are located all over the US. Included among these libraries are three in the state of SC: Charleston, Columbia, and Greenville.

In addition to the above collections, there are SC record collections in a number of large genealogical libraries (LGL) around the country, especially those in states near SC. Other collections, usually with an emphasis on a particular section of SC, are located in several good regional libraries (RL) in SC. All pre-1785 governmental records of genealogical significance for SC are available at SCDA, and many pre-1860 records of the counties and districts are also there, either the originals, microfilm copies, printed copies, or transcripts. Numerous county records after 1860 are also in SCDA. In the nearby SCL is the largest collection of non-governmental SC records in existence. This means that the resources of the SCDA and SCL should be used first, then if necessary, research can be continued in the appropriate court house (CH). Finally, local libraries (LL) in the county seats and cities which are not county seats often have good materials relating to their own areas. All of the archives, repositories, and libraries mentioned above will be discussed in detail in Chapter 3.

In this chapter, the many types of records which are available for SC genealogical research are discussed. Those records which are essentially _national_ or _statewide_ in scope will be treated in detail. Please recall that all pre-1785 governmental records for SC are state-wide. Records which are basically _county_ or _district_ records will be mentioned and treated only generally, but detailed lists of them will be given in Chapter 4, where the major local records available for each of the 46 SC counties will be presented. Record types and locations for defunct counties and districts will also be indicated.

2. <u>Bible records</u>

During the past 200 years it was customary for families with religious affiliations to keep vital statistics on their members in the family Bible. These records vary widely, but among the items that may be found are names, dates, and places of birth, christening, baptism, marriage, death, and sometimes military service. Although most Bibles containing recorded information probably still remain in private hands, some of the information has been submitted for publication and some has been filed in libraries and archives. Bible records may be found in libraries and archives throughout SC. You should inquire about such records at every possible library and archives in and near your ancestor's county or district, especially the RL and the LL. Sometimes there will be indexes or the records will be arranged alphabetically. RL will be listed in Chapter 3, section 7, and LL will be listed under the counties in Chapter 4. You should not overlook the possibility that Bible records may be listed in indexes or in files labelled something other than Bible records. The most likely ones are family records, genealogies, manuscripts, names, surnames. Also do not fail to look in the major card index of each library for the names you are seeking.

There are a few published compilations of Bible records which contain SC records. Among those you should examine are:
__DAR, Ann Pamela Cunningham Chapter, SC BIBLE RECORDS, The Chapter, Columbia, SC, 1962, 2 volumes.
__M. A. Lester, OLD SOUTHERN BIBLE RECORDS, Genealogical Publishing Co., Baltimore, MD, 1856-62 (1974).
In addition, there are some index volumes which lead to Bible records (along with other records):
__J. H. Moore, RESEARCH MATERIALS IN SC, University of SC Press, Columbia, SC, 1967. [Check the manuscript listings.]
__R. N. Cote, LOCAL AND FAMILY HISTORY IN SC: BIBLIOGRAPHY, Southern Historical Press, Easley, SC, 1981. [Check the index for names.]
__E. K. Kirkham, AN INDEX TO SOME OF THE BIBLE AND FAMILY RECORDS OF THE SOUTHERN STATES, Everton Publishers, Logan, UT, 1980.

And there are also some folders and three volumes of
Bible records in the SCL:
___L. Andrea, THE LEONARDO ANDREA GENEALOGICAL COLLECTION,
   SCL, Columbia, SC, look under Bible Records and the
   surnames you are interested in.
Bible records also appear in genealogical periodical
articles and in published family genealogies. These two
types of records, as well as details on manuscript
sources will be discussed in sections 18, 19, 23, and 32
of this chapter.

3. Biographies

   There are several major national biographical works
which contain sketches on nationally-prominent SC
personages. There are also numerous good biographical
compilations for the state of SC or for sections of it.
These volumes list persons who have attained some
prominence in the fields of law, agriculture, business,
politics, medicine, engineering, science, military,
teaching, public service, or philanthropy. Fifty-three
of these national and SC biographical works have been
indexed in the following excellent compilation:
___R. N. Cote and P. H. Williams, THE DICTIONARY OF SC
   BIOGRAPHY, Southern Historical Press, Easley, SC, 1984,
   volume 1, others to follow.
If you know or suspect that your ancestor was fairly well
known, be certain to consult this volume. If you find
your forebear in it (or in the further volumes of the
series), you will be referred to the books in which the
biographical sketches occur. The index volume and most
of the books it refers to will be found in SCL and SCHS.
Many are also available in RL in SC and some are
available in LGL and GSU (and thus BLGSU).

   In addition to the above national, state, and
regional biographical works, there are some local
(county, district, city, and professional) biographical
volumes. If these are available, this fact will be
indicated under the counties/districts in Chapter 4.
These works are available in SCL and SCHS, and those
pertaining to specific counties, districts, cities, and
towns are generally on the shelves of RL and LL in the
corresponding places. There are also some special
biographical collections and some unpublished
compilations in several SC libraries. Do not fail to

inquire in libraries near your ancestor's homeplace. Numerous other volumes carrying varying amounts of SC biographical data are listed in:
__R. N. Cote, LOCAL AND FAMILY HISTORY IN SC: A BIBLIOGRAPHY, Southern Historical Press, Easley, SC, 1981, pp. 196-9.

And there is a very useful card index to biographical volumes and will records in the SCDA which you should be sure to consult:
__BIOGRAPHICAL INDEX, SCDA, Columbia, SC. [Check under surname]

4. Birth records

SC state law required births to be registered with the state beginning in 1915, but it was 1919 before the registration reached a 90% complete level. Copies of birth certificates may be obtained by authorized persons from:
__Division of Vital Records, Bureau of Health Measurement, SC Department of Health and Environmental Control, 2600 Bull St., Columbia, SC 29201.

A fee is charged for this service. With four exceptions, no district, county, or city governmentally-collected birth records were kept in SC prior to 1915. The exceptions are as follows: City of Aiken (1909-10), City of Charleston (1877-1926), City of Florence (1895-1914), City of Newberry (late 1800s-1914). The Aiken records are available at SCDA, the Charleston records at Charleston County Library (404 King St., Charleston, SC 29403), and the Florence and Newberry records may be obtained from the respective County Health Departments. When writing for birth records, be sure and give them as many of the following as you can: full name, sex, race, names of parents, maiden name of mother, approximate or exact birth date, approximate or exact place of birth, your relationship to the person, and the reason you want the record (namely, genealogical research).

Prior to the time when SC required birth registration (1915), other records may yield dates and places of birth along with names of parents: Bible, biographical, cemetery, census, church, death, divorce, manuscript, marriage, military, mortuary, newspaper, pension, and published records. These are all discussed in other sections of this chapter. The finding of birth

record articles in genealogical periodicals is also described in a separate section in this chapter. Some of these other sources of birth records along with their locations are listed in:
__J. D. and E. D. Stemmons, THE VITAL RECORDS COMPENDIUM, Everton Publishers, Logan, UT, 1979.
__M. J. Brown, HANDY INDEX TO THE HOLDINGS OF THE GENEALOGICAL SOCIETY OF UT, VOLUME 3: SOUTHERN STATES, Everton Publishers, Logan, UT, 1984.
__R. N. Cote, LOCAL AND FAMILY HISTORY IN SC: A BIBLIOGRAPHY, Southern Historical Press, Easley, SC, 1981.
__J. H. Moore, RESEARCH MATERIALS IN SC, University of SC Press, Columbia, SC, 1967.

5. **Cemetery records**

If you know or suspect that your ancestor was buried in a certain SC cemetery, the best thing to do is to write the caretaker of the cemetery, enclose an SASE and ask if the records show your forebear. If no luck is had, or no official caretaker can be located, try writing the local genealogical society, the local historical society, or the LL, inquiring about records for cemeteries in the area. Addresses for these organizations will be presented under the appropriate counties in Chapter 4.

Another important cemetery record source is the numerous collections of cemetery records which have been made by the DAR, by the WPA, by state, regional, and local genealogical and historical societies, and by individuals. Sizable listings of many of these available cemetery records will be found in:
__J. D. and E. D. Stemmons, THE CEMETERY RECORD COMPENDIUM, Everton Publishers, Logan, UT, 1979.
__M. J. Brown, HANDY INDEX TO THE HOLDINGS OF THE GENEALOGICAL SOCIETY OF UT, VOLUME 3: SOUTHERN STATES, Everton Publishers, Logan, UT, 1984.
__R. N. Cote, LOCAL AND FAMILY HISTORY IN SC, University of SC Press, Columbia, SC, 1967, pp. 66-138.
__BOOK AND MANUSCRIPT CARD CATALOGS, SCL, Columbia, SC, check for microfilms and transcripts of epitaphs under surname, county or district name, church name, and cemetery name.
__PUBLICATIONS, MANUSCRIPTS, WPA TOMBSTONE, and

CHARLESTON TOMBSTONE INSCRIPTION CARD CATALOGS, SC Historical Society, Charleston, SC, check surnames, and county, district, church and cemetery names.

The above references indicate that the main sources of SC cemetery records are SCL, SCHS, GSU, and BLGSU. In addition, LL often have records of the cemeteries of their own counties and districts, and RL libraries often have those in their regions. Some LGL outside of SC may also have records. The genealogical periodicals published in or near SC quite frequently carry cemetery listings (see section 19 in this chapter). Notable among SC cemetery record compilations are the many volumes by the WPA, cemeteries in practically every county being included.

In Chapter 4, those counties for which local cemetery record compilations exist in printed, filmed, typed, or written form are indicated. Instructions for locating the above records will be presented in Chapter 3. Instructions for finding cemetery records in genealogical periodical articles are given in section 19 of this chapter.

6. <u>Census records</u>

Excellent ancestor information is available in eight types of census reports which have been accumulated for SC: some early lists for the period 1670-1788, regular (R), agricultural (A), industrial (I), mortality (M), slaveholder (S), the special 1840 Revolutionary War pension census (P), the special 1890 Union Civil War veteran census (C), and some state censuses (X).

The <u>early lists</u> during 1670-1788, even though incomplete, are valuable because they provide useful data during the colonial period. Among the most important of these are:
_1670 FIRST RESIDENTS, SC Historical and Genealogical Magazine, volume 70, pp. 101-5.
_1716-7 PETITIONERS, SC Historical and Genealogical Magazine, volume 62, pp. 89-95.
_M. B. Warren, CITIZENS AND IMMIGRANTS: SC, 1768, Heritage Papers, Danielsville, GA, 1980.
_1775 RESIDENTS, National Genealogical Society Quarterly, volume 18, pp. 1-2.
_1776 RESIDENTS, American Archives, 4th Series, volume

5, pp. 622-5.
__1781 HEADS OF FAMILIES, SC Historical and Genealogical Magazine, volume 34, pp. 78-83.
__LOYALISTS OF 1783, SC Historical and Genealogical Magazine, volume 14, pp. 37-43.
__GERMAN PROTESTANTS OF 1788, SC Historical and Genealogical Magazine, volume 47, pp. 195-204.

Regular census records (R) are available for practically all of SC in 1790, 1800, 1810, 1820, 1830, 1840, 1850, 1860, 1870, 1880, 1890, 1900, and 1910, the exceptions being that the records for Clarendon District in 1820, 1830, 1840, and 1850 are missing. The 1840 census and all before it listed the head of the household plus a breakdown of the number of persons in the household according to age and sex brackets. Beginning in 1850, the names of all persons were recorded along with age, sex, occupation, real estate, marital, and other information, including the state of birth. With the 1880 census and thereafter, the birthplaces of the mother and father of each person are also shown. Chapter 4 lists the regular census records (R) available for each of the 46 SC counties.

Census data for SC are reproduced in the following microfilm and transcript copies of the original records:
__US Bureau of the Census, HEADS OF FAMILIES AT THE FIRST CENSUS OF THE US, 1790, SC, Genealogical Publishing Co., Baltimore, MD, 1908 [1978].
__US Bureau of the Census, FIRST CENSUS OF THE US, 1790, SC, The National Archives, Washington, DC, Microfilm M637, Roll 11, or Microfilm T498, Roll 3.
__US Bureau of the Census, SECOND CENSUS OF THE US, 1800, SC, The National Archives, Washington, DC, Microfilm M32, Rolls 47-50.
__US Bureau of the Census, THIRD CENSUS OF THE US, 1810, SC, The National Archives, Washington, DC, Microfilm M251, Rolls 60-62.
__US Bureau of the Census, FOURTH CENSUS OF THE US, 1820, SC, The National Archives, Washington, DC, Microfilm M33, Rolls 118-121. [Clarendon missing]
__US Bureau of the Census, FIFTH CENSUS OF THE US, 1830, SC, The National Archives, Washington, DC, Microfilm M19, Rolls 169-173. [Clarendon missing]
__US Bureau of the Census, SIXTH CENSUS OF THE US, 1840, SC, The National Archives, Washington, DC, Microfilm

M704, Rolls 507-516. [Clarendon missing]
__US Bureau of the Census, SEVENTH CENSUS OF THE US, 1850, SC, The National Archives, Washington, DC, Microfilm M432, Rolls 848-60 (free), 861-8 (slaveholder). [Clarendon missing]
__US Bureau of the Census, EIGHTH CENSUS OF THE US, 1860, SC, The National Archives, Washington, DC, Microfilm M653, Rolls 1212-28 (free), 1229-38 (slaveholder).
__US Bureau of the Census, NINTH CENSUS OF THE US, 1870, SC, The National Archives, Washington, DC, Microfilm 593, Rolls 1481-1512.
__US Bureau of the Census, TENTH CENSUS OF THE US, 1880, SC, The National Archives, Washington, DC, Microfilm T9, Rolls 1217-43.
__US Bureau of the Census, TWELFTH CENSUS OF THE US, 1900, SC, The National Archives, Washington, DC, Microfilm T623, Rolls 1514-45.
__US Bureau of the Census, THIRTEENTH CENSUS OF THE US, 1910, SC, The National Archives, Washington, DC, Microfilm T624, Rolls 1446-74.

The 1790 census records are indexed in the published volume and Microfilm T498 mentioned above, and indexes have been printed for the 1800, 1810, 1820, 1830, 1840, 1850, and 1860 census records. Chief among these state-wide indexes are:
__B. H. Holcomb, INDEX TO THE 1800 CENSUS OF SC, Genealogical Publishing Co., Baltimore, MD, 1980. [30,000 names]
__R. V. Jackson, SC 1800 CENSUS INDEX, Accelerated Indexing Systems, Bountiful, UT, 1973. [Over 35,000 entries.]
__R. V. Jackson, SC 1810 CENSUS INDEX, Accelerated Indexing Systems, Bountiful, UT, 1976. [Over 40,000 entries.]
__R. V. Jackson, SC 1820 CENSUS INDEX, Accelerated Indexing Systems, Bountiful, UT, 1976. [Over 64,000 entries.]
__G. B. Platt, SC INDEX TO THE US CENSUS OF 1820, GAM Publications, Tustin, CA, 1972.
__R. V. Jackson, SC 1830 CENSUS INDEX, Accelerated Indexing Systems, Bountiful, UT, 1976. [Over 47,000 entries.]
__J. P. Hazelwood, INDEX TO THE 1830 CENSUS, SC, GenRePut, Ft. Worth, TX, 1973. [Over 47,000 entries.]
__R. V. Jackson, SC 1840 CENSUS INDEX, Accelerated

Indexing Systems, Bountiful, UT, 1976. [Over 51,000 entries.]
__R. V. Jackson, SC 1850 CENSUS INDEX, Accelerated Indexing Systems, Bountiful, UT, 1976. [Over 70,000 entries.]
__J. P Arnold, INDEX TO THE 1860 FEDERAL CENSUS OF SC, A Press, Greenville, SC, 1982.

There are as yet no state-wide indexes to the 1870 censuses. However, a few district and county census indexes have been published. These are listed in:
__R. N. Cote, LOCAL AND FAMILY HISTORY IN SC, Southern Historical Press, Easley, SC, 1981, pp. 10-12.

In addition to the above bound indexes, there is a microfilm index which contains only those families with a child 10 or under in the 1880 census. There are also complete microfilm indexes to the 1900 and 1910 censuses. All three of these microfilms are indexed by a code called Soundex. Librarians and archivists can show you how to use it. The indexes are:
__US Bureau of the Census, SOUNDEX INDEX TO THE 1880 POPULATION SCHEDULES, SC, The National Archives, Washington, DC, Microfilm T771, Rolls 1-56.
__US Bureau of the Census, SOUNDEX INDEX TO THE 1900 POPULATION SCHEDULES, SC, The National Archives, Washington, DC, Microfilm T1070, Rolls 1-124.
__US Bureau of the Census, SOUNDEX INDEX TO THE 1910 POPULATION SCHEDULES, SC, The National Archives, Washington, DC, Microfilm T1275, Rolls 1-93.

The indexes listed in the two previous paragraphs are exceptionally valuable as time-saving devices. However, some of the computer-printed volumes have enough errors in them that you need to use them with caution. If you do not find your ancestor in them, do not conclude that he or she is not in the state; this may mean only that your forebear has been accidentally omitted or that the name has been misread or misprinted. Once you have located a name in the indexes, you can go directly to the reference in the census microfilms and read the entry. When an index is not available (chiefly 1870, and partially 1880), it is necessary for you to go through the census listings entry-by-entry. This can be essentially prohibitive for the entire state, so it is necessary for you to know the county in order to limit your search. Both the census records and the indexes are

available in SCDA, the National Archives in Washington, DC, GSU (thus BLGSU), and in some LGL, RL, and LL. Other LGL, RL, and LL have the printed indexes but not the microfilmed indexes or censuses. The Regional Branches of the National Archives also have the microfilmed indexes and censuses. They are located in or near Boston, New York, Philadelphia, Chicago, Atlanta, Kansas City, Fort Worth, Denver, San Francisco, Los Angeles, and Seattle. Their exact locations and telephone numbers can be obtained from telephone directories in these cities or from the pamphlet:
__National Archives, REGIONAL BRANCHES OF THE NATIONAL ARCHIVES, Leaflet No. 22, The Archives, Washington, DC, 1980.
Also, the microfilmed census records and the microfilmed indexes may be borrowed for you by your local library through interlibrary loan [from AGLL, PO Box 244, Bountiful, UT 84010]. There is a charge of a few dollars per roll.

Agricultural census records (A), also known as farm and ranch census records, are available for 1850, 1860, 1870, and 1880 for SC. These records list the name of the owner, size of farm or ranch, value of the property, crops, livestock, and other details. If your ancestor was a farmer (quite likely), it will be worthwhile to seek him in these records. No indexes are available, but you will probably know the county, so your entry-by-entry search should be fairly easy. The original records and microfilm copies of them are available in the SCDA:
__US Bureau of the Census, AGRICULTURE, INDUSTRY, SOCIAL STATISTICS, AND MORTALITY SCHEDULES FOR SC, 1850-80, SCDA, Columbia, SC, Microcopy 2, Agriculture Rolls 1-2 (1850), 3-4 (1860), 5-6 (1870), 7-15 (1880).

Industrial census records (I) are available for 1850, 1860, 1870, and 1880. There were fragmentary records of this sort in 1810 (added to the regular census), and a short record was taken in 1820. The records, particularly the later ones (1850, 1860, 1870, 1880), list manufacturing firms which produced articles having an annual value of $500 or more. Given in the later records are the name of the firm, the owner, the product(s), the machinery, number of employees, and other details. No indexes except for 1820 are available, so knowledge of the county is helpful. The originals of the

1820 records are in the National Archives, Washington, DC, and they have been microfilmed as:
__US Bureau of the Census, RECORDS OF THE 1820 CENSUS OF MANUFACTURES, The National Archives, Washington, DC, Microfilm M279, 27 Rolls, Index on each roll.

The original records and microfilm copies of them are available in the SCDA:
__US Bureau of the Census, AGRICULTURE, INDUSTRY, SOCIAL STATISTICS, AND MORTALITY SCHEDULES FOR SC, 1850-80, SCDA, Columbia, SC, Microcopy 2, Industry Roll 1 (1850, 1860, 1870), Roll 2 (1880).

Mortality census records (M) are available for the one year periods 01 June (1849, 1859, 1869, 1879) to 31 May (1850, 1860, 1870, 1880). The records give information on persons who died in the year preceding the 1st of June of each of the census years 1850, 1860, 1870, 1880. The data contained in the compilations include name, age, sex, occupation, place of birth, and other information. The original records or microfilm copies of them are available at the National Archives, Washington, DC, and at SCDA:
__US Bureau of the Census, MORTALITY CENSUS SCHEDULE MICROFILM 1850, 1860, 1870, 1880, SC, The National Archives, Washington, DC, Microfilm GR22, Rolls 1-3.
__US Bureau of the Census, AGRICULTURE, INDUSTRY, SOCIAL STATISTICS, AND MORTALITY SCHEDULES FOR SC, 1850-80, SCDA, Columbia, SC, Microcopy 2, Mortality Roll 1 (1850, 1860), 2 (1870), 3 (1880).

Indexes for two of these years are available:
__B. H. Holcomb, INDEX TO THE 1850 FEDERAL CENSUS MORTALITY SCHEDULES OF SC, Southern Historical Press, Easley, SC, 1980.
__J. P. Arnold, INDEX TO THE 1860 MORTALITY SCHEDULE OF SC, A Press, Greenville, SC, 1982.

Slaveholder census records (S) for 1850 and 1860 are available. The records list the names of slaveholders along with the number of slaves, but no names of slaves are given. No indexes have been compiled, so it is important to know the county. The microfilmed records are available in SCDA, the National Archives in Washington, DC, Regional Branches of the National Archives, GSU, BLGSU, and in some LGL, RL, and LL. The microfilms are:
__US Bureau of the Census, SEVENTH CENSUS OF THE US,

1850, SC, The National Archives, Washington, DC, Microfilm M432, Rolls 861-8.
__US Bureau of the Census, EIGHTH CENSUS OF THE US, 1860, SC, The National Archives, Washington, DC, Microfilm M653, Rolls 1229-38.

Revolutionary War pensioners (P) were included in a special census taken in 1840. This compilation was an attempt to list all pension holders, however, there are some omissions and some false entries. The list and an index have been published:
__CENSUS OF PENSIONERS FOR REVOLUTIONARY OR MILITARY SERVICE, SIXTH CENSUS, 1840, INDEXED, Genealogical Publishing Co., Baltimore, MD, 1841 (1965, 1974).
This volume is available in SCDA, SCL, SCHS, GSU, BLGSU, in most LGL, in many RL, and in some LL.

Civil War Union veterans (C) were included in a special census taken in 1890, as were widows of the veterans. A few numerators have also inadvertently listed some Confederate veterans. These records are arranged by county, so it is well if you know your ancestor's county. However, since there is only one roll, it is relatively easy to go through. Microfilm copies of the records are available at SCDA, the National Archives in Washington, DC, GSU, BLGSU, most LGL, and some RL. These records show the veteran's name, widow's name (if applicable), rank, company, regiment or ship, and other pertinent military data. The microfilms are:
__Veterans Administration, SPECIAL SCHEDULES OF THE ELEVENTH CENSUS (1890) ENUMERATING UNION VETERANS AND WIDOWS OF THE CIVIL WAR, The National Archives, Washington, DC, Microfilm M1231, SC, 1 roll.

State census records (X) for SC were taken several times, but a number of the records no longer exist. Among those which are presently available in SCDA are the 1829 schedules for Fairfield and Kershaw Districts, the 1839 schedules for Chesterfield and Kershaw Districts, the 1869 schedules for all counties except Clarendon, Oconee, and Spartanburg; and the 1875 schedules are complete for Clarendon, Newberry, and Marlboro Counties, and partial for Abbeville, Beaufort, Fairfield, Lancaster, and Sumter Counties. These documents are:
__SCDA, STATE POPULATION CENSUS SCHEDULES, SCDA, Columbia, SC, under Secretary of State Records

Deposited for Security and Records of the Office of the Commissioner of the Department of Agriculture, 95 volumes not all of which contain the population schedules.

Because of the complicated district/county/parish structure of SC, the subdivisions in the SC census schedules are often difficult to understand and locate. This thorny problem has been largely solved by an excellent set of maps which clearly show the enumeration subdivisions for each Federal census 1790-1920.
__W. Thorndale and W. Dollarhide, MAP GUIDE TO THE FEDERAL CENSUSES, SOUTH CAROLINA, 1790-1920, Dollarhide Systems, Bellingham, WA, 1984.

These excellent maps also give a summary of which schedules have been lost.

7. <u>Church records</u>

Many SC families were affiliated with a church, and so for these families, there is the possibility of valuable records. The Anglican (Episcopal) Church was the established church of colonial times, but very early numerous other denominations began to come into the colony. The major denominations of SC are Baptist, Disciples of Christ (Christian Church), Episcopal, Jewish, Lutheran, Methodist, Presbyterian, and Roman Catholic. The records of these churches often prove very useful since they frequently contain information on one or more of the following items: births, christenings, baptisms, confirmations, marriages, deaths, burials, admissions, dismissals, reprimands, contributions, officers, ministers. The data are particularly important for those years before county or state vital records were kept. Some of the church records have been inventoried, some have been copied into books or microfilmed, some have been deposited in denominational or state or private archives, but most remain in the individual churches.

Should you have the good fortune to know your ancestor's church, you can write directly. Send an SASE, a check for $5, your ancestor's name, and the pertinent dates, and request a search of the records, or information on the location of the records if they no longer have them. If they neither have them nor know where the records are, dispatch a letter of inquiry to the SC denominational depository or headquarters, enclose an SASE, and ask them if they know where the records are. The names of these depositories or headquarters will be given later. Another step you might take if you know the church is to examine the following:

__R. N. Cote, LOCAL AND FAMILY HISTORY IN SC, Southern Historical Press, Easley, SC, 1981, pp. 15-47, 381-419.
__A. H. Stokes, Jr., A GUIDE TO THE MANUSCRIPT COLLECTION OF THE SOUTH CAROLINIANA LIBRARY, University of SC, Columbia, SC, 1982.
__J. H. Moore, RESEARCH MATERIALS IN SC, University of SC Press, Columbia, SC, 1967, pp. 18, 21-28, 32, 36-37, 45-46, 55-61, 66-138, 148, 154, 174.
__Publication, manuscript, and tombstone card indexes in SCDA, SCL, SCHS, RL. Look under county, church name, and denomination.

These volumes and indexes list many published and microfilmed church records, church record manuscripts, and church record surveys and inventories. They also indicate the locations of these materials, the chief ones being SCDA, SCL, SCHS, RL, various denominational repositories, and some college libraries.

If, as is often the case, you do not know your ancestor's church, you will need to dig deeper. Knowing your ancestor's nationality, his SC county, where in the county he lived, and perhaps some other pertinent details, you should make a good guess about his denomination. You may then write the SC depository or headquarters of that denomination, enclosing an SASE, and asks them what churches of their denomination were in your ancestor's section of the county during his dates there. Also request from them information on the locations of the records of these churches. If you are not sure of the denomination, you might examine maps of your ancestor's county which show churches. You can then observe the churches which are near your forebear's property, and you can write the appropriate denominations. Suitable maps for this purpose are listed in section 17 of this chapter, especially those maps available from the US Geological Survey. The names and addresses of the SC denominational depositories or headquarters will now be given for each major denomination, along with pertinent notes concerning the denominations. These denominations will be treated alphabetically.

The oldest <u>Baptist</u> church in SC was established in Charleston in 1783. The archives for the churches of the Southern Baptist Convention is:
__SC Baptist Historical Society, Furman University, Greenville, SC 29613.
A listing of the church records available in this repository has been published:
__Journal of the SC Baptist Historical Society, Volume 3 (1977), pp. 32-43.
Useful histories of Baptists in SC include:
__J. M. King, A HISTORY OF SC BAPTISTS, Bryan Co., Columbia, SC, 1964.
__L. L. Owens, SAINTS OF CLAY, THE SHAPING OF SC BAPTISTS, Bryan Co., Columbia, SC, 1971.
__L. Townsend, SC BAPTISTS, 1670-1805, Genealogical Publishing Co., Baltimore, MD, 1935 [1978]. [7000 persons]

The <u>Disciples of Christ</u> (Christian Church) came into being as the Campbellites who split from the Baptists in 1832, after having also had some earlier Presbyterian affiliation. Their repository is:
__Disciples of Christ Historical Society, 1101 Nineteenth Ave., Nashville, TN 37212.
Their history in SC is recounted in:
__C. C. Ware, SC DISCIPLES OF CHRIST, A HISTORY, Christian Churches of SC, Charleston, SC, 1967.

In 1681/2 the first <u>Episcopal</u> parish, St. Phillip´s, was established in Charleston. Many early parish registers have been published both in book form and in the SC Historical and Genealogical Magazine. These may be found in SCL, SCHS, Charleston Library Society, some RL, and some LL in SC. Many of the original manuscripts are in SCHS. The historical society and library of the Diocese of SC (which include the entire state until 1922) is located as follows:
__Dalcho Historical Society, Episcopal Diocese of SC, 1020 King St., Charleston, SC 29403.
Histories of the denomination which are useful to genealogists include:
__J. S. Anderson, THE HISTORY OF THE CHURCH OF ENGLAND IN THE COLONIES, Rivington, London, England, 1856, 3 volumes.

__P. G. Clarke, Jr., ANGLICISM IN SC, 1660-1976, Southern Historical Press, Easley, SC, 1977.
__F. Dalcho, AN HISTORICAL ACCOUNT OF THE PROTESTANT EPISCOPAL CHURCH IN SC, 1670-1820, Arno Press, New York, NY, 1820 [1970].
__A. S. Thomas, AN HISTORICAL ACCOUNT OF THE PROTESTANT EPISCOPAL CHURCH IN SC, 1820-1857, Bryan Co., Columbia, SC, 1957.

The Hugenot Church (French Protestant) in Charleston, SC, and dating from 1687, is the only active Hugenot church in the US. Its early records have been lost, but the cemetery records have been published by the following society which has a sizable Hugenot genealogical record collection:
__The Hugenot Society of SC, 25 Chalmers St., Charleston, SC 29401.
The society publishes an annual periodical which contains genealogies, records, and history articles:
__TRANSACTIONS OF THE HUGENOT SOCIETY OF SC, The Society, Charleston, SC, 1889-, volumes 1-, annual.
Useful volumes on Hugenot genealogy and history in SC include:
__H. A. Davis, SOME HUGENOT FAMILIES OF SC AND GA, The Author, Washington, DC, 1927, 1937, 2 volumes.
__S. Dubose and F. A. Porcher, A CONTRIBUTION TO THE HISTORY OF THE HUGENOTS OF SC, Bryan Co., Columbia, SC, 1887 [1972].
__A. H. Hirsch, THE HUGENOTS OF COLONIAL SC, Archon Books, Hamden, CT, 1928 [1973].
__Mrs. M. D. MacDowell, HISTORY OF HUGENOTS OF SC, The Author, Aiken, SC, 1887 [1972].

The Jewish congregation K. K. Beth Elohim was founded in Charleston in 1750, thereby becoming the second in the US. The records of Jewish congregations in SC remain in the individual congregations in practically all cases. Volumes of use for SC Jewish history and genealogy are:
__B. A. Elzas, JEWS OF SC FROM THE EARLIEST TIMES TO THE PRESENT DAY, Lippincott, New York, NY, 1905.
__B. A. Elzas, JEWISH MARRIAGE NOTICES FROM THE NEWSPAPER PRESS OF CHARLESTON, SC, 1775-1906, Bloch, New York, NY, 1917.
__B. A. Elzas, THE JEWISH CEMETERIES OF SC: AN INDEX TO INSCRIPTIONS ON THEIR TOMBSTONES, The Author,

Charleston, SC, 1911.

Lutheran people entered the SC area when German and Swiss settlers came in the early eighteenth century. The majority of SC Lutheran churches are affiliated with the Lutheran Church in America. The synod headquarters in Columbia has very few individual church records, but some will be found in:
_Lutheran Theological Seminary Library, Columbia, SC 29203.
This repository also has collections of Baptist, Methodist, and German Pietist records. There are several histories of SC Lutherans which will be valuable to you if your forebear was a member of this denomination:
_G. D. Bernheim, HISTORY OF THE GERMAN SETTLEMENTS AND OF THE LUTHERAN CHURCH IN NC AND SC, Reprint Co., Spartanburg, SC, 1872 [1972].
_S. J. Hallman, editor, Lutheran Church in the US, Synod of SC, HISTORY OF THE EVANGELICAL LUTHERAN SYNOD OF SC, 1824-1924, The Synod, Columbia, SC, 1924.
_Lutheran Church in America, SC Synod, A HISTORY OF THE LUTHERAN CHURCH IN SC, The Synod, Columbia, SC, 1971.

Methodist churches in SC date back into the late eighteenth century. A collection of conference records, histories, biographical works, manuscripts, and some church records will be found in:
_SC Conference Historical Society, United Methodist Church, Wofford College Library, Spartanburg, SC 29302.
They have an obituary card index to the Methodist publication, the SOUTHERN CHRISTIAN ADVOCATE (1837-1908). Histories of SC Methodists are:
_A. D. Betts, HISTORY OF SC METHODISM, Advocate Press, Columbia, SC, 1952.
_A. M. Chreitzberg, EARLY METHODISM IN THE CAROLINAS, Methodist Publishing House, Nashville, TN, 1897.
_J. B. Hilson, HISTORY OF THE SC CONFERENCE OF THE WESLEYAN METHODIST CHURCH, Light and Life Press, Winona Lake, IN, 1950.
_A. M. Shipp, THE HISTORY OF METHODISM IN SC, Reprint Co., Spartanburg, SC, 1883 [1972].

Presbyterians entered SC early in the eighteenth century. The SC record repository for both the Presbyterian Church in the US and the Associate Reformed Presbyterian Church is:

__The Historical Foundation of the Presbyterian and
  Reformed Churches, Montreat, NC 28757.
The foundation has copies of records for well over 100 SC
Presbyterian churches, manuscripts, histories,
biographical materials, and pamphlets. A description of
the repository and its holdings is available:
__T. H. Spence, THE HISTORICAL FOUNDATION AND ITS
  TREASURES, The Historical Foundation, Montreat, NC,
  1960.
Two other record collections will be found at:
__Presbyterian College Library, Clinton, SC 29325.
__Erskine College Library, Due West, SC 29639.
  [Associate Reformed Presbyterian materials.]
Among the most valuable SC Presbyterian history works
are:
__G. Howe, HISTORY OF THE PRESBYTERIAN CHURCH IN SC,
  Presbyterian Synod of SC, Columbia, SC, 1870 [1965], 2
  volumes.
__F. D. Jones, HISTORY OF THE PRESBYTERIAN CHURCH IN SC
  SINCE 1850, Bryan Co., Columbia, SC, 1926.

Roman Catholic parish records are for the most part
in the custody of the individual churches. Catholicism
in SC dates from the founding of the state's first
Catholic church in Charleston in 1789. The following
archives has some records of defunct churches,
biographical materials, and diocesan records:
__Archives, Diocese of Charleston, Chancery Office, 119
  Broad St., Charleston, SC 29401.
A good history of SC Roman Catholics is:
__J. J. O'Connell, CATHOLICITY IN THE CAROLINAS AND GA,
  1820-75, Reprint Co., Spartanburg, SC, 1879 [1972].

An exceptionally useful genealogical guide to
Charleston and Charleston County lists the church records
available in both the city and the county for churches
established before 1900:
__R. N. Cote, THE GENEALOGISTS GUIDE TO CHARLESTON
  COUNTY, SC, Cote Genealogical Publications, Ladson, SC,
  1978.
Please recall that the major sources of collected church
records in SC are SCDA, SCL, SCHS, Charleston Library
Society, RL, denominational depositories, and some
college libraries.

Many SC city and county histories contain histories of individual churches. These city and county histories are discussed in section 9 of this chapter. These city and county histories may be located in SCL and SCHS, some are found in LGL, and those pertaining to their regions are in RL and LL. They may be located by looking under the city and county names in the card catalogs of these libraries.

8. City directories

During the 19th century many larger cities in the US began publishing city directories. These volumes usually appeared erratically at first, but then began to come out annually a little later on. They usually list heads of households and workers plus their home addresses and their occupations, and sometimes the names and addresses of their place of employment. Businesses, institutions, churches, and organizations are also usually listed. Notable among the SC city directories are those of Charleston. These are available for 1782, 5, 6, 8, 1790, 4, 6, 1801, 2, 3, 6, 7, 8, 9, 1822, 4, 9, 1831, 5, 6, 7, 1840, 9, 1852, 5, 9, 1860, 6, 7, 9, 1872, 4, 5, 6, 7, 8, 9, 1881, and on to the present. City directories for Columbia begin in 1859, appeared erratically at first, then more regularly. In general, the other cities and towns of SC did not begin regular city directories until very late in the 19th century or in the 20th century. Many of these directories are available in SCL, SCHS, and the Library of Congress in Washington, DC. Those for Charleston are also in the Charleston Library Society, 164 King St., Charleston, SC 29401. City directories for other places in SC should be sought in RL and LL in the pertinent area.

The telephone was invented in 1876-7, underwent rapid development, and became widespread fairly quickly. By the late years of the century telephone directories were coming into existence. Older issues can often be found in LL, and as the years have gone on, they have proved to be ever more valuable genealogical sources.

9. City and county histories

Histories for many SC counties/districts and numerous SC cities have been published. These volumes

usually contain biographical data on leading citizens, details about early settlers, histories, organizations, businesses, trades, and churches, and often list clergymen, lawyers, physicians, teachers, governmental officials, farmers, military men, and other groups. Several works which list many of these histories are:
_M. J. Kaminkow, US LOCAL HISTORIES IN THE LIBRARY OF CONGRESS, Magna Carta, Baltimore, MD, 1975, 4 volumes.
_C. S. Peterson, BIBLIOGRAPHY OF LOCAL HISTORIES, Genealogical Publishing Co., Baltimore, MD, 1966-7, 2 volumes.
_R. N. Cote, LOCAL AND FAMILY HISTORY IN SC, Southern Historical Press, Easley, SC, 1981.

Most of the SC volumes in these bibliographies can be found in SCL, SCHS, and the Library of Congress in Washington, DC, and some are usually in LGL. RL and LL are likely to have those relating to their particular areas. In Chapter 4, you will find listed under the counties/districts various recommended histories. Not all are listed, only the better one(s) for each county/district. There will also be an indication under each county/district which has city and/or town histories available.

10. Colonial record compilations

The colonial period for SC extended from 1670 until 1775, during which time the area was a colony either sponsored by or directly related to Great Britain. Many other sections in this chapter describe specific types of records relating to colonial SC, particularly sections 3, 5, 7, 9, 11, 15, 16, 17, 18, 22, 23, 25, 31, 32, and 35. This section, therefore, will be made up of two sub-sections, one dealing with general reference materials to all the colonies (including SC), a second dealing with general reference materials to colonial SC.

Among the important genealogical materials relating to all the colonies are the following. They should be consulted as you search for your colonial SC ancestor. However, some of the volumes must be used with care, since some of the information in them is not from original sources, and is therefore often inaccurate.
_F. A. Virkus, THE ABRIDGED COMPENDIUM OF AMERICAN GENEALOGY, Genealogical Publishing Co., Baltimore, MD,

1968 (1925-42), 7 volumes. [425,000 names of colonial people]
__G. M. MacKenzie and N. O. Rhoades, COLONIAL FAMILIES OF THE USA, Genealogical Publishing Co., Baltimore, MD, 1966 (1907-20), 7 volumes. [125,000 names]
__H. Whittemore, GENEALOGICAL GUIDE TO THE EARLY SETTLERS OF AMERICA, Genealogical Publishing Co., Baltimore, MD, 1967 (1898-1906).
__T. P. Hughes and others, AMERICAN ANCESTRY, Genealogical Publishing Co., Baltimore, MD, 1968 (1887-9), 12 volumes.
__BURKE´S DISTINGUISHED FAMILIES OF AMERICA, Burke´s Peerage, London, England, 1948.
__W. M. Clemens, AMERICAN MARRIAGE RECORDS BEFORE 1699, Genealogical Publishing Co., Baltimore, MD, 1867 (1926-30). [10,000 entries]
__C. E. Banks, PLANTERS OF THE COMMONWEALTH, Genealogical Publishing Co., Baltimore, MD, 1972.
__G. R. Crowther, III, SURNAME INDEX TO 65 VOLUMES OF COLONIAL AND REVOLUTIONARY PEDIGREES, National Genealogical Society, Washington, DC, 1964.
__M. B. Colket, Jr., FOUNDERS OF EARLY AMERICAN FAMILIES, Order of Founders and Patriots of America, Cleveland, OH, 1975.
__H. K. Eilers, NSDAC BICENTENNIAL ANCESTOR INDEX, National Society Daughters of American Colonists, Ft. Worth, TX, 1976.
__National Society of Daughters of Founders and Patriots of America, FOUNDERS AND PATRIOTS OF AMERICA INDEX, The Society, Washington, DC, 1975.
__National Society of the Colonial Dames of America, REGISTER OF ANCESTORS, The Society, Richmond, VA, 1979.
__N. Currer-Briggs, COLONIAL SETTLERS AND ENGLISH ADVENTURERS, Genealogical Publishing Co., Baltimore, MD, 1971.
__P. W. Filby and M. K. Meyer, PASSENGER AND IMMIGRATION LIST INDEX, Gale Research Co., Detroit, MI, 1981, 3 volumes, plus supplements. [400 sources, 600,000 names]
__W. A. Crozier, KEY TO SOUTHERN PEDIGREES, Southern Book Co., Baltimore, MD, 1953 (1911). [7000 listings]
__G. F. T. Sherwood, AMERICAN COLONISTS IN ENGLISH RECORDS, Sherwood, London, England, 1932, 2 volumes.
__P. W. Coldham, ENGLISH ESTATES OF AMERICAN COLONISTS, Genealogical Publishing Co., Baltimore, MD, 1980-1, 3 volumes.
__J. C. Hotten, THE ORIGINAL LISTS OF PERSONS OF QUALITY,

Genealogical Publishing Co., Baltimore, MD, 1980 (1874).
__S. P. Hardy, COLONIAL FAMILIES OF THE SOUTHERN STATES OF AMERICA, Genealogical Publishing Co., Baltimore, MD, 1981 (1958).
__National Society Colonial Daughters of the 17th Century, LINEAGE BOOK, The Society, Rotan, TX, 1982 (1979). [2000 names]
__E. K. Kirkham, AN INDEX TO SOME OF THE FAMILY RECORDS OF THE SOUTHERN STATES, Everton Publishers, Logan, UT, 1980.
__Daughters of the American Revolution, DAR PATRIOT INDEX, The Daughters, Washington, DC, 1966, 1979, 2 volumes.
__National Genealogical Society, INDEX OF REVOLUTIONARY WAR PENSION APPLICATIONS IN THE NATIONAL ARCHIVES, The Society, Washington, DC, 1976.
__F. Rider, THE AMERICAN GENEALOGICAL BIOGRAPHICAL INDEX, Godfrey Memorial Library, Middletown, CT, 1942-52, 48 volumes; also F. Rider, AMERICAN GENEALOGICAL BIOGRAPHICAL INDEX, Godfrey Memorial Library, Middletown, CT, new series, 1952-, in process, over 130 volumes published.

There are also important genealogial and historical compendia and indexes relating specifically to colonial SC which you should search. The most important of these is:
__THE COMBINED ALPHABETICAL INDEX, Microfilm Finding Aid, Search Room, SCDA, Columbia, SC.
This microfilm index brings together in alphabetical order persons and places mentioned in a very large number of SC records, including a large number of colonial records. The chief record series containing colonial references are land plats (1680-1926), land grants (1694-1776), land memorials (1731-75), land conveyances (1719-76), court of common pleas petitions to practice law (1752-78), court of common pleas renunciations of dower (1726-75), court of common pleas judgment rolls (1703-90), bills of sale (1773-1840), and others are being continually added. A second very important colonial record source which must under no circumstances be missed is a compilation of records relating to SC which have been abstracted from materials in the British Public Record Office. There are 38 volumes in the record group, the last two being a person, place, and topic

index. These volumes contain information on military matters, land grants, warrants, petitions, correspondence, land entry, plantations, licenses, trade, affidavits, and other topics which could contain references to your ancestor(s). The volumes have been microfilmed by SCDA as:

__RECORDS IN THE BRITISH PUBLIC RECORD OFFICE RELATING TO SC, 1663-1782, Microcopy No. 1, SCDA, Columbia, SC, 1973, 12 rolls, index of persons, places, and topics in the 12th roll.

In addition, other colonial compilations of relevance to SC are:

__A. L. Baldwin, FIRST SETTLERS OF SC, 1670-80, University of SC Press, Columbia, SC, 1969.

__J. H. Easterby and others, THE JOURNAL OF THE COMMONS HOUSE OF ASSEMBLY, 1736-54, Historical Commission of SC, Columbia, SC, 1951-83, 12 volumes. Index in each volume.

__A. K. Gregorie, RECORDS OF THE COURT OF CHANCERY OF SC, 1671-1779, American Historical Association, Washington, DC, 1950.

__B. H. Holcomb, NC LAND GRANTS IN SC, A Press, Greenville, SC, 1980.

__B. H. Holcomb, PROBATE RECORDS OF SC, 1746-1821, Southern Historical Press, Easley, SC, 1977-9, 3 volumes.

__Mrs. F. H. Horlbeck, REGISTER OF NATIONAL SOCIETY OF COLONIAL DAMES OF THE 17TH CENTURY IN THE STATE OF SC, Waverly Press, 1945.

__M. L. Houston, INDEXES TO THE COUNTY WILLS OF SC, 1766-1853, Genealogical Publishing Co., Baltimore, MD, 1939 (1970).

__R. V. Jackson, EARLY SC RECORDS, 1600-1799, Accelerated Indexing Systems, Bountiful, UT, 1980.

__J. B. Landrum, COLONIAL AND REVOLUTIONARY HISTORY OF UPPER SC, Reprint Co., Spartanburg, SC, 1897 (1959).

__C. T. Moore, ABSTRACTS OF THE WILLS OF SC, 1670-1800, Bryan Co., Columbia, SC, 1960-74, 5 volumes.

__C. T. Moore, ABSTRACTS OF RECORDS OF THE SECRETARY OF THE PROVINCE OF SC, 1692-1721, Bryan Co., Columbia, SC, 1978. (Wills, administrations, bonds, bills of sale, powers of attorney.)

__R. P. Morgan, A PRELIMINARY BIBLIOGRAPHY OF SC IMPRINTS, 1731-1800, Clemson University, Clemson, SC, 1966.

__J. Revill, A COMPILATION OF THE ORIGINAL LISTS OF

PROTESTANT IMMIGRANTS TO SC, Genealogical Publishing Co., Baltimore, MD, 1939 (1981).
_A. S. Salley, Jr., ELIGIBILITY LIST OF THE NATIONAL SOCIETY OF THE COLONIAL DAMES IN SC, The Author, Columbia, SC, 1962.
_A. S. Salley, Jr., RECORDS OF THE SECRETARY OF THE PROVINCE AND REGISTER OF THE PROVINCE OF SC, 1671-5, SC Archives, Columbia, SC, 1944.
_A. S. Salley, Jr., and M. L. Webber, DEATH NOTICES IN THE SC GAZETTE, 1732-75, Ethra, Inc., Miami, FL, 1917 (1976).
_SC GENEALOGIES, Reprint Co., Spartanburg, SC, 1984, 5 volumes. (30,000 individuals, 3000 families.)
_SC Historical Society, INDEXES TO THE SC HISTORICAL AND GENEALOGICAL MAGAZINE, The Society, Charleston, SC, index to volumes 1-40, subject index to volumes 1-61, index to volumes 41-71.
_SC TREASURY LEDGERS AND JOURNALS, Microcopy No. 5, SCDA, Columbia, SC, 1973, 4 rolls, index in 1st roll.
_M. B. Warren, CITIZENS AND IMMIGRANTS, 1768, Heritage Papers, Danielsville, GA, 1980.
_M. B. Warren, SC JURY LISTS 1718-83, Heritage Press, Danielsville, GA, 1977.
_F. L. Weis, THE COLONIAL CLERGY OF VA, NC, AND SC, Genealogical Publishing Co., Baltimore, MD, 1976.
_P. H. Wood, BLACK MAJORITY: NEGROES IN COLONIAL SC, 1670 THROUGH THE STONO REBELLION, Knopf, New York, NY, 1974.
_P. Young, EARLY SETTLERS OF SC, The Author, Columbia, SC, 1954.

11. Court records

Among the most unexplored genealogical source materials are the court records of SC. They are often exceptionally valuable, giving information that is often unavailable anywhere else. It is therefore of great importance that you carefully examine all available court records. It is also important for you to remember that there were no local courts of any importance outside of the Charleston region until 1773, and even then, practically all court records were sent to and kept in Charleston until 1781. Further, some courts, most notably equity (or chancery) courts, were not held anyplace other than Charleston until after 1791. In other words, if you are seeking your ancestor in court records anytime prior to 1799 (even as late as 1798), all Charleston court records must be among those which you examine. This is particularly true because when SC courts were spread outside of Charleston (beginning in the 1770s), the process was often so erratic and/or delayed that records may have been kept at the same time in both Charleston and in the local place, or even in a couple of local places.

Now, before we discuss the court records, it will be helpful to you to understand the origin of the SC court system. This is closely related to the somewhat complicated county and district origins discussed in section 11 of the previous chapter. There the generalization is stated: Up until 1785, all the governmental records of SC were kept for the entire colony (state) in Charleston. Essentially no county, district, or regional records were kept during this time (1670-1785) because of the strong centralized governmental structure. The only change needed in these generalizations for court records is that you read "about 1785" instead of "1785".

When the first governor was sent to Carolina in 1670 by the proprietors (owners of the province), he formed a Council composed of eight representatives of the proprietors and of eight freemen of the province. At first, the Governor and his Council exercised all governmental powers, including the judiciary (court activities). By 1682, the Governor had dispersed these powers by appointing a Chief Judge, four other judges, an itinerant judge, and some justices of the peace. The Justices of the Peace (Magistrates) dealt with minor civil and criminal cases. The Chief Judge and the four other judges constituted a County Court (Chief Judge's Court) that sat sometimes as a Court of Pleas (or Common Pleas) dealing with civil matters (persons or private organizations against persons or private organizations) and sometimes sat with the itinerant judge as a Court of Sessions (or General Sessions or Assize Court) dealing with criminal matters (the colony or state against persons or private organizations). The Governor and his Council sometimes sat as a Court of Equity (Chancery) dealing with partitions of land, divisions of estates, slaves, and other property matters; they sometimes sat as a Court of Appeals for cases from the County Court; and they sometimes sat as a Court of Admiralty dealing with affairs of the sea and ships. The Governor sat as a Court of Probate (of Ordinary) dealing with wills, estates, and guardianships. In 1697, the Court of Admiralty was made separate.

When the SC government was transferred to the King from the proprietors in the 1720s, the Royal Colony essentially retained the previous types of courts: Courts of Justices of Peace (Magistrates), Court of Common Pleas, Court of General Sessions, Court of Equity (Chancery), Court of Appeals, Court of Admiralty, and Court of Probate (Ordinary). These have remained the basic courts in SC to the present day. Of course some others were added and some of these were split as time went on and the population increased. Some of these were the County and Intermediate Court, Court of Errors, Court of Appeals in Law, Court of Appeals in Equity, Supreme Court, Municipal Courts, and District Courts. The Court of Admiralty was turned over to US jurisdiction in 1790. We will now discuss what sorts of records courts kept and then we will indicate details of the records which still exist for each major type of court. The main exception will be the Courts of Probate (Ordinary) since they will be treated later in a separate section entitled Wills and Probate Records.

Sometimes you will find <u>indexes</u> to court records, but in the majority of cases, there will be none, or they will be partial or incomplete. Practically every court maintained a <u>docket</u> which was simply a chronological listing of the cases the court heard. A case was entered on the docket when the court agreed to entertain it. When indexes do not exist, the docket can be scanned to see if you can pick up your ancestor's name. Be careful to examine all dockets, since courts often kept several kinds dealing with different sorts of cases. In some instances, you may have the good fortune to discover that the docket is indexed. The next type of record kept by courts is called the <u>minutes</u>, these being brief notes describing the actions of the court in chronological order. These records are usually not indexed, but they are of exceptional value because they can be searched through fairly readily because of their brevity. In many courts, more detailed accounts of the court activities are kept in volumes called <u>journals</u>, and there may also

be other specialized books dealing with specific types of
court actions (judgments, decrees, orders, writs, fines,
opinions, reports, petitions, bills, jury lists, and
others). Finally, there are the case files or papers
which are the original materials which the court
considered as it acted upon the case. These are usually
of exceptional genealogical value because they often have
a great deal of detailed family information in them.
They consist of copies of evidence, testimony, court
proceedings, and other information too voluminous to
record in the minutes, journals, or other volumes.
Information provided in the dockets and/or the minutes
and/or journals, especially the dates on which cases were
heard, will lead you to the papers. Now let us consider
the major courts.

Until 1772, a Court of Common Pleas and a Court of
General Sessions existed only in Charleston. All cases
had to be brought there. In 1769, SC was divided into
seven judicial districts and a Circuit Court (combined
Court of Common Pleas and Court of General Sessions) was
established in each in 1772. The district names (with
the towns where the courts met) were Charleston District
(Charleston), Beaufort District (Beaufort), Georgetown
District (Georgetown), Orangeburg District (Orangeburg),
Camden District (Camden), Cheraws District (Long Bluff),
and Ninety-Six District (Ninety-Six). The Circuit Court
in each district had all the powers of the Courts in
Charleston, both civil and criminal. However, all
records of these Circuit Courts were kept in Charleston,
and other courts (Equity, Appeals, Admiralty, Probate)
continued to be found only in Charleston. In 1785, SC
laid out counties in each of the seven districts,
authorized each to have a Court of Common Pleas and a
Court of General Sessions, or a County and Intermediate
Court and instructed them to keep their own records. The
counties in Charleston, Beaufort, and Georgetown
Districts declined to function, and those in the
Orangeburg District functioned only until about 1791.
Thus, the courts sat and their records were kept at the
district level (as indicated in section 11, Chapter 1)
for Charleston District (1785-99), Beaufort District
(1785-99), Georgetown District (1785-99), and Orangeburg
District (1791-99). In the other districts (Camden,
Cheraws, Ninety-Six) during 1785-99 and in the Orangeburg
District during 1785-91, the courts sat and records were

kept at the county level (see section 11, Chapter 1 for the counties) _and_ at the district level. In 1799/1800, as you will remember (section 11, Chapter 1), the 37 existing counties (some functioning, some not) in the nine _old_, _large_ districts were changed into 25 _new_, _smaller_ districts. Many of these new districts, particularly in the Up Country, were simply re-designated counties (see charts 1-7, section 11, Chapter 1). Each of these 25 new districts got its own Court of Common Pleas and Court of General Sessions, both keeping their own records. As the years went on, the districts split, and each of the resulting districts got these courts and kept their own records. In 1868, the districts were called counties but the courts continued as before.

Records of the _Court of Common Pleas_ and the _Court of General Sessions_ in Charleston apply to the entire colony (state) until 1785. These records are:
_JOURNALS OF THE GRAND COUNCIL, 1671-92, 2 volumes, SCDA, Columbia, SC.
_HIS MAJESTY'S COUNCIL JOURNALS, 1721-74, PAPERS, 1706-53, SCDA, Columbia, SC.
_SC COURT OF COMMON PLEAS JOURNALS, 1713-69, 3 volumes, JUDGMENT ROLLS, 1703-90, 171 file boxes, JUDGMENT BOOKS, 1733-71, 16 volumes, JUDGMENT DOCKETS, 1739-73, 2 volumes, WRITS OF PARTITION, 1749-77, 1 file box and 1 volume, RENUNCIATIONS OF DOWER, 1726-75, 10 volumes, all at SCDA, Columbia, SC.
_SC COURT OF GENERAL SESSIONS JOURNALS, 1796-76, CHARGES TO THE GRAND JURY 1758, 1776, SCDA, Columbia, SC.
Between 1785 and 1800, Courts of Common Pleas and General Sessions were held and records were kept at Charleston for the Charleston District, at Beaufort for the Beaufort District, at Georgetown for the Georgetown District, and in the individual county court houses of the Camden, Cheraws, Ninety-Six, Pinckney, and Pendleton Districts, as well as sometimes in the districts. Courts were held and records were kept in the counties of the Orangeburg District 1785-91, then at Orangeburg for 1791-1800. The district records for this period (1785-1800) which have survived include:
_CHARLESTON DISTRICT IN SC COURT OF COMMON PLEAS ROLLS, 1785-90, latter ones of the 171 file boxes, SCDA, Columbia, SC.
_CAMDEN DISTRICT COURT OF COMMON PLEAS JOURNALS, 1786-99, 2 volumes, MINUTES, 1782-95, 5 volumes,

PLEADINGS AND JUDGMENTS, 1790-98, 4 volumes and 2 microfilms, ABSTRACTS OF JUDGMENTS, 1790-1800, ISSUE DOCKETS, 1794-1800, 3 volumes, TRIAL AND APPEARANCE DOCKETS, 1790-9, APPEARANCES, 1789-99, 2 volumes, ABSTRACT OF DECREES, 1790-1805, 3 volumes, later dates for all of these are in Kershaw County records, SCDA, Columbia, SC.
__PINCKNEY DISTRICT COURT OF COMMON PLEAS, COMMON PLEAS MINUTES, 1792-4, SCDA, Columbia, SC, 1 microfilm roll.
__Pendleton District records included in Anderson County. Among the available county records for this period (1785-1800) are the records of the County and Intermediate Courts of these counties: Chester (1785-8), Edgefield (1785-95), Fairfield (1785-99), Kershaw (1791-9), Marlboro (1785-99), Newberry (1785-98), Pendleton (1790-3), Spartanburg (1785-99), Union (1785-99), Winton (1785-91), and York (1785-98). All of these are available in SCDA as the originals, and all have been published and thus are available in the SCL and many other libraries. These courts were not only minor civil and criminal courts, they also dealt with deeds, wills, probate, licenses, and other matters. After 1800, each district had its own Courts of Common Pleas and General Sessions, as did the counties which succeeded the districts in 1868. The records available in SCDA are listed under the counties in Chapter 4 and others may be sought in the county courthouses (CH).

Prior to 1791, all equity (chancery) matters were handled in the <u>Court</u> <u>of</u> <u>Equity</u> (<u>Chancery</u>) at Charleston. For many of these records, consult
__A. K. Gregorie, RECORDS OF THE COURT OF CHANCERY OF SC, 1671-1799, American Historical Assn., Washington, DC, 1950.
For 1791-9, districts were set up for equity courts: Lower Equity District (Charleston, Beaufort, and Georgetown Districts with the court sitting at Charleston), Middle Equity District (Orangeburg, Camden, and Cheraws Districts with the court sitting at Columbia), Upper Equity District (Ninety-Six, Pinckney, then Washington Districts with the court sitting at Cambridge). For 1799-1808, the equity districts were rearranged: Northern Section of Eastern Equity District (Marion and Georgetown Districts with the court sitting at Charleston), Northern Section of Northern Equity District (Chesterfield, Darlington, and Marlboro

Districts with the court sitting at Greenville), Southern Section of Northern Equity District (Lancaster, Fairfield, Kershaw, Richland, and Sumter Districts with the court sitting at Camden), Eastern Section of the Southern Equity District (Orangeburg and Barnwell Districts with the court sitting at Orangeburg), Western Section of the Southern Equity District (Abbeville, Edgefield, and Pendleton Districts with the court sitting at Abbeville), Northern Section of Western Equity District (Spartanburg, York, Chester, and Union Districts with the court sitting at Union), and Southern Section of the Western Equity District (Greenville, Laurens, and Newberry Districts with the court sitting at Laurens). During 1801-21, the equity districts were as follows: Charleston Equity District (Charleston, Colleton, and Beaufort Districts with the court sitting at Charleston), Georgetown Equity District (Georgetown, Horry, Marion, and Williamsburg Districts with the court sitting at Georgetown), Cheraws Equity District (Chesterfield, Darlington, and Marlboro Districts with the court sitting at Greenville), Camden Equity District (Kershaw, Lancaster, and Sumter Districts with the court sitting at Camden), Pinckney Equity District (Chester, Spartanburg, Union, and York Districts with the court sitting at Union), Washington Equity District (Greenville, Laurens, and Newberry Districts with the court sitting at Laurens), Ninety-Six Equity District (Abbeville, Edgefield, and Pendleton Districts with the court sitting at Abbeville), Columbia Equity District (Fairfield, Richland, and Lexington Districts with the court sitting at Columbia), and Orangeburg Equity District (Orangeburg and Barnwell Districts with the court sitting at Orangeburg). In 1821, all Districts received an Equity Court except for those in the Cheraws Equity District. It was not until later that these Districts got separate Equity Courts. In general, equity (chancery) records should be looked for in the county/district records of the places where the courts sat, but records in other counties/districts in the Equity Districts should not be overlooked.

Numerous actions of local and regional courts were appealed to higher courts. Many of these have been indexed in the following volume:
__WEST'S SC DIGEST, 1783-date, West Publishing Co., St. Paul, MN, volume 20 [Indexes by plaintiff and

defendant.]
Do not fail to look your SC ancestor up in this volume.
It will be found in most law libraries in SC and in
larger law libraries outside the state. The book refers
you to printed detailed descriptions of the cases.
Original records of higher courts in SC will be found in
SCDA and are listed in:
__M. C. Chandler and E. W. Wade, THE SC ARCHIVES: A
SUMMARY GUIDE, SCDA, Columbia, SC, 1985/6.
Also listed in this guide under the appropriate
county/district headings are records of Magistrate's
Courts, Municipal Courts, and a few other courts. Thus,
records of these courts should be ought in SCDA and in
the local CH. Records for the SC Court of Admiralty are
to be found in SCDA:
__JOURNALS OF THE SC COURT OF VICE-ADMIRALTY, 1716-63, 3
microfilm rolls, SCDA, Columbia, SC.
The probate (ordinary) courts will be treated later in a
section entitled Wills and Probate Records.

12. Death records

SC state law required deaths to be registered with
the state beginning in 1915, and compliance was so good
that by 1916 the registrations reached a 90% complete
level. Copies of death certificates may be obtained by
relatives of the deceased from:
__Division of Vital Records, Bureau of Health
Measurement, SC Department of Health and Environmental
Control, 2600 Bull St., Columbia, SC 29201.
A fee is charged for this service. With four exceptions,
no district, county, or city governmentally-collected
death records were kept in SC prior to 1915. The
exceptions are as follows: City of Aiken (1903-15), City
of Charleston (1821-1926), City of Florence (1895-1914),
City of Newberry (late 1800s-1914). The Aiken records
are available at SCDA, the Charleston records at
Charleston County Library (404 King St., Charleston, SC
29403), and the Florence and Newberry records may be
obtained from the respective County Health Departments.
When writing for death records, be sure and give them as
many of the following as you can: full name, sex, race,
names of parents, name of spouse, approximate or exact
death date, approximate or exact place of death, your
relationship to the person, and the reason you want the
record (namely, genealogical research).

Prior to the time when SC required death registation (1915), other records may yield dates and places of death along with other details: Bible, biographical, cemetery, census, church, manuscript, military, mortuary, newspaper, pension, published records, and wills and probate records. These are all discussed in other sections of this chapter. Special attention should be paid to the numerous compilations of death data from newspapers (section 30 of this chapter) and to wills and probate records (section 34, this chapter). The finding of death record articles in genealogical periodicals is also described in a separate section in this chapter. Some of these other sources of death records are listed in:
__J. D. and E. D. Stemmons, THE VITAL RECORDS COMPENDIUM, Everton Publishers, Logan, UT, 1979.
__M. J. Brown, HANDY INDEX TO THE HOLDINGS OF THE GENEALOGICAL SOCIETY OF UT, VOLUME 3: SOUTHERN STATES, Everton Publishers, Logan, UT, 1984.
__R. N. Cote, LOCAL AND FAMILY HISTORY IN SC: A BIBLIOGRAPHY, Southern Historical Press, Easley, SC, 1981.
__J. H. Moore, RESEARCH MATERIALS IN SC, University of SC Press, Columbia, SC, 1967.

13. Divorce records

Since divorce was not legal in SC until 1949, there are essentially no official divorce records before that date. Records of divorces since April, 1949 are in the custody of the Clerk of Court in the county where the divorce was granted. Since July, 1962, duplicate records have been filed with the state, and authorized persons may obtain copies for a fee from:
__Division of Vital Records, Department of Health and Environmental Control, 2600 Bull St., Columbia, SC 29201.
Some divorces which seem to have been granted in 1869-70 during the Reconstruction Period were probably actually only separations.

14. Emigration and immigration

Since SC was one of the thirteen original colonies, many early settlers came in (immigrated) and many of them or their descendants moved out (emigrated) chiefly to the

west and southwest. There are a number of good volumes available which list <u>immigrants</u> to the US. You should consult these volumes because they include both people who came directly to SC and people who came to some other colony or state and then to SC. The first set of volumes is an index to hundreds of ship passenger lists and contains over 900,000 listings. Each listing gives the full name of the immigrant, the names of accompanying relatives, ages, the date and port of arrival, and the source of the information. These volumes are:
_P. W. Filby and M. K. Meyer, PASSENGER AND IMMIGRATION LISTS INDEX, Gale Research Co., Detroit, MI, 1981, 1982, 1984, 5 volumes.

Also of imortance for locating passenger lists are:
_H. Lancour, R. J. Wolfe, and P. W. Filby, BIBLIOGRAPHY OF SHIP PASSENGER LISTS, 1538-1900, Gale Research Co., Detroit, MI, 1981.
_US National Archives and Records Service, GUIDE TO GENEALOGICAL RESEARCH IN THE NATIONAL ARCHIVES, The Service, Washington, DC, 1982, pp. 41-57. [Refers to National Archives, CUSTOMS PASSENGER LISTS, CHARLESTON (1820-28), PORT ROYAL (1865), Microfilm M575, and STATE DEPARTMENT TRANSCRIPT OF IMMIGRATION PASSENGER LISTS, CHARLESTON (1820-29), with INDEX, Microfilm M334.]

A very important work for SC immigration and emigration is one which describes the migration routes and patterns into, out of, and within the state:
_M. W. Lewis, THE DEVELOPMENT OF EARLY IMMIGRANT TRAILS IN THE US EAST OF THE MS RIVER, National Genealogical Society, Washington, DC, 1962.

Then you can look into some works dealing exclusively with <u>immigration</u> to SC. Among these are:
_L. Andrea, IMMIGRANTS FROM GREAT BRITAIN TO SC, 1763-73, SCL, Columbia, SC, 1974.
_A. L. Baldwin, THE FIRST SETTLERS OF SC, 1670-80, University of SC Press, Columbia, SC, 1969.
_L. E. Ivers, COLONIAL FORTS IN SC, 1670-1775, GA Genealogical Society Quarterly, Vol. 7, No. 1, p. 88.
_H. B. Johnston, NORTH CAROLINIANS TO SC, GA Genealogical Magazine, No. 40, p. 191.
_R. L. Meriwether, THE EXPANSION OF SC, 1729-65, Southern Publishers, Kingsport, TN, 1940.
_NATURALIZATION REGISTER OF SC, 1792-1800, National Genealogical Quarterly, Vol. 30, p. 125.

__M. L. Pettus, EUROPEAN IMMIGRATION TO SC, 1881-1908, MA Thesis, University of SC, Columbia, SC, 1954.
__D. Ramsey, THE HISTORY OF SC FROM ITS FIRST SETTLEMENT IN 1670 TO THE YEAR 1808, Heritage Series, Newberry, SC, 1858.
__A. S. Salley, NARRATIVES OF EARLY CAROLINA, 1650-1708, Barnes and Noble, New York, NY, 1911 (1967).
__W. R. Smith, SC AS A ROYAL PROVINCE, 1719-76, Macmillan, New York, NY, 1903.
__SC NATURALIZATIONS, Microfilm, University of GA Library, Athens, GA.
__M. B. Warren, CITIZENS AND IMMIGRANTS, SC, 1768, Heritage Papers, Danielsville, GA, 1980.
__P. Young, EARLY SETTLERS OF SC, The Author, Columbia, SC, 1954.
Additional source materials will be found in the next section as well as in the books by Miller and Cote mentioned at the end of this section.

In addition to works on immigration, there are also several volumes on _emigration_, that is, movements out of SC to settle areas to the west and southwest. Among those which might help you in your search for a migratory SC progenitor are:
__W. W. Lynch, THE WESTWARD FLOW OF SOUTHERN COLONISTS BEFORE 1861, Journal of Southern History, Vol. 9, 1943, pp. 313-27.
__R. L. Meriwether, THE EXPANSION OF SC, 1729-65, Southern Publishers, Kingsport, TN, 1940.
__A. Pitts, EMIGRATION FROM SC, 1820-50, Manuscript in Coker College Library, Hartsville, SC, no date.
__J. C. Pruitt, MIGRATIONS OF SOUTH CAROLINIANS ON NATCHEZ TRACE, The Author, Fairfax, VA, 1949.
__C. H. Robertson, KS TERRITORIAL SETTLERS OF 1860 WHO WERE BORN IN TN, VA, NC, AND SC, Genealogical Publishing Co., Baltimore, MD, 1976.
__LIST OF PIONEERS WHO MOVED FROM OLD NINETY-SIX DISTRICT, SC, 1780-1850, TO GA AND AL, Microfilm No. 27409, Pt. 7, Genealogical Society of UT Library, Salt Lake City, UT.
Other materials on emigration and immigration relating to SC may be found in:
__O. K. Miller, MIGRATION, EMIGRATION, IMMIGRATION, Everton Publishers, Logan, UT, 1974, 1981, 2 volumes.
__R. N. Cote, LOCAL AND FAMILY HISTORY IN SC: A BIBLIOGRAPHY, Southern Historical Press, Easley, SC,

1981, pp. 13-47.
The above books are almost all in SCL, some are in RL, LGL, and LL, and many are in GSU, thus being obtainable through BLGSU.

15. Ethnic records

   In addition to the English, many other ethnic groups were involved quite early in the settlement of SC, as Chapter 1 indicated. Since most of these groups adhered to particular religious affiliations, many publications relating to them need to be sought among church records and histories. Instructions for locating these were presented in section 7 of this chapter. Among the larger ethnic groups were the French Hugenots (1680-6), Quakers (1680), the Scottish (1684), the German-Swiss (1732-5), the Irish (1732), the German (1734), the Welsh (1736), and later Scotch-Irish, Catholics, and Jews. A succinct outline history of the major ethnic group settlement is provided in:
__E. K. Kirkham, A GENEALOGICAL AND HISTORICAL ATLAS OF THE USA, Watkins and Sons, Providence, UT, 1980.
Among the useful volumes relating to these groups are:
__G. D. Bernheim, HISTORY OF THE GERMAN SETTLEMENTS AND OF THE LUTHERAN CHURCH IN NC AND SC, Reprint Co., Spartanburg, SC, 1872 (1972).
__K. L. Carroll, JOSEPH NICHOLS AND THE NICHOLITES: THE NEW QUAKERS OF MD, DE, NORTH AND SC, Easton, MD, 1962.
__H. A. Davis, SOME HUGENOT FAMILIES OF SC AND GA, Washington, DC, 1926.
__B. A. Elzas, THE JEWS OF SC, FROM THE EARLIEST TIMES TO THE PRESENT DAY, Reprint Co., Spartanburg, SC, 1972.
__G. J. Gongaware, THE HISTORY OF THE GERMAN FRIENDLY SOCIETY OF CHARLESTON, 1766-1916, Garrett and Massie, Richmond, VA, 1935.
__A. H. Hirsch, THE HUGENOTS OF COLONIAL SC, Archon Books, Hamden, CT, 1962.
__G. Howe, THE SCOTCH-IRISH AND THEIR FIRST SETTLEMENTS IN SC, Southern Guardian Steam Power Press, Columbia, SC, 1861.
__D. Ravenel, LISTE DES FRANCOIS ET SUISSES, Genealogical Publishing Co., Baltimore, MD, 1888 (1968). [List of French and Swiss Protestant settlers on Santee River and in Orange Quarter who sought naturalization.]
__J. Revill, A COMPILATION OF THE ORIGINAL LISTS OF PROTESTANT IMMIGRANTS TO SC, 1768-73, Genealogical

Publishing Co., Baltimore, MD, 1939 (1974).
__J. Revill, LIST OF IRISH IMMIGRANTS WHO CAME TO SC IN 1768, Columbia, SC, 1937.
__SC GERMAN PROTESTANTS, 1788, SC Historical and Genealogical Magazine, Volume 47, pp. 195-204.
__J. Stephenson, SCOTCH-IRISH MIGRATION TO SC, 1772, Hotaling, Vienna, VA, 1971.
Other useful records will be found listed in:
__O. K. Miller, MIGRATION, EMIGRATION, IMMIGRATION, Everton Publishers, Logan, UT, 1974, 1981, 2 volumes.
The Indians of SC constituted a notable ethnic group. There are a number of federal, state, and county records which are pertinent to genealogical searchers. These records are described or referenced in:
__National Archives and Records Service, GUIDE TO GENEALOGICAL RESEARCH IN THE NATIONAL ARCHIVES, The Service, Washington, DC, 1982, Chapter 11, pp. 159-170.
__E. E. Hill, GUIDE TO RECORDS IN THE NATIONAL ARCHIVES RELATING TO AMERICAN INDIANS, National Archives and Records Service, Washington, DC, 1982.
__R. N. Cote, LOCAL AND FAMILY HISTORY IN SC: A BIBLIOGRAPHY, Southern Historical Press, Easley, SC, 1981.
__J. H. Moore, RESEARCH MATERIALS IN SC, University of SC Press, Columbia, SC, 1967.
__M. C. Chandler and E. W. Wade, THE SC ARCHIVES: A SUMMARY GUIDE, SCDA, Columbia, SC, 1985/6.

The blacks of SC constitute another important ethnic group. Again there are sizable federal, state, county, and private records which are especially pertinent to blacks. Details and/or listings of many of these records are given in the following:
__National Archives and Records Service, GUIDE TO GENEALOGICAL RESEARCH IN THE NATIONAL ARCHIVES, The Service, Washington, DC, 1982, Chapter 12, pp. 173-185.
__The three books by Cote, Moore, and Chandler and Wade mentioned in the previous paragraph.

16. Gazetteers, atlases, and maps

Detailed information regarding SC geography is exceptionally useful to the genealogical searcher, especially with regard to land records. They usually mention locations in terms requiring an understanding of local geographical features. Several sorts of geographical aids are useful in this regard: gazetteers, atlases, and maps. Gazetteers are volumes which list geographical features (towns, villages, crossroads, settlements, districts, rivers, streams, creeks, hills, mountains, valleys, coves, lakes, ponds), locate them, and sometimes give a few details concerning them. An atlas is a collection of maps in book form. Among the better gazetteer-type materials for SC are:

__M. Cropper, SC WATERWAYS, Accelerated Indexing Systems, Bountiful, UT, 1977. [Index to waterways in Mill's ATLAS to be mentioned below.]

__C. N. Neuffer, NAMES IN SC, University of SC, Columbia, SC, Volumes 1-, 1959-, continuing series with indexes. [Over 15,000 place and family names.]

__Works Progress Administration, PALMETTO PLACE NAMES, Reprint Co., Spartanburg, SC, 1941 (1975).

__W. G. Simms, THE GEOGRAPHY OF SC, Babcock, Charleston, SC, 1843.

__SCDA Staff, LOOSE-LEAF GAZETTEER, SCDA, Columbia, SC. Lists rivers, streams, creeks, places, also an alphabetical listing of the places in Mill's 1825 ATLAS.

A useful atlas for early nineteenth-century SC, the contents of which are broadly applicable to earlier and later years, is:

__R. Mills, ATLAS OF THE STATE OF SC, Bostick and Thornley, Columbia, SC, 1825 (1938). [39 maps, name and place index.]

A very useful set of maps outlining census districts and/or counties for every ten years 1790-1920 is available:

__W. Thorndale and W. Dollarhide, MAP GUIDE TO THE US FEDERAL CENSUS OF SC, 1790-1920, Dollarhide Systems, Bellingham, WA, 1984.

There are several books which list SC maps and indicate sources of them or which give descriptions of map collections:

__W. P. Cumming, THE SOUTHEAST IN EARLY MAPS, University of NC Press, Chapel Hill, NC, 1958.

__L. C. Karpinski, EARLY MAPS OF CAROLINA AND ADJOINING REGIONS, Carolina Art Association, Charleston, SC, 1937.

__National Archives and Records Service, GUIDE TO CARTOGRAPHIC RECORDS IN THE NATIONAL ARCHIVES, The Service, Washington, DC, 1971.

__J. J. Petty, A BIBLIOGRAPHY OF THE GEOGRAPHY OF THE STATE OF SC, University of SC, Columbia, SC, 1952.
__P. Smith, EARLY MAPS OF CAROLINA AND ADJOINING REGIONS, University of SC, Columbia, SC, 1930.
__SC LAND GRANT MAPS, 1752-66, 1786-1820, Union County Historical Foundation, Union, SC, 1979.
__J. R. Hebert, PANORAMIC MAPS OF ANGLO-AMERICAN CITIES IN THE LIBRARY OF CONGRESS, The Library, Washington, DC, 1974. [Maps available for Charleston (1872) and Columbia (1872).]
__R. W. Stephenson, LAND OWNERSHIP MAPS IN THE LIBRARY OF CONGRESS, The Library, Washington, DC, 1967. [County maps which show names of owners on their land: Abbeville (1895), Anderson (1877), Beaufort (1873), Dorchester (1900), Fairfield (1876), Greenville (1882), Laurens (1883), Marion (1882), Newberry (1887), Richland (1897).]
__National Archives and Records Service, GUIDE TO GENEALOGICAL RESEARCH IN THE NATIONAL ARCHIVES, The Service, Washington, DC, 1982, pp. 255-262.
__Library of Congress, FIRE INSURANCE MAPS IN THE LIBRARY OF CONGRESS, The Library, Washington, DC, 1981, pp. 580-6. [Maps in SCL.]

Several sources of detailed maps of SC counties can provide you with excellent assistance as you attempt to locate your progenitor's land and as you look for streams, roads, bridges, churches, cemeteries, towns, and villages in the vicinity. The _first_ of these sources is the US Geological Survey, which has mapped the whole state of SC and has issued a series of hundreds of detailed maps. These maps are available at very reasonable cost. Write the following address and ask for the Index to Topographic Maps of SC and a Map Order Form:
__Branch of Distribution, Eastern Region, US Geological Survey, 1200 South Eads St., Arlington, VA 22202.
Another source is the SC Department of Highways. They have published highway maps of the SC counties, and these are available for purchase from:
__Map Sales, SC Department of Highways and Public Transportation, 955 Park St., Box 191, Columbia, SC 29202.

The two best collections for genealogically-related maps of SC are SCDA and SCL. SCDA has over 3000 maps, 25% of them being pre-1800, and 50% dating 1800-99. SCL has over 1500 maps, 23% being pre-1800, and 33% dating 1800-99. Other notable SC map collections are to be found in the Library of Clemson University, Clemson, SC 29631, in the Department of Geography, Geography Map Depository, Columbia, SC 29208, in the Map Library, Byrnes International Center, University of SC, Columbia, SC 29208, and at the SC State Development Board, Division of Geology, Harbison Forest Rd., Columbia, SC 29210. Most of the volumes mentioned in this section are available in SCL, and some may be found in SCHS, RL, LGL, GSU, and through BLGSU.

An utterly invaluable set of maps which is of exceptional help in interpreting SC place locations during the period 1790-1920 has already been mentioned under section 6. These maps give the census enumeration subdivisions and clearly show land locations for those listed in the census schedules:
_W. Thorndale and W. Dollarhide, MAP GUIDE TO THE US FEDERAL CENSUSES, SC, 1790-1920, Dollarhide Systems, Bellingham, WA, 1984.

17. <u>Genealogical indexes for SC</u>

There are a number of genealogical indexes for the colony and state of SC which list very large numbers of names. These are of considerable utility because they may save you going through many small volumes and detailed records as you search for your SC forebears:
_CENSUS INDEXES FOR SC, 1768, 1790, 1800, 1810, 1820, 1830, 1840, 1850, 1860, 1880, 1900, 1910 (see section 6, this chapter).
_COMBINED ALPHABETICAL INDEX, SCDA, Columbia, SC.
_SURNAME INDEX and INTERNATIONAL GENEALOGICAL INDEX at GSU, Salt Lake City, UT, and BLGSU (see section on GSU in Chapter 3).
_FAMILY GROUP RECORDS ARCHIVES, TEMPLE RECORDS INDEX BUREAU, and FAMILY REGISTER, GSU, Salt Lake City, UT.
_BOOK DIVISION CARD CATALOG and MANUSCRIPTS DIVISION CARD CATALOG, SCL, Columbia, SC.
_PUBLICATIONS CARD CATALOG, MANUSCRIPTS CARD CATALOG, and WPA TOMBSTONE INDEX, SCHS, Charleston, SC.
_US War Department, GENERAL INDEX TO COMPILED MILITARY SERVICE RECORDS OF REVOLUTIONARY WAR SOLDIERS, SAILORS, AND MEMBERS OF ARMY STAFF DEPARTMENTS, The National Archives, Washington, DC, Microfilm Publication M860,

58 rolls.
___US War Department, INDEX TO COMPILED SERVICE RECORDS OF CONFEDERATE ARMY VOLUNTEERS FROM SC, The National Archives, Washington, DC, Microfilm Publication M381, 35 rolls.
___F. Rider, AMERICAN GENEALOGICAL-BIOGRAPHICAL INDEX, Godfrey Memorial Library, Middletown, CT, 1942-52, 1st series, 48 volumes; new series, in progress, over 130 volumes so far.
___P. W. Filby and M. K. Meyer, PASSENGERS AND IMMIGRATION LISTS INDEX, Gale Research Co., Detroit, MI, 1981-4, 6 volumes.
___W. M. Clemens, NORTH AND SC MARRIAGE RECORDS, Genealogical Publishing Co., Baltimore, MD, 1977.
___G. L. C. Hendrix and M. M. Lindsay, THE JURY LISTS OF SC, 1778-9, Genealogical Publishing Co., Baltimore, MD 1980.
___G. L. C. Hendrix, M. M. Lindsay, and others, SC LINEAGE CHARTS, SC Genealogical Society, Greenville Chapter, Greenville, SC, 1976-80, 5 volumes.
___B. H. Holcomb, PROBATE RECORDS OF SC, Southern Historical Press, Easley, SC, 1977-9 (1981), 3 volumes.
___B. H. Holcomb, SC MARRIAGES, 1688-1799, Genealogical Publishing Co., Baltimore, MD, 1980.
___M. L. Houston, INDEXES TO THE COUNTY WILLS OF SC, 1766-1853, Genealogical Publishing Co., Baltimore, MD, 1939 (1970).
___S. E. Lucas, Jr., AN INDEX TO THE DEEDS OF THE PROVINCE AND STATE OF SC, 1719-85, AND CHARLESTON DISTRICT, 1785-1800, Southern Historical Press, Easley, SC, 1977 (1980).
___C. T. Moore and A. A. Simmons, ABSTRACTS OF THE WILLS, STATE OF SC, 1670-1800, The Author, Charleston, SC, 1960-78, 5 volumes.
___B. Moss, ROSTER OF SC PATRIOTS IN THE AMERICAN REVOLUTION, Genealogical Publishing Co., Baltimore, MD, 1983.
___J. Revill, SC WILLS, 1672-1730, The Author, Sumter, SC, 1939.
___SC HISTORICAL AND GENEALOGICAL MAGAZINE, CONSOLIDATED INDEXES, VOLUMES 1-71, The Society, Charleston, SC, 1900-.
___J. E. Wooley, A COLLECTION OF UPPER SC GENEALOGICAL AND FAMILY RECORDS, Southern Historical Press, Easley, SC, 1980-, several volumes.
___R. N. Cote, LOCAL AND FAMILY HISTORY IN SC, Southern

Historical Press, Easley, SC, 1981, pp. 421-98.
_A. H. Stokes, A GUIDE TO THE MANUSCRIPT COLLECTION OF THE SOUTH CAROLINIANA LIBRARY, University of SC, Columbia, SC, 1982.
The published works mentioned above will be found in SCL and SCHS. Many of them are in GSU (thus available through BLGSU), LGL, and RL.

18. Genealogical periodicals

Several genealogical periodicals and history periodicals carrying some genealogical data have been or are being published for SC. These journals or newsletters contain genealogies, local histories, genealogical records, family queries and answers, book reviews, and other pertinent information. If you had a SC progenitor, you will find it of great value to subscribe to one or more of the state-wide periodicals, as well as any periodicals published in the region or county where he/she lived. The major SC genealogical periodicals include:
_BULLETIN OF THE CHESTER COUNTY GENEALOGICAL SOCIETY, The Society, Richburg, SC, 1978-, quarterly.
_BULLETIN OF THE DARLINGTON COUNTY HISTORICAL SOCIETY, The Society, Darlington, SC, irregular.
_BULLETIN OF THE NEWBERRY COUNTY GENEALOGICAL SOCIETY, The Society, Newberry, SC, 1970-, semiannual.
_CAROLINA HERALD, SC Genealogical Society, Columbia, SC, 1972-, quarterly.
_CAROLINA GENEALOGIST, Heritage Papers, Danielsville, GA, 1970-, quarterly.
_CAROLINAS GENEALOGICAL SOCIETY BULLETIN, Carolinas Genealogical Society, Monroe, NC, 1974-, three times each year.
_GA GENEALOGICAL MAGAZINE, Southern Historical Press, Easley, SC, 1961-, quarterly. [Much SC material.]
_GA GENEALOGIST, Heritage Papers, Danielsville, GA, 1969-, quarterly.
_INDEPENDENT REPUBLIC QUARTERLY, Horry County Historical Society, Conway, SC, 1967-, quarterly.
_LEXINGTON GENEALOGICAL EXCHANGE, Lexington County Genealogical Association, Lexington, SC.
_NEWSLETTER OF THE SC GENEALOGICAL SOCIETY, The Society, Charleston, SC, 1972-.
_ORANGEBURG HISTORICAL AND GENEALOGICAL RECORD, Orangeburg County Historical and Genealogical Register,

Orangeburg, SC, 1969-, quarterly.
__PEE DEE QUEUE, Pee Dee Chapter, SC Genealogical Society, Marion, SC, 1977-, monthly.
__PIEDMONT HISTORICAL SOCIETY QUARTERLY, The Society, Spartanburg, SC, quarterly.
__SC AND ITS PEOPLE, edited by P. Young, Liberty, SC, 1952-4, 3 volumes.
__SC GENEALOGICAL REGISTER, Epes, AL, 1963-, quarterly.
__SC HISTORICAL MAGAZINE, formerly SC HISTORICAL AND GENEALOGICAL MAGAZINE, SCHS, Charleston, SC, 1900-, quarterly.
__SC MAGAZINE OF ANCESTRAL RESEARCH, A Press, Greenville, SC, 1973-, quarterly.
__SOUTHERN ECHOES, Augusta Genealogical Society, Augusta, GA, 1979-, quarterly. [Much SC material.]
__TRANSACTIONS OF THE HUGENOT SOCIETY OF SC, The Society, Charleston, SC, 1889-, annual.

The above periodicals will be found in SCL and SCHS. Many of them are in LGL and RL, some in GSU (and thus through BLGSU), and those for local areas are in LL. Other journals, transactions, newsletters, and periodic publications of SC organizations are listed in:
__R. N. Cote, LOCAL AND FAMILY HISTORY IN SC, Southern Historical Press, Easley, SC, 1981.

Not only do articles pertaining to SC genealogy appear in the above publications, they are also printed in other genealogical periodicals. Fortunately, indexes to major genealogical journals are available:
__For periodicals published 1858-1952, consult D. L. Jacobus, INDEX TO GENEALOGICAL PERIODICALS, Genealogical Publishing Co., Baltimore, MD, 1973.
__For periodicals published 1957-62, consult the annual volumes by I. Waldenmaier, ANNUAL INDEX TO GENEALOGICAL PERIODICALS AND FAMILY HISTORIES, The Author, Washington, DC, 1957-8-9-60-1-2.
__For periodicals published 1962-9 and 1974-80, consult the annual volumes by various editors, E. S. Rogers, G. E. Russell, L. C. Towle, and C. M. Mayhew, GENEALOGICAL PERIODICAL ANNUAL INDEX, various publishers, most recently Heritage Books, Bowie, MD, 1962-3-4-5-6-7-8-9, 1974-5-6-7-8-9-80.

These index volumes will be found in SCL, and GSU (available through BLGSU), most LGL, some RL, and a few LL. In them, you should consult all general SC listings, then all listings under the counties and/or districts which concern you, as well as listings under family names (if included in the indexes).

19. Genealogical societies

In the state of SC various societies for the study of genealogy, the discovery of hereditary lineages, the accumulation of data, and the publication of the materials have been organized. Among the state-wide organizations are:

__SC GENEALOGICAL SOCIETY, PO Box 2266, Charleston, SC 29403.
__HUGENOT SOCIETY OF SC, 25 Chalmers St., Charleston, SC 29401.
__SOCIETY OF FIRST FAMILIES OF SC, PO Box 30153, Charleston, SC 29417.
__SONS OF CONFEDERATE VETERANS, FT. SUMTER CAMP, 8 Legare St., Charleston, SC 29401.
__SC SOCIETY COLONIAL DAMES XVII CENTURY, 124 Dunbarton Cr., Aiken, SC 29801.
__NATIONAL SOCIETY OF THE COLONIAL DAMES OF AMERICA IN SC, 79 Cumberland St., Charleston, SC 29401.
__SC STATE SOCIETY, NATIONAL SOCIETY DAUGHTERS OF THE AMERICAN COLONISTS, 235 Shareditch Rd., Columbia, SC 29210.
__SC SOCIETY, SONS OF THE AMERICAN REVOLUTION, 2102 Forest Dr., Camden, SC 29020.
__NATIONAL SOCIETY DAUGHTERS OF THE AMERICAN REVOLUTION, 104 Sandy Creek Ct., Greer, SC 29651.

There are also genealogical societies whose interests are more local, most usually county-wide. Some of the organizations publish regular journals or newsletters containing data they have gathered, queries from their members, book reviews, and items of general interest. The members of regional and local societies are generally well informed about the genealogical resources of their regions, and often can offer considerable help to non-residents who had progenitors in the area. Among the major regional and county genealogical societies are:

__CHARLESTON CHAPTER, SC Genealogical Society, PO Box 2266, Charleston, SC 29403.
__COLUMBIA CHAPTER, SC Genealogical Society, PO Box 11353, Columbia, SC 29211.
__GREENVILLE CHAPTER, SC Genealogical Society, PO Box

16236, Greenville, SC 29606.
__GREENWOOD CHAPTER, SC Genealogical Society, 243 Dogwood Dr., Greenwood, SC 29646.
__PEE DEE CHAPTER, SC Genealogical Society, 829 N. Main St., Marion, SC 29571.
__PENDLETON CHAPTER, SC Genealogical Society, PO Box 1406, Clemson, SC 29631.
__PINCKNEY CHAPTER, SC Genealogical Society, 2352 Bruce Ave., Spartanburg, SC 29302.
__SUMTER CHAPTER, SC Genealogical Society, PO Box 2543, Sumter, SC 29150.
__CHESTER COUNTY GENEALOGICAL SOCIETY, PO Box 336, Richburg, SC 29729.
__HILTON HEAD ISLAND GENEALOGICAL SOCIETY, 10 Pelican Rd., Hilton Head Island, SC 29928.
__LEXINGTON COUNTY GENEALOGICAL ASSOCIATION, PO Box 1442, Lexington, SC 29072.
__ORANGEBURG HISTORICAL AND GENEALOGICAL SOCIETY, Route 1, Box 1069-C, Orangeburg, SC 29115.

It is advisable for you to join the SC GENEALOGICAL SOCIETY as well as any regional and/or county organization which is in your ancestor's area. All correspondence with such societies should be accompanied by an SASE.

20. Historical societies

In addition to genealogical societies, SC has numerous historical societies. Some of these organizations, but not all, deal with genealogical interests in addition to their historical pursuits. Even if they do not do much genealogical work as such, their efforts will be of considerable interest to you, since they deal with the historical circumstances through which your ancestor lived. It is often well for you to dispatch an SASE and an inquiry to one or more asking about membership, genealogical interests if any, and publications. Every one of the 46 SC counties has at least one historical organization (association, commission, foundation, society), most having more than one. These are listed in the following publication which also gives their addresses and their officers:
__SCDA, 1984 DIRECTORY SC HISTORICAL ORGANIZATIONS, SCDA, Columbia, SC, 1984.

21. **Land records**

One of the most important types of SC genealogical records is that type that deals with land. This is because SC throughout most of its history has been predominantly an agricultural state with its population largely rural. In addition, land up to the present century was widely available and quite inexpensive. This means that many South Carolinians owned land and therefore their names appear in land records. The only caution that needs to be exercised here is to remember that SC had numerous large plantations worked by laborers who did not own the land, and thus whose names will not turn up on land ownership records. There are basically three types of land records in SC. (1) The _first_ kind involves the transactions by which the government originally transferred the land to its first private owner. These transactions made use of documents and records called petitions or applications for land, warrants or precepts, plats or surveys, and grants. (2) The _second_ kind of land records are those by which one private owner transferred the land to another private owner. These transactions were evidenced by documents and records called deeds (conveyances) and mortgages. (3) The _third_ kind of land records are memorials, a type unique to SC. They will be discussed at the end of this section.

The _first_ category of land records (transfers from the proprietary, colonial, or state government to the first private owner) dates from 1670. In the period 1670-1719, the proprietors granted land, then the royal colony granted land until 1776, then the state from 1776 to the present. The steps in the granting process usually involved these steps. (1) The person desiring land made a petition or application for the piece of property he wanted. (2) The land officer then issued a warrant, which was an order to the surveyor to survey the land and describe it with a small map called a plat. (3) The plat was then recorded. (4) And finally, a grant for the land was given to the new owner with a copy being recorded. In SC's earlier days, many grants were awarded to men and their families, 50 acres being given for the man and 50 acres for each dependent, including slaves. SC also awarded headright grants in which land was given to persons who paid transportation costs for people brought over from Europe. The allotment was 50 acres per person (or head).

The land grants are in SCDA and microfilm copies of them are at SCDA, and GSU and thus available through BLGSU. Included are:
__Secretary of State, LAND GRANTS, COLONIAL SERIES, 1731-76, SCDA, Columbia, SC, 56 volumes, indexed.*
__Secretary of State, LAND GRANTS, COLONIAL SERIES, COPIES, 1694-1776, SCDA, Columbia, SC, 43 volumes, indexed.*
__Secretary of State, TOWNSHIP GRANTS, 1735-62, SCDA, Columbia, SC, indexed.*
__Secretary of State, TOWN LOT GRANTS, 1735-75, SCDA, Columbia, SC, indexed.*
__Grand Council of SC, GRAND COUNCIL JOURNAL, 1671-80, SCDA, Columbia, SC, 1 volume.
__His Majesty's Council of SC, JOURNALS OF HIS MAJESTY'S COUNCIL, 1721-74, SCDA, Columbia, SC, 27 volumes.
__Secretary of State, LAND GRANTS, CHARLESTON SERIES, 1st Series (1784-1841, 40 volumes), 2nd Series (1790-1820, 38 volumes), 3rd Series (1822-45, 9 volumes), SCDA, Columbia, SC, indexed.
__Secretary of State, LAND GRANTS, COLUMBIA SERIES, 1st Series (1784-1821, 77 volumes), 2nd Series (1822-45, 9 volumes), 3rd Series (1841-82, 7 volumes), 4th Series (1884-1936, 1 volume), SCDA, Columbia, SC, indexed.

There are also some important publications that refer to land grants which you should search thoroughly:
__B. H. Holcomb, NC LAND GRANTS IN SC, 1745-73, A Press, Greenville, SC, 1980.
__R. V. Jackson, INDEX TO SC LAND GRANTS, 1784-1800, Accelerated Indexing Systems, Bountiful, UT, 1977.
__A. S. Salley, Jr., and R. N. Olsberg, WARRANTS FOR LANDS IN SC, 1672-1711, University of SC Press, Columbia, SC, 1910-15 (1973).
__A. S. Salley, Jr., JOURNAL OF THE GRAND COUNCIL OF SC, 1671-80, 1692, Historical Commission of SC, Columbia, SC, 1907, 2 volumes.
__C. N. Smith, COLONIAL LAND GRANTS IN THE CAROLINAS, Westland Publications, McNeal, AZ, 1981.

In addition to the land grant records, there are also many plat records in the SCDA. Quite a number of these have been microfilmed and are available at SCDA, and GSU and therefore through BLGSU.

__Office of the Surveyor General, COLONIAL PLATS, DUPLICATES, 1731-75, SCDA, Columbia, SC, 78 file boxes.
__Office of the Surveyor General, COLONIAL PLATS, RECORDED COPIES, 1731-75, SCDA, Columbia, SC, 21 volumes, indexed.*
__Office of the Surveyor General, COLONIAL PLATS, COPIES, 1731-75, SCDA, Columbia, SC, 22 volumes, indexed.*
__His Majesty´S Council of SC, JOURNALS OF HIS MAJESTY´S COUNCIL, 1721-74, SCDA, Columbia, SC, 27 volumes. To be used in conjunction with the above plat records.
__Office of the Surveyor General, STATE PLATS, 1st Series (1784-1847, 43 volumes), 2nd Series (1796-1840, 17 volumes), 3rd Series (1840-82, 7 volumes), 4th Series (1878-1932, 3 volumes), SCDA, Columbia, SC.
__Office of the Surveyor General, UNRECORDED PLATS FOR LAND NOT GRANTED, 1730-1855, SCDA, Columbia, SC, indexed.*

The major colonial grants and plats are indexed in a very large and very useful finding aid in SCDA. Those included in this index are marked with an asterisk * in this paragraph and the preceding paragraph. If your ancestor lived in the colonial period, this index should be examined first, and only afterwards should the other records be looked into.
__COMBINED ALPHABETICAL INDEX, SCDA, Columbia, SC.

The <u>second</u> category of land records (transfers between individual private persons or groups) consists of deeds and mortgages. In SC, these transactions are usually referred to as conveyances (conveying land from one owner to another) or as mesne (pronounced "mean") conveyances. Until 1785 all deeds (conveyances) were recorded in Charleston. After that they began to be recorded in districts or counties, as described in section 11, Chapter 1. As you seek conveyance (deed) records after 1785, especially in the difficult period 1785-1810, careful attention needs to be paid to the descriptions and charts of section 11, Chapter 1. One of the safest approaches is to search out the records of Charleston District, the district of your ancestor´s residence, neighboring districts, the county of your ancestor´s residence, and neighboring counties during 1785-1810. In the SCDA are early conveyance records, as well as mortgage records from 1736 forward:
__Register of the Province, CONVEYANCES, 1694-1712, SCDA, Columbia, SC, 4 volumes.

__Secretary of State, MORTGAGES, CHARLESTON SERIES, 1736-1867, SCDA, Columbia, SC, 53 volumes, indexed. Those volumes after 1785 apply only to the Charleston District.

The original conveyance (deed, mortgage, lease, plat) records for all of SC during 1719-85 are in one series of volumes located in the Office of the Register of Mesne Conveyances in Charleston (County Office Building, 2 Court House Square, Room 201, Charleston, SC 29401). There are also indexes to grantors for deeds and mortgages (1719-), and a separate index to plats (1742-). Microfilm copies of these are available at SCDA, GSU, and through BLGSU.

__Register of Mesne Conveyance, SC LAND RECORDS (Deeds, Mortgages, Leases, Plats), 1719-1881, Charleston County, Charleston, SC. Only records through 1785 are state-wide. Microfilm copy in SCDA.

__Register of Mesne Conveyance, DIRECT INDEXES TO DEEDS AND MORTGAGES, 1719-1800, Charleston County, Charleston, SC. Microfilm copy in SCDA.

__Register of Mesne Conveyance, PLAT INDEX, 1800-1881 [actually 1742-1881], Charleston County, Charleston, SC. Microfilm copy in SCDA.

Access to many of these records is made easy through the use of several published volumes:

__S. E. Lucas, Jr. and B. H. Holcomb, AN INDEX TO THE DEEDS OF THE PROVINCE AND STATE OF SC, 1719-85, AND CHARLESTON DISTRICT, 1785-1800, Southern Historical Press, Easley, SC, 1977.

__C. B. Langley, SC DEED ABSTRACTS, 1719-72, Southern Historical Press, Easley, SC, 1983-4, 4 volumes.

After 1785, as we have mentioned above, deeds, mortgages, and other conveyance records were recorded in the appropriate districts or counties. In Chapter 4, the available records for each county/district will be listed.

There is a _third_ intriguing type of land record which is unique to SC. These records are known as land memorials. A land memorial is a document which traces the history of a piece of land back through each owner to the person who originally was granted the land by the colony or state. The original records are in SCDA:

__Auditor General, MEMORIAL BOOKS, 1731-75, SCDA, Columbia, SC, 16 volumes, indexed.*

A published work and microfilm copies of these records

are also available:
- K.-P. W. Esker, SC MEMORIALS, 1731-76, Polyanthos, Cottonport, LA, 1977, 2 volumes.
- SCDA, MEMORIALS OF THE 17TH AND 18TH CENTURY SC LAND TITLES, Microcopy No. 12, SCDA, Columbia, SC, 1984, 12 rolls, with index.

These materials can be of exceptional value because they pick up transfers of land which were not recorded, as well as land passed on by inheritance or marriage.

A _final_ and often overlooked category of land records for SC are records of land transfers (both grants and deeds or conveyances) issued in NC for land which is now in SC. The reason for this seemingly strange situation is that the NC-SC border in the center and western sections of the state was not surveyed and agreed upon by NC and SC until the period 1764-72. Prior to this time, a goodly portion of what is now in SC was considered to be NC territory and records therefore have to be sought in NC. The SC counties to which this applies include (moving E to W) Marlboro, Chesterfield, Lancaster, York, Chester, Union, Spartanburg, Greenville, and parts of Newberry and Laurens. The NC counties in which land records need to be sought during this period of time are Bladen (1745-9), Anson (1749-64), Mecklenburg (1763-72), and Tryon (1769-72). If you suspect your ancestor to have been in this area during this time, do not fail to check the records of the NC counties mentioned above. Much of the material on land grants and deeds has been published, as well as wills and estates which also often refer to SC residents:
- B. H. Holcomb, ANSON COUNTY, NC, WILLS AND ESTATES, 1749-95, The Author, Clinton, SC, 1975.
- B. H. Holcomb, BLADEN COUNTY, NC ABSTRACTS OF EARLY DEEDS, 1738-1804, Southern Historical Press, Easley, SC, 1979.
- B. H. Holcomb, DEED ABSTRACTS OF TRYON, LINCOLN, AND RUTHERFORD COUNTIES, NC, 1769-86, AND TRYON WILLS AND ESTATES, Southern Historical Press, Easley, SC, 1977.
- B. H. Holcomb, MECKLENBURG COUNTY, NC, ABSTRACTS OF EARLY WILLS, 1763-90, A Press, Greenville, SC, 1980.
- B. H. Holcomb, MECKLENBURG COUNTY, NC, DEED ABSTRACTS, 1763-79, Southern Historical Press, Easley, SC, 1979.
- B. H. Holcomb, NC LAND GRANTS IN SC, 1745-73, A Press, Greenville, SC, 1980.
- B. H. Holcomb, ANSON COUNTY, NC, DEED ABSTRACTS,

Genealogical Publishing Co., Baltimore, MD, 1980.

22. Manuscripts

One of the most useful and yet one of the most unused sources of genealogical data are the various manuscript collections relating to SC. These collections will be found in state, regional, and private libraries, archives, museums, and repositories located in numerous places in SC, including universities and colleges. Manuscript collections consist of all sorts of records of religious, educational, patriotic, business, social, civil, professional, governmental, and political organizations; documents, letters, memoirs, notes, and papers of early settlers, ministers, politicians, business men, educators, physicians, dentists, lawyers, judges, and farmers; records of churches, cemeteries, mortuaries, schools, corporations, and industries; works of artists, musicians, writers, sculptors, photographers, and architects; and records, papers, letters, and reminiscences of participants in various wars, as well as records of military organizations and campaigns.

The major sources of manuscripts relating to SC are SCL, SCHS, and the Southern Historical Collection in the Wilson Library at the University of NC, Chapel Hill, NC 27514. The holdings of these repositories are described in the following volumes:
_A. H. Stokes, Jr., A GUIDE TO THE MANUSCRIPT COLLECTION OF THE SCL, SCL, University of SC, Columbia, SC, 1982.
_D. Moltke-Hansen and S. Dosser, SCHS MANUSCRIPT GUIDE, SCHS, Charleston, SC, 1979. Supplements published in SC HISTORICAL MAGAZINE, SCHS, Charleston, SC, 1979-.
_S. S. Blosser and C.N. Wilson, Jr., THE SOUTHERN HISTORICAL COLLECTION: A GUIDE TO MANUSCRIPTS, University of NC Library, Chapel Hill, NC, 1970; and E. H. Smith, III, THE SOUTHERN HISTORICAL COLLECTION: SUPPLEMENTARY GUIDE TO MANUSCRIPTS, 1970-5, University of NC library, Chapel Hill, NC, 1971.
Many of the more important genealogically-related materials in the SCL and SCHS are indexed in:
_R. N. Cote, LOCAL AND FAMILY HISTORY IN SC: A BIBLIOGRAPHY, Southern Historical Press, Easley, SC, 1981.

Many of the manuscripts mentioned in the above works, many in smaller repositories in SC, and many outside the state of SC may be located in:

___US Library of Congress, THE NATIONAL UNION CATALOG OF MANUSCRIPT COLLECTIONS, The Library, Washington, DC, annual volumes since 1959-, index in each volume, also cumulative indexes, of names, places, and historical periods.

___P. M. Hamer, A GUIDE TO ARCHIVES AND MANUSCRIPTS IN THE US, Yale University Press, New Haven, CT, 1961.

___US National Historical Publications and Records Commission, DIRECTORY OF ARCHIVES AND MANUSCRIPT REPOSITORIES IN THE US, The Commission, Washington, DC, 1978.

___J. B. Howell, SPECIAL COLLECTIONS IN LIBRARIES OF THE SOUTHEAST, Southeastern Library Association, Jackson, MS, 1978.

___M. F. Hollings, DESCRIPTIVE INVENTORY OF THE CITY OF CHARLESTON DIVISION OF ARCHIVES AND RECORDS, The Division, Charleston, SC, 1979.

___R. Chepesink, GUIDE TO THE MANUSCRIPT AND ORAL HISTORY COLLECTIONS IN THE WINTHROP COLLEGE ARCHIVES AND SPECIAL COLLECTIONS, Dacus Library, Winthrop College, Rock Hill, SC, 1978.

___R. Chepesink, MASTER SURNAME INDEX TO GENEALOGICAL HOLDINGS OF THE WINTHROP COLLEGE ARCHIVES, Dacus Library, Winthrop College, Rock Hill, SC, 1983.

Included in the smaller, but nonetheless important, repositories in SC are some of the RL mentioned in Chapter 3.

The reference books mentioned in the previous paragraphs are available in SCL, SCHS, and in many larger libraries including LGL and RL. If you find in these volumes materials which you suspect may relate to your ancestor, write to the appropriate repository asking for details. Don't forget to send an SASE and to ask them for names of researchers if you cannot go in person. In SCL, SCHS, and some other SC manuscript repositories there are special indexes and other finding aids which facilitate your search. In some cases, there are several indexes, not just one, so you need to be careful to examine all of them.

23. Marriage records

Marriage records for SC have been recorded at the state level since July 1950. These records are in the custody of:
__Office of Vital Records and Public Health Statistics, SC Department of Health and Environmental Control, 2600 Bull St., Columbia, SC 29201.
Since July 1911, marriages have been recorded in the county where the license was issued. The records are in the custody of the Probate Judge in each of the counties. A major exception is Charleston. Marriage licenses are available beginning in 1879. The licenses and a computer index by both bride and groom are in Room 104 of the Charleston County courthouse.

Prior to July 1911 marriage information must be sought in various places including a few governmental agencies for short periods of time, Bible records, church records, court records, land records, manuscripts, military records (especially pension applications), mortuary records, newspaper records, and wills. These record types are treated in separate sections of this chapter. The most important source of SC marriage data prior to 1911 is newspapers. Marriage notices in many early SC newspapers have been compiled and published with indexes. A large number of these are listed in section 30 of this chapter. Newspapers in the years prior to 1880 tended to cover regions (several districts/counties) and those published in Columbia and Charleston often contained marriages from all over the state. Newspapers issued by various religious denominations also often contained many marriage notices.

Numerous sources of SC marriage information, including church records, minister's records, Bible records, and newspaper accounts, are listed in:
__J. D. Stemmons and E. D. Stemmons, THE VITAL RECORD COMPENDIUM, The Authors, Salt Lake City, UT, 1979.
In SCDA, there are marriage-related records which could be of value to you:
__SC Court of Common Pleas, RENUNCIATIONS OF DOWER, Record Group 0151, Series 006, 1726-75, Record Group B1AE, Series 017, 1775-1887, SCDA, Columbia, SC.
These documents are indexed in:
__SCDA, COMBINED ALPHABETICAL INDEX, SCDA, Columbia, SC.

There are also a number of published volumes of marriage data which you should not overlook:

___W. M. Clemens, NC AND SC MARRIAGE RECORDS: FROM THE EARLIEST TIMES TO THE CIVIL WAR, Genealogical Publishing Co., Baltimore, MD, 1927 (1975).

___B. H. Holcomb, SC MARRIAGES, 1688-1820, Genealogical Publishing Co., Baltimore, MD, 1980-1, 2 volumes.

___B. H. Holcomb, PROBATE RECORDS OF SC, JOURNAL OF THE COURT OF ORDINARY, 1764-71, Southern Historical Press, Easley, SC, 1979, 3rd volume in the series. See end of the journal for list of marriages.

___B. H. Holcomb, UPPER SC MARRIAGE AND DEATH NOTICES, 1843-65, Southern Historical Press, Easley, SC, 1977 (1979).

___S. E. Lucas, Jr., OLD NINETY-SIX AND ABBEVILLE DISTRICT MARRIAGES, 1777-1852, Southern Historical Press, Easley, SC, 1979.

___L. Pursley, 7500 MARRIAGES FROM NINETY-SIX AND ABBEVILLE DISTRICTS, 1774-1890, Southern Historical Press, Easley, SC, 1980.

___M. Waddell, A REGISTER OF MARRIAGES SOLEMNIZED BY MOSES WADDELL IN SC AND GA, 1795-1836, Heritage Papers, Danielsville, GA, 1967.

24. **Military records: colonial**

Before going into detail on sources of military records (sections 24, 25, 26, 27), you need to understand the types of records which are available and what they contain. There are five basic types which are of value to genealogists: (a) service, (b) pension, (c) bounty land, (d) claims, and (e) military unit history. Service records contain a number of the following: name, rank, military unit, personal description, plus dates and places of enlistment, mustering in, payrolls, wounding, capture, death, imprisonment, hospital stay, release, oath of allegiance, desertion, promotion, battles, heroic action, re-enlistment, leave of absence, mustering out, and discharge. Pension records (applications and payment documents) contain a number of the following: name, age, rank, military unit, personal description, name of wife, names and ages of children, residences during pension period, plus dates and places of service, wartime experiences, birth, marriage, pension payments, and death. Bounty land records (applications and awards of land) contain the same sort of data that pension records do. **Claims** of military participants for back pay and of civilians for supplies or services contain some of the following: name, details of claim, date of claim, witnesses to claim, documents supporting claim, action on claim, amount awarded. **Military unit history** records trace the detailed events of the experiences of a given military unit throughout a war, often referring to officers, enlisted personnel, battles, campaigns, deaths, plus dates and places of organization, mustering in, reorganization, mustering out and other pertinent events. Now, with this background, you are ready to learn where these records may be found.

Beginning in earliest colonial times, SC maintained loosely-organized local civilian military units called militia. These local units were parts of an overall state militia which was subject to call by the governor. In times of disaster, insurrection, riot, or invasion, the militia could be employed. Very few data on these militia have survived.

Not too many records are extant from the SC wars of the pre-Revolutionary period. The major ones of these wars were Queen Anne's War (1702-14), the Tuscarora Indian War (1711-15), the Yemassee-Creek Indian Wars (1715-8), the Spanish Alarm (1739-48) which was made up of two wars called the War of Jenkin's Ear and King George's War, and the French and Indian War (1754-63), with SC's participation consisting of frontier conflicts with the Cherokees and a more intense period of warfare called the Cherokee Indian War (1760-1). The few records which survive carry very little information, usually only the name and the military unit. Nonetheless, they can often help to locate an ancestor, that is, give a clue to his place of residence. Among the available materials listing names or giving related information are:
__D. Cole, THE ORIGIN AND DEVELOPMENT OF THE SC MILITIA, manuscript volume, SCL, Columbia, SC, 1948; also D. Cole, A BRIEF OUTLINE OF THE SC COLONIAL MILITIA SYSTEM, Proceedings of the SC Historical Association, 1954, pp. 14-23.
__M. J. Clark, COLONIAL SOLDIERS OF THE SOUTH, Genealogical Publishing Co., Baltimore, MD, 1983.
__SCDA, CARD FILE INDEX TO PAY LISTS FOR THE 1759-60 CHEROKEE EXPEDITION, SCDA, Columbia, SC.
__THE TUSCARORA EXPEDITION LETTERS OF COLONEL JOHN

BARNWELL, SC Historical and Genealogical Magazine, Volume 9, pp. 28-54.
__R. D. McDowell, JOHN BARNWELL AND THE TUSCARORAS, Paper No. 14, Beaufort County Historical Society, Beaufort, SC.
__F. M. Kirk, THE YEMASSEE WAR, 1715-8, Society of Colonial Wars, Mt. Pleasant, SC, 1970.
__C. Langdon, A LETTER FROM CAROLINA IN 1715 AND JOURNAL IN THE YEMASSEE INDIAN WAR, City of Charleston Yearbook, 1894, pp. 313-54.
__E. L. Pennington, THE SC INDIAN WAR OF 1715, SC Historical and Genealogical Magazine, Volume 32, pp. 251-69.
__J. T. Lanning, THE ST. AUGUSTINE EXPEDITION OF 1740, SCDA, Columbia, SC, 1954.
__OFFICERS OF THE SC REGIMENT IN THE CHEROKEE WAR, SC Historical and Genealogical Magazine, Volume 3, pp. 202-6.
__CHEROKEE WAR: FRONTIER FORTS PAYMENTS, Carolina Genealogist, Volume 21, pp. 1-4.
__COLONIAL GOVERNOR CORRESPONDENCE, CHIEFLY MILITARY, 1742-62, British Public Record Office, Documents CO5/13-20, as transcribed in SCDA, RECORDS IN THE BRITISH PUBLIC RECORD OFFICE RELATING TO SC, 1663-1782, SCDA, Microcopy 1, 12 rolls, indexes to persons, places, and topics in 12th roll.

25. **Military records: Revolutionary War**

As mentioned in Chapter 1, SC had a heavy involvement in the American War of Independence, particularly in the latter years. Over 6000 SC patriots fought with the Continental (united colonies) Army and many militia members participated on the home front. Quite a large number of records, which you should investigate, are available for this War: national service records, national pension records, national bounty land records, and state payment records for military service, for goods applied to the armed forces, and for annuities paid to wounded and disabled soldiers, widows, and orphans. There are also records of state pension applications and payments. As you begin your quest, one very important thing that you need to realize is that you will find both national and state records on Continental personnel, but there are only state records (no national ones) on the militia.

The _first_ step you should take in searching for your SC ancestor who served in this War or gave public service or provided support of the War is to employ the following nation-wide record sources and look for him in them:

__National Archives, GENERAL INDEX TO COMPILED SERVICE RECORDS OF REVOLUTIONARY WAR SOLDIERS, The Archives, Washington, DC, Microfilm Publication M860, 58 rolls. [Continental only; copies in SCDA, National Archives, Regional Branches of the National Archives, GSU (BLGSU)].

__National Archives, INDEX TO COMPILED SERVICE RECORDS OF AMERICAN NAVAL PERSONNEL DURING THE REVOLUTIONARY WAR, The Archives, Washington, DC, Microfilm Publication M879, 1 roll. [Also includes Marines; copies in SCDA, National Archives, Regional Branches of the National Archives, GSU (BLGSU)].

__National Genealogical Society, INDEX OF REVOLUTIONARY WAR PENSION APPLICATONS IN THE NATIONAL ARCHIVES, The Society, Washington, DC, 1976. [Also includes bounty land records; copies in SCDA, SCL, SCHS, LGL, some RL, GSU (BLGSU)].

__F. Rider, AMERICAN GENEALOGICAL INDEX, Godfrey Memorial Library, Middletown, CT, 1942-52, 48 volumes; and F. Rider, AMERICAN GENEALOGICAL AND BIOGRAPHICAL INDEX, Godfrey Memorial Library, Middletown, CT, 1952-84, over 125 volumes, more to come. [Continental and militia.]

__US Pay Department, War Department, REGISTERS OF CERTIFICATES ISSUED BY JOHN PIERCE TO OFFICERS AND SOLDIERS OF THE CONTINENTAL ARMY, Genealogical Publishing Co., Baltimore, MD, 1973.

__National Society of the DAR, DAR PATRIOT INDEX, The Society, Washington, DC, 1966, 1979, 2 volumes. [Continental, militia, public service, military aid.]

If you discover from these sources that your forebear served in the Continental forces, then you may proceed to obtain his records from the National Archives. Write them at the following address and ask for three copies of NATF Form 80:

__Reference Service Branch (NNIR), National Archives and Records Service, 8th and PA Ave., NW, Washington, DC 20408.

Upon receiving the forms, fill them out, check the box on one for military service, on another for pension records, and on the third one for bounty land, and mail them back. If the Archives staff finds the records, they will send you a notification of the cost. Upon receipt of the

money, you will receive the materials. The Archives is very busy, and thus the filling of your order may be slow. If you want faster service, you can go to the Archives in person, or you can hire a researcher in Washington, DC, to do the work for you. Researchers and their addresses may be found in:
__V. N. Chambers, editor, THE GENEALOGICAL HELPER, Everton Publishers, Logan, UT, latest September-October issue.

The _service_ records (not pension or bounty land) have been microfilmed by the National Archives (M881, 1097 rolls and M880, 4 rolls) and these are available at GSU (BLGSU) and Regional Branches of the National Archives.

The _second_ step that you should take, especially if you failed to find your progenitor in the first step is to look into the state sources. Even if you did find your ancestor in the first step, you should not neglect this second possible source of data. Some original sources in the SCDA are indexed in:
__SCDA, THE COMBINED ALPHABETICAL INDEX, SCDA, Columbia, SC, leads to Comptroller General, ACCOUNTS AUDITED OF CLAIMS GROWING OUT OF THE REVOLUTION, SCDA, Columbia, SC, 328 file boxes, or Microcopy No. 8, SCDA, Columbia, SC, 165 rolls, arranged alphabetically.

Another very important set of records which should be delved into is:
__Office of the Commissioners of the Treasury, STUB INDENTS AND INDEXES, 1779-91, SCDA, Columbia, SC, 22 volumes.

These records include payments for service, goods given to the military, annuities, pensions, and there are also pension applications. Other original SC records which may be examined in SCDA and two in SCL include:
__SCDA, SC CONTINENTAL LINE SERVICE LIST, SCDA, Columbia, SC, 1 volume.
__SCDA, MUSTER ROLL OF REVOLUTIONARY OFFICERS, SCDA, Columbia, SC, 1 volume.
__Office of Treasurer of the Lower Division, REVOLUTIONARY PENSION LIST, 1828-38, SCDA, Columbia, SC, 1 volume.
__Office of Treasurer of the Lower Division, REVOLUTIONARY WAR ANNUITIES LIST, 1799-1857, SCDA, Columbia, SC, 1 volume.
__Office of Treasurer, LIST OF CLAIMS AGAINST THE STATE, 1791-1820, SCDA, Columbia, SC, 3 volumes.

___SC DAR, RECORDS OF REVOLUTIONARY WAR SOLDIERS BURIED IN SC, 1 microfilmed manuscript volume, SCL, Columbia, SC, Entry No. 1962.
___SC ROYALIST TROOPS, MUSTER ROLLS, 1777-83, 2 microfilm rolls, SCL, Columbia, SC, Entry No. 1985.

Printed sources in which references to your ancestor may appear include:

___J. D. Bailey, SOME HEROES OF THE AMERICAN REVOLUTION, Southern Historical Press, Easley, SC, 1924 (1976).
___W. W. Boddie, MARION'S MEN: A LIST OF 2500, Heisser Printing Co., Charleston, SC, 1938.
___A. W. Burns, SC PENSION ABSTRACTS OF THE REVOLUTIONARY WAR, WAR OF 1812 AND INDIAN WARS, The Author, Washington, DC, 1935, 12 volumes. [Use cautiously.]
___M. J. Clark, LOYALISTS IN THE SOUTHERN CAMPAIGN OF THE REVOLUTIONARY WAR, Genealogical Publishing Co., Baltimore, MD, 1980, volume 1.
___D. Dandridge, AMERICAN PRISONERS OF THE REVOLUTION, Genealogical Publishing Co., Baltimore, MD, 1967.
___W. G. DeSaussure, OFFICERS WHO SERVED IN THE SC REVOLUTIONARY WAR REGIMENTS, Charleston Yearbook 1893, Charleston, SC, pp. 205-37.
___S. S. Ervin, SOUTH CAROLINIANS IN THE REVOLUTION, Genealogical Publishing Co., Baltimore, MD, 1949 (1976).
___Mrs. G. D. Foxworth, ROSTER AND ANCESTRAL ROLL OF THE SC DAR, Bryan Co., Columbia, SC, 1954.
___W. E. Hemphill, EXTRACTS FROM THE JOURNALS OF THE PROVINCIAL CONGRESSES OF SC, 1775-6, University of SC Press, Columbia, SC, 1960.
___J. T. Maddox and M. Carter, SC REVOLUTIONARY SOLDIERS, PATRIOTS, SAILORS, AND DESCENDANTS, GA Pioneers Publishing Co., Irwinton, GA, 1976.
___J. C. Pruitt, REVOLUTIONARY WAR PENSION APPLICANTS WHO SERVED FROM SC, The Author, Fairfax County, VA, 1946.
___RECORDS OF THE SC TREASURY, 1775-80, Microcopy No. 4, SCDA, Columbia, SC, 1969, 6 rolls, partial index in front of each volume, but should be searched entry by entry.
___J. Revill, COPY OF THE ORIGINAL INDEX BOOK SHOWING REVOLUTIONARY CLAIMS FILED IN SC, 1783-6, Genealogical Publishing Co., Baltimore, MD, 1941 (1969).
___A. S. Salley, Jr., ACCOUNTS AUDITED OF REVOLUTIONARY CLAIMS AGAINST SC, Department of Archives, Columbia, SC, 1935-43, 3 volumes.
___A. S. Salley, Jr., SC PROVINCIAL TROOPS IN PAPERS OF

THE FIRST COUNCIL OF SAFETY, 1775 Genealogical Publishing Co., Baltimore, MD, 1900-2 (1977).
__A. S. Salley, Jr., RECORDS OF THE REGIMENTS OF THE SC LINE IN THE REVOLUTIONARY WAR, Genealogical Publishing Co., Baltimore, MD, 1977.
__A. S. Salley, Jr. and W. A. Wates, STUB ENTRIES TO INDENTS ISSUED IN PAYMENT OF CLAIMS AGAINST SC GROWING OUT OF THE REVOLUTION, University of SC Press, Columbia, SC, 1910-27, 12 volumes.
__PAPERS OF THE FIRST AND SECOND COUNCILS OF SAFETY OF SC, 1775-6, SC Historical and Genealogical Magazine, 1900-3, volumes 1-4.
__JOURNAL ARTICLES ON LOYALISTS: SC Historical and Genealogical Magazine, Volume 14, pp. 37-43; Proceedings of the SC Historical Association, 1936, pp. 3-17, and 1937, pp. 34-46.
__US Census Bureau, A CENSUS OF PENSIONERS 1840 FOR REVOLUTIONARY WAR OR MILITARY SERVICE, Genealogical Publishing Co., Baltimore, MD, 1841 (1974).
All of the above books are in SCL, many are available in SCHS, LGL, and RL, and some can be obtained at GSU (and through BLGSU) and LL.

For considerably more detail about genealogical data which can be gleaned from Revolutionary War records, you may consult a book especially dedicated to this:
__Geo. K. Schweitzer, REVOLUTIONARY WAR GENEALOGY, $8 postpaid from Geo. K. Schweitzer, 7914 Gleason, C-1136, Knoxville, TN 37919.
This volume goes into detail on local, state, and national records, discusses both militia and Continental Army service, deals in detail with service, pension, bounty land, and claims records, and treats the subjects of regimental histories, battle accounts, medical records, courts-martial, foreign participants, Loyalist data, maps, museums, historic sites, patriotic organizations, and many other related topics.

26. Military records: 1812-60

In the period 1812-60, the US was involved in two major foreign wars: The War of 1812 (1812-5) and the Mexican War. In addition, there was a series of conflicts which began during this period called the Indian Wars (1817-98). A number of SC men were participants in the War of 1812. As was the case with

the Revolutionary War, three types of _national_ records should be sought: military service, pension, and bounty land. To obtain these records, request three copies of NATF Form 80 from:
__Reference Services Branch (NNIR), National Archives and Records Service, 8th and PA Ave., NW, Washington, DC 20408.

When you receive them, fill all three out, check the box for military records on one, the box for pension records on another, and the box for bounty land records on the third one. Then mail all three back. The Archives staff will check their records, send you a reply, and if records were found will tell you what copies will cost. Upon receipt of your money, your copies will be made and dispatched to you. Because of their heavy backlog, the National Archives is often slow. If you want faster service, hire a researcher in Washington, DC, to do the work for you. Such researchers may be found in:
__V. N. Chambers, editor, THE GENEALOGICAL HELPER, Everton Publishers, Logan, UT, latest Sep-Oct issue.

Among the microfilm indexes and alphabetical files which the National Archives employees will search or which your hired researcher should search are:
__The National Archives, INDEX TO COMPILED SERVICE RECORDS OF SC VOLUNTEER SOLDIERS WHO SERVED DURING THE WAR OF 1812, Microfilm Publication M652, The Archives, Washington, DC, 7 rolls.
__The National Archives, INDEX TO WAR OF 1812 PENSION APPLICATION FILES, Microfilm Publication M313, The Archives, Washington, DC, 102 rolls.
__The National Archives, WAR OF 1812 MILITARY BOUNTY LAND WARRANTS (WITH INDEXES), 1815-58, Microfilm Publication M848, The Archives, Washington, DC, 14 rolls.
__The National Archives, POST-REVOLUTIONARY WAR BOUNTY LAND WARRANT APPLICATION FILE, arranged alphabetically, National Archives, Washington, DC.

Copies of the three microfilm publications mentioned above are available at some LGL, at Regional branches of the National Archives, and at GSU (and through BLGSU). The first and third are at SCDA. Records of volunteer service in the FL Seminole War (1812) and the Creek Indian War (1813-4) are included in the above materials.

Among published _national_ sources for War of 1812 information are:
__F. I. Ordway, Jr., REGISTER OF THE GENERAL SOCIETY OF

THE WAR OF 1812, The Society, Washington, DC, 1972.
__F. S. Galvin, 1812 ANCESTOR INDEX, National Society of US Daughters of 1812, Washington, DC, 1970.
__C. S. Peterson, KNOWN MILITARY DEAD DURING THE WAR OF 1812, The Author, Baltimore, MD, 1955.

In addition, there are a number of state source volumes, manuscripts, and microfilms for SC:
__Mrs. J. H. Sams, PAY ROLLS, MUSTER ROLLS OF SC MILITIA IN 1812-5, US Daughters of 1812, Columbia, SC, no date, 2 volumes.
__A. W. Burns, INDEX TO THE PENSION LIST OF THE WAR OF 1812, SCL, Columbia, SC, 9 volumes.
__R. Nash, OFFICERS AND MEN IN THE WAR OF 1812, SC, typed manuscript, SCL, Columbia, SC, Entry No. 1542.
__US Daughters of 1812, SC Society, Andrew Jackson Chapter, RECORDS, 1812-5, 5 manuscript volumes, SCL, Columbia, SC, Entry No. 2171. Regimental rolls, lineages of members.
__SC MILITIA, FIRST AND SECOND REGIMENTS, 1812, ROLL BOOK, SCL, Columbia, SC, Entry No. 1977.
__SC MILITIA, SECOND REGIMENT, PAYMASTER AND OTHER WAR OF 1812 RECORDS, 113 items, SCL, Columbia, SC, Entry No. 1980.
__THIRD REGIMENT, SC STATE TROOPS, WAR OF 1812, ROLL BOOK AND ORDER BOOK, 2 manuscript volumes, SCL, Columbia, SC, Entry No. 2096.
__THIRD REGIMENT, STATE TROOPS, ORDER BOOK, 1812-4, manuscript volume, SCL, Columbia, SC, Entry No. 2291.
__SC MILITIA, SIXTH MILITARY DISTRICT, ADJUTANT GENERAL'S OFFICE, 1814-5, ORDER BOOK, manuscript volume, SCL, Columbia, SC, Entry No. 1981.
__US ARMY, EIGHTH INFANTRY, RECORD BOOK, 1812-21, manuscript volume, SCL, Columbia, SC, Entry No. 2163. Contains SC recruiting returns.
__SC MILITIA, FORT MARION, BEAUFORT, 1814-5, REPORTS AND RECORDS, 21 microfilmed items, SCL, Columbia, SC, Entry No. 1978.

For considerably more detail about genealogical information which can be derived from War of 1812 records, you may consult a book especially dedicated to this:
__Geo. K. Schweitzer, WAR OF 1812 GENEALOGY, $7 postpaid from Geo. K. Schweitzer, 7914 Gleason, C-1136, Knoxville, TN 37919.

This volume goes into detail on local, state, and national records, discusses service, pension, bounty land, and claims records, and treats the subjects of regimental histories, hospital records, courts-martial, prisoners, militia activity, battle sites, museums, officer biographies and many other related topics.

During the Indian Wars period (1817-98), some SC personnel were involved in several of the conflicts. The National Archives has military service, pension, and bounty land application records, plus indexes to all three. NATF Form 80 should be obtained and used or a researcher hired in accordance with the previously-given instructions (1st paragraph, this section). The National Archives indexes which lead to the records and some alphabetized records are as follows:
__National Archives, INDEX TO COMPILED SERVICE RECORDS OF VOLUNTEER SOLDIERS WHO SERVED DURING INDIAN WARS, Microfilm Publication M629, The Archives, Washington, DC, 42 rolls.
__National Archives, INDEX TO INDIAN WARS PENSION FILES, Microfilm Publication T318, The Archives, Washington, DC, 12 rolls.
__National Archives, POST-REVOLUTIONARY WAR BOUNTY LAND APPLICATION FILE, arranged alphabetically, National Archives, Washington, DC.
The two microfilm indexes are available in Regional Branches of the National Archives, some LGL, and GSU (and through BLGSU).

The Mexican War was fought 1846-8. As before, NATF Form 80 should be obtained and used or a researcher hired as indicated in previously-given instructions (1st paragraph, this section). Again, military service, pension, and bounty land records should be asked for. The National Archives indexes which lead to the records and some alphabetized records are:
__The National Archives, INDEX TO THE COMPILED SERVICE RECORDS OF VOLUNTEER SOLDIERS DURING THE MEXICAN WAR, Microfilm Publication M616, The Archives, Washington, DC, 41 rolls.
__The National Archives, INDEX TO MEXICAN WAR PENSION FILES, Microfilm Publication T317, The Archives, Washington, DC, 14 rolls.
__The National Archives, POST-REVOLUTIONARY WAR BOUNTY LAND APPLICATION FILE, arranged alphabetically, National Archives, Washington, DC.
An exceptionally valuable publication is a complete

roster of both regular and volunteer troops in the Mexican War:
__W. H. Roberts, MEXICAN WAR VETERANS, 1846-8, Washington, DC, 1887.
Also useful is:
__C. S. Peterson, KNOWN MILITARY DEAD DURING THE MEXICAN WAR, The Author, Baltimore, MD, 1957.
A useful book and a noteworthy manuscript on SC in the Mexican War are:
__R. G. M. Dunovant, THE PALMETTO REGIMENT, SC VOLUNTEERS, 1846-8, Walker, Evans, and Cogswell Co., Charleston, SC, 1897.
__SC VOLUNTEERS, PALMETTO REGIMENT, MEMORANDUM BOOK, 1846-8, manuscript volume, SCL, Columbia, SC, Entry No. 2002.

27. Military records: Civil War

Records which are available for SC participants in the Civil War (1861-5) include national service records for soldiers, sailors and marines, SC state pension records and SC state military histories. No bounty land awards were made by either the federal or the state government for service in the Civil War. A major index lists SC military service records which are in the National Archives:
__INDEX TO THE COMPILED SERVICE RECORDS OF CONFEDERATE SOLDIERS WHO SERVED IN ORGANIZATIONS FROM THE STATE OF SC, Microfilm Publication M381, The Archives, Washington, DC, 35 rolls.
This index leads to the compiled service records which have been reproduced on microfilm. In addition, service records of Confederate naval and marine personnel may be readily found because they are arranged alphabetically in the second item below:
__The National Archives, COMPILED SERVICE RECORDS OF CONFEDERATE SOLDIERS WHO SERVED IN ORGANIZATIONS FROM THE STATE OF SC, Microfilm Publication M267, The Archives, Washington, DC, 392 rolls.
__The National Archives, (SERVICE) RECORDS RELATING TO CONFEDERATE NAVAL AND MARINE PERSONNEL, Microfilm Publications M260, The Archives, Washington, DC, 7 rolls, arranged alphabetically by name.
These indexes and records may be examined in the National Archives, their Regional Branches, or in the SCDA. Or you may write for NATF Form 80 and use it, or hire a

researcher in Washington, DC, or Columbia, SC, to look into these records for you. Details for these procedures were given previously (1st paragraph, section 26). Don't forget that the US did not award Confederate pensions, so do not request pension records for Confederates from the National Archives.

There are several _published_ state sources for information on SC Confederate veterans and their military units. The most important of these are:

_A. S. Salley, Jr., SC TROOPS IN CONFEDERATE SERVICE, Bryan Co., Columbia, SC, 1913-4, 1930, 3 volumes.
_E. Capers, CONFEDERATE MILITARY HISTORY, SC, VOLUME 5, Confederate Publishing Co., Atlanta, GA, 1899.
_E. Capers, SC CONFEDERATE MILITARY HISTORY (EXTENDED EDITION), Confederate Publishing Co., Atlanta, GA, 1899.
_C. E. Dornbusch, MILITARY BIBLIOGRAPHY OF THE CIVIL WAR, NY Public Library, New York, NY, 1967, Volume 2, pp. 84-90. [References to SC regimental histories.]

These volumes are in SCL, SCHS, GSU, (BLGSU), many LGL, many RL, and some LL.

Among the _state of SC_ records are the very important Confederate pension records. In 1882 the SC State Legislature ordered the Adjutant and Inspector General to prepare a list of all SC Civil War veterans along with details of their service and to prepare a brief history of every regiment. These data provided the basis for a state law passed in 1887 which awarded pensions to permanently disabled, needy SC veterans and to widows of men who lost their lives in service. Application for the pensions were to be made through the Clerks of the County Courts of Common Pleas who then forwarded the applications to the Comptroller General of the State. Both the county and the state were directed to keep records of the applications and the action taken on them. Applications had to be renewed each year. In 1888, a County Pension Application Examining Board was set up in each county to assist the Clerk, and a State Board of Pensions was established to assist the Comptroller General, which resulted in pensions first being awarded on 08 February 1889. In 1895, 1896, 1900, 1903, and 1910, the pension laws were gradually broadened so that pensions could be applied for by widows of disabled veterans, then all veterans over 60, then all veterans, then all veterans who gave service in any Confederate state, then all needy widows, then all widows. Finally, in 1919, a complete revision of the pension laws was passed. A Confederate Pension Department was set up, a State Pension Commissioner was appointed, County Pension Boards were reorganized, pensions were provided for practically all veterans and their widows, but everyone had to reapply. Lists by county of approved pensions (and often disapproved ones) were published yearly beginning in 1888:

__REPORTS AND RESOLUTIONS OF THE GENERAL ASSEMBLY OF THE STATE OF SC, Woodrow, Columbia, SC, Report of the Comptroller General 1888 (p. 429), 1889 (p. 370), 1890 (p. 357), 1891 (p. 1,), 1892 (p. 1), 1893 (p. 417), 1894 (p. 1), 1895 (p. 428), 1896 (p. 428), 1897 (p. 1179), 1898 (p. 1077), 1899 (p. 787), 1900 (p. 1), 1901 (p. 1), 1902 (p. 19), 1903 (p. 19), 1904 (p. 20), 1905 (p. 19), 1906 (p. 19), 1907 (p. 19), 1908 (p. 12), 1909 (p. 21), 1910 (p. 21), 1911 (p. 20), 1912 (p. 21), 1913 (p. 21), 1914 (p. 1011), 1915 (p. 21), 1916 (p. 191), 1917 (p. 7), 1918 (p. 5), 1919 (p. 5), 1920 (p. 11), Report of the Pension Commissioner 1921 (p. 3), Report of the Comptroller General 1922 (p. 3), 1924 (p. 1), 1925 (p. 5), etc.

There is in SCDA an index which leads to the pension applications which were filed 1919-26. This index is:

__CARD FILE INDEX OF 1919-26 SC CONFEDERATE PENSION APPLICATIONS, SCDA, Columbia, SC. Leads to applications.

Also in SCDA are applications which wounded and incapacitated Confederate veterans could submit for artificial limbs and relief. These documents are filed alphabetically:

__APPLICATIONS OF CONFEDERATE VETERANS FOR ARTIFICIAL LIMBS AND RELIEF, 1879-1907, SCDA, Columbia, SC. Arranged alphabetically.

Details of further Civil War records which are in the National Archives will be found in:

__National Archives Staff, GUIDE TO GENEALOGICAL RESEARCH IN THE NATIONAL ARCHIVES, The Archives, Washington, DC, 1982, Chapters 4-10, 16.

For a detailed in-depth discussion of Civil War records as genealogical sources, consult:

__Geo. K. Schweitzer, CIVIL WAR GENEALOGY, $8 from Geo. K. Schweitzer, 7914 Gleason, C-1136, Knoxville, TN

37919.
This book treats local, state, and national records, service and pension records, regimental and naval histories, enlistment rosters, hospital records, court-martial reports, burial registers, national cemeteries, gravestone allotments, amnesties, pardons, state militias, discharge papers, officer biographies, prisons, prisoners, battle sites, maps, relics, weapons, museums, monuments, memorials, deserters, black soldiers, Indian soldiers, and many other topics.

There is in the National Archives an index to service records of the Spanish-American War (1898-9):
___The National Archives, GENERAL INDEX TO COMPILED SERVICE RECORDS OF VOLUNTEER SOLDIERS WHO SERVED DURING THE WAR WITH SPAIN, Microfilm Publication M871, The Archives, Washington, DC, 126 rolls, leads to service records.

Again a properly submitted NATF Form 80 (see 1st paragraph of section 26 for instructions) will bring you both military service and pension records (there were no bounty land awards). Or you may choose to hire a researcher, or even go yourself. The pension records are indexed in:
___The National Archives, GENERAL INDEX TO PENSION FILES, 1861-1934, Microfilm Publication T288, The Archives, Washington, DC, 544 rolls.

Two volumes which you should not overlook are:
___J. W. Floyd, HISTORICAL ROSTER AND ITINERARY OF SC VOLUNTEER TROOPS, WAR BETWEEN US AND SPAIN, 1898, Bryan Co., Columbia, SC, 1901.
___HISTORICAL SKETCH AND ROSTER OF INDEPENDENT BATTALION, SC VOLUNTEER INFANTRY, USA, SPANISH-AMERICAN WAR, 1898-9, Bryan Co., Columbia, SC, 1901.

In the manuscript archives of the SCL there is:
___UNITED STATES ARMY, COMPANY E, FIRST SC REGIMENT, US VOLUNTEER INFANTRY, 1898 MUSTER ROLL, SCL, Columbia, SC, ENTRY NO. 2494.

And in the SCDA, you will find:
___SPANISH-AMERICAN WAR VETERANS FILE, 1898, 2 drawers, SCDA, Columbia, SC.

Some records for World War I and subsequent wars may be obtained from the following address. However, many documents were destroyed by an extensive fire in 1972. Write for Form 180:

___National Personnel Records Center (MPR), 9700 Page Blvd., St. Louis, MO 63132.

Draft records for World War I are in Record Group 163 (Records of the Selective Service System of World War I) at

___Archives Branch, Federal Archives and Records Center, 1557 St. Joseph Ave., East Point, GA 30344.

28. Mortuary records

Very few SC mortuary records have been transcribed or microfilmed, even though a few are to be found in manuscripts. This means that you must write directly to the mortuaries which you know or suspect were involved in burying your ancestor. Sometimes a death certificate will name the mortuary; sometimes it is the only one nearby; sometimes you will have to write several to ascertain which one might have done the funeral arrangements. You may discover that the mortuary that was involved is now out of business, and so you will have to try to discover which of the existing ones inherited the records. Mortuaries for SC with their addresses are listed in the following volume:

___C. O. Kates, editor, THE AMERICAN BLUE BOOK OF FUNERAL DIRECTORS, Kates-Boyleston Publications, New York, NY, latest issue.

This reference book will usually be found in the offices of most mortuaries. In all correspondence with mortuaries be sure to enclose an SASE.

29. Naturalization records

In the earliest years of the colonial period, the major immigrants to the territory that later became the US were from the British Isles and since the colonies were British, they were citizens. When immigrants of other nationalities began to arrive, English traditions, customs, governmental structures, and language had become firmly established. In spite of this English dominance, many early foreign SC settlers simply did not bother to change their citizenships. This was particularly the case in frontier areas and when foreigners set up separate communities of their own as several did in SC. However, those who chose or were pressed to do so could swear loyalty to the British sovereign before a court and thereby become official citizens. Others never went through a formal procedure and functionally became citizens simply by conforming to the laws and entering into community activity. In 1740, the English Parliament passed a law which set requirements for naturalization: 7 years residence in one colony plus an oath of allegiance to the Crown. The oath was sometimes certified by a court.

In 1776-7, all those who supported the Revolution were automatically considered to be citizens. Then, in 1788, the Articles of Confederation made all citizens of states citizens of the new nation. The US Congress in 1790 enacted a national naturalization act which required one year's state residence, two years' US residence, and a loyalty oath taken in a court. In 1795, a five years' residence came to be required along with a declaration of intent three years before the oath. Then in 1798, these times became 14 and 5 years respectively. Revised statutes of 1802 reverted to the 5 and 3 years of 1795. The declaration and oath could be carried out in any court of record (US, SC, district, local). Wives and children of naturalized males usually became citizens automatically. And persons who gave military service to the US and received an honorable discharge also received citizenship.

In 1906, the Bureau of Immigration and Naturalization was set up, and this agency has kept records on all naturalizations since then. Thus, if you suspect your ancestor was naturalized after September 1906, write to the following address for a Form 6641 which you can use to request records:
__Immigration and Naturalization Service, 425 I St., Washington, DC 20536.
For naturalization records before October 1906, you need to recall that the process could have taken place in any court and, in addition, in the colonial and early state legislatures. Unfortunately, locating naturalization records before 1906 means going through all possible court and some legislative records for the time period you consider proper. The most likely places to find these records are the Secretary of State (Province) Records, the Federal Courts, the District Courts, and the County Courts. Some of the pertinent materials and finding aids are:
__Secretary of State (Province), MISCELLANEOUS RECORDS,

MAIN SERIES, 1671-1971, COLUMBIA SERIES, 1776-1875, 183 volumes, 2 cartons, 1 box, SCDA, Columbia, SC.
__CARD FILE INDEX TO LEGISLATIVE PETITIONS FOR NATURALIZATION, SCDA, Columbia, SC.
__M. R. Hemperley, FEDERAL NATURALIZATION OATHS, CHARLESTON, SC, 1790-1860, SC Historical and Genealogical Magazine, Volume 66, pp. 112-24, 183-92, 218-28.
__US District Court, Eastern District of SC, Charleston, NATURALIZATION RECORDS, Alphabetical indexes, 1790-1906, to MINUTE BOOKS, which show name of naturalized person, age, country of origin, occupation, date and place of arrival, and date of oath, Federal Archives and Records Center, National Archives and Records Service, 1557 St. Joseph Ave., East Point, GA 30344, microfilmed as National Archives Microfilm M1183, 1 roll.
Naturalizations (often called citizenship) records have been gathered and indexed by some county/district courts. These will be noted under the county/district listings in Chapter 4.

30. Newspaper records

A number of original and microfilmed newspapers are available for towns, cities, counties, and districts of SC. These newspapers date from 1732 and carry valuable information including national news, local news, ads, marriages, and deaths. Before about 1860, the newspapers of Charleston and Columbia tended to cover the entire state, and those of other places were often regional in scope (covering several counties/districts). The largest collections of newspapers and microfilms of them are to be found in SCL (largest collection), the Charleston Library Society in Charleston (2nd largest collection) [164 King St., Charleston, SC 29401], and the SCDA. Other collections with good local holdings are located in The College of Charleston Library in Charleston [Charleston, SC 29401], Clemson University Library [Clemson, SC 29631], Presbyterian College Library [Clinton, SC 29325], Horry County Memorial Library [Conway, SC 29526], Darlington Public Library [Darlington, SC 29532], Florence Public Library [Florence, SC 29501], Georgetown County Memorial Library [Georgetown, SC 29440], Furman University Library [Greenville, SC 29613], Winthrop College Library [Rock

Hill, SC 29733], and Wofford College Library [Spartanburg, SC 29301]. The contents of these various collections are listed in
__ J. H. Moore, RESEARCH MATERIALS IN SC, University of SC Press, Columbia, SC, 1967, pp. 14-16, 18, 30, 32, 47, 138-147, 150, 152, 154-5, 169-70, 174.

Other important guides which refer to SC newspapers in SC repositories and in a number of places outside the state include:
__ C. S. Brigham, HISTORY AND BIBLIOGRAPHY OF AMERICAN NEWSPAPERS, 1690-1820, American Antiquarian Society, Worcester, MA, 1961, 2 volumes.
__ W. Gregory, AMERICAN NEWSPAPERS, 1821-1936, H. W. Wilson Co., New York, NY 1937.

Unfortunately, not too many newspapers have been completely indexed, so it is necessary that you have some idea of the time span of your ancestor, which will facilitate your page by page search. However, many early newspapers have been partly indexed as indicated in the next paragraph. Some existing indexes are listed in:
__ A. C. Milner, NEWSPAPER INDEXES, Scarecrow Press, Metuchen, NJ, 1977-81, 3 volumes.
__ B. M. Jarboe, OBITUARIES: A GUIDE TO SOURCES, Hall, Boston, MA, 1982.

There is also an index volume of marriage, death, and other notices in all extant SC newspapers during 1733-83:
__ MARRIAGE AND DEATH NOTICES IN SC NEWSPAPERS, 1733-83, Heritage Papers, Danielsville, GA, 1983.

The above publications are located in SCL, SCHS, GSU, LGL, many RL and some LL.

As you have realized from previous sections in this chapter, not many death and marriage records are available for SC before the 20th century. This, however, is partially redressed by the fact that SC newspapers in early years listed these very valuable records, death and marriage. Several extremely dedicated workers have compiled many of these newspaper notices which they have published in journals and as books. Among the important ones are:
__ J. G. B. Bullock, EXTRACTS FROM THE SC GAZETTE, 1732-81, National Genealogical Society Quarterly, Volume 2 (1914), p. 47.
__ H. Cohen, THE SC GAZETTE, 1732-75, University of SC Press, Columbia, SC, 1953.
__ E. Curry, DEATH NOTICES FROM THE SC GAZETTE, 1781-5,

National Genealogical Society Quarterly, Volume 11 (1923), pp. 53-7.

__E. Curry, EARLY SC MARRIAGES AND DEATH NOTICES FROM THE SC WEEKLY MUSEUM, 1797, National Genealogical Society Quarterly, Volume 11 (1923), pp. 47-8.

__C. M. Elliott, MARRIAGE AND DEATH NOTICES FROM THE KEOWEE COURIER, 1849-51, 1857-61, 1865-71, Southern Historical Press, Easley, SC, 1979.

__B. A. Elzas, JEWISH MARRIAGE NOTICES FROM THE NEWSPAPER PRESS OF CHARLESTON, 1775-1906, Bloch, New York, NY, 1917.

__E. D. English, MARRIAGE AND DEATH NOTICES FROM THE EDGEFIELD HIVE, 1830, SC Historical Magazine, Volume 42 (1941), pp. 25-7.

__I. H. Griffin, MARRIAGE AND DEATH NOTICES FROM THE CHARLESTON GAZETTE, THE CITY GAZETTE, AND THE COMMERCIAL DAILY ADVERTISER, 1825-8, SC Historical Magazine, Volume 60, pp. 43-7, 107-10, 170-2, 228-36, Volume 62, pp. 55-7, 115-7, 183-4, 238-40, Volume 63, pp. 52-4, 112-4, 182-4, Volume 64, pp. 114-6, 178-80, 227-9, Volume 65, pp. 48-51, 114-7, 233-5, Volume 66, pp. 125-9, Volume 67, pp. 46-9, Volume 75, pp. 184-6.

__J. E. Hart, Jr., MARRIAGE AND DEATH NOTICES FROM YORKVILLE NEWSPAPERS, The Author, typed copy, York County Library, Rock Hill, SC, 1971, 2 volumes.

__I. Hayne, RECORDS KEPT BY ISAAC HAYNE (NEWSPAPERS, 1740-76), SC Historical Magazine, Volume 10 (1909), pp. 145-70.

__E. D. Herd, MARRIAGE AND DEATH NOTICES FROM THE ABBEVILLE BANNER, 1846-60, The Author, Abbeville, SC, 1980.

__B. H. Holcomb, MARRIAGE AND DEATH NOTICES FROM BAPTIST NEWSPAPERS OF SC, 1835-65, Reprint Co., Spartanburg, SC, 1981.

__B. H. Holcomb, MARRIAGE AND DEATH NOTICES FROM CAMDEN NEWSPAPERS, 1816-65, Southern Historical Press, Easley, SC, 1978.

__B. H. Holcomb, MARRIAGE AND DEATH NOTICES FROM THE CHARLESTON OBSERVER, 1827-45, A Press, Greenville, SC, 1980. [7900 names]

__B. H. Holcomb, MARRIAGE AND DEATH NOTICES FROM THE CHARLESTON TIMES, 1800-21, Genealogical Publ. Co., Baltimore, MD, 1979. [4000 notices]

__B. H. Holcomb, MARRIAGE AND DEATH NOTICES FROM COLUMBIA NEWSPAPERS, 1792-1839, Southern Historical Press, Easley, SC, 1981. [1000 notices]

__B. H. Holcomb, MARRIAGE, DEATH, AND ESTATE NOTICES FROM GEORGETOWN NEWSPAPERS, 1791-1861, Southern Historical Press, Easley, SC, 1978.
__B. H. Holcomb, MARRIAGE AND DEATH NOTICES FROM LUTHERAN OBSERVER AND THE SOUTHERN LUTHERAN, 1831-65, Southern Historical Press, Easley, SC, 1979.
__B. H. Holcomb, MARRIAGE AND DEATH NOTICES FROM THE PENDLETON MESSENGER, 1807-51, Southern Historical Press, Easley, SC, 1977.
__B. H. Holcomb, MARRIAGE AND DEATH NOTICES FROM THE SOUTHERN CHRISTIAN ADVOCATE, 1837-67, Southern Historical Press, Easley, SC, 1979-80, 2 volumes. [100,000 individuals]
__B. H. Holcomb, MARRIAGE AND OBITUARY NOTICES FROM THE UNIONVILLE JOURNAL AND UNIONVILLE TIMES, 1852-68, SC Magazine of Ancestral Research, Volume 3 (1975), p. 214.
__B. H. Holcomb, MARRIAGE AND DEATH NOTICES FROM THE UP COUNTRY OF SC, 1826-63, A Press, Greenville, SC, 1978.
__B. H. Holcomb, UPPER SC MARRIAGE AND DEATH NOTICES, 1843-65, Southern Historical Press, Easley, SC, 1977. [5200 notices]
__B. H. Holcomb, YORK NEWSPAPERS: MARRIAGE AND DEATH NOTICES, 1823-65, A Press, Greenville, SC, 1981.
__E. H. Jervey, DEATH NOTICES FROM THE GAZETTE OF THE STATE OF SC, 1777-85, SC Historical Magazine, Volume 50 (1949), pp. 127-30, 204-8, Volume 51 (1950), pp. 24-8, 97-102, 164-70.
__E. H. Jervey, MARRIAGE AND DEATH NOTICES FROM THE CHARLESTON COURIER, 1806, SC Historical Magazine, Volume 29 (1928), pp. 258-63.
__E. H. Jervey, MARRIAGE AND DEATH NOTICES FROM THE CITY GAZETTE, SC Historical Magazine, long series in Volumes 35-58.
__J. M. Lesesne, MARRIAGE AND DEATH NOTICES FROM THE GREENVILLE MOUNTAINEER, 1826-36, SC Historical Magazine, Volume 49 (1948), pp. 57-60, 119-22, Volume 50, pp. 101-5, 156-62, 216-20.
__J. M. Lesesne, MARRIAGE AND DEATH NOTICES FROM THE PENDLETON MESSENGER, 1807-23, SC Historical Magazine, Volume 47 (1946), pp. 29-31, 109-16, 163-70, 228-31, Volume 48, pp. 35-9, 112-4.
__S. E. Lucas, Jr., OLD NINETY-SIX AND ABBEVILLE DISTRICT MARRIAGES, 1777-1852, Southern Historical Press, Easley, SC, 1979.
__MARRIAGE AND DEATH NOTICES FROM CHERAW INTELLIGENCER

(1825-6), CHESTER STANDARD (1855-62), COLUMBIA TELESCOPE (1826-33), EARLY COLUMBIA NEWSPAPERS (1819-29), DARLINGTON FLAG (1851-2), EDGEFIELD ADVERTISER (1836-9), GREENVILLE MOUNTAINEER (1836-45), MARION STAR (1852-6), SC STATE JOURNAL (1826-33), SOUTHERN CHRISTIAN HERALD (1834-8), SOUTHERN ENTERPRISE (1854-7), SOUTHERN REGISTER (1825-6), SUMTER GAZETTE (1831-3), UNIONVILLE JOURNAL (1851-2), SC Magazine of Ancestral Research, Volumes 1, 2, 4, 5, 9.

__MARRIAGE NOTICES FROM NEGRIN'S SOCIABLE MAGAZINE, 1804, SC Historical magazine, Volume 63, pp. 238-9.

__C. T. McClendon, EDGEFIELD DEATH NOTICES AND CEMETERY RECORDS, Hive Press, Columbia, SC, 1977.

__J. Revill, MARRIAGE AND DEATH NOTICES ABSTRACTED FROM NEWSPAPERS PUBLISHED IN CAMDEN, 1822-42, The Author, Columbia, SC, 1936.

__J. Revill, ABSTRACT OF MARRIAGES AND DEATHS FROM THE KEOWEE COURIER, 1852-71, The Author, Columbia, SC, 1935.

__J. Revill, MARRIAGE AND DEATH NOTICES FROM NEWSPAPERS ON FILE IN THE SCL, 1804-71, THE AUTHOR, COLUMBIA, SC, 1935-6, 2 VOLUMES.

__J. Revill, THE PENDLETON MESSENGER: ABSTRACT DATA FROM THE MARRIAGE AND DEATH NOTICES, 1826-51, The Author, Sumter, SC, 1956.

__A. S. Salley, Jr., MARRIAGE NOTICES IN THE CHARLESTON COURIER, 1803-8, Genealogical Publishing Co., Baltimore, MD, 1919 (1976).

__A. S. Salley, Jr., MARRIAGE NOTICES IN THE SC AND AMERICAN GENERAL GAZETTE, 1766-82, Genealogical Publ. Co., Baltimore, MD, 1914 (1976).

__A. S. Salley, Jr., MARRIAGE NOTICES IN THE SC GAZETTE, COUNTY JOURNAL, AND CHARLESTON GAZETTE, 1765-75, 1778-80, The Author, Columbia, SC, 1904.

__A. S. Salley, Jr., MARRIAGE NOTICES IN THE SC GAZETTE AND ITS SUCCESSORS, 1732-1801, Genealogical Publ. Co., Baltimore, MD, 1902 (1965).

__A. S. Salley and M. L. Webber, DEATH NOTICES IN THE SC GAZETTE, 1732-75, Ethra, Miami, FL, 1917 (1976).

__G. S. Schorn, MARRIAGES AND DEATHS FROM THE PENDLETON MESSENGER, Tulsa Annals, Volume 9 (1974), pp. 48-56.

__R. F. Simpson, Jr., and Mrs. C. R. Barham, SOME SC MARRIAGES AND OBITUARIES FROM GREENVILLE AND LAURENSVILLE NEWSPAPERS, 1826-54, The Authors, Memphis, TN, 1978.

__SC MARRIAGES, Southern Historical Press, Easley, SC,

1980-1, Volume 1 (1688-1799), Volume 2 (1800-20).
__M. L. Webber, DEATH NOTICES FROM THE SC AND AMERICAN GENERAL GAZETTE (1766-82), SC GAZETTE (1766-74), CHARLESTON MORNING POST AND DAILY ADVERTISER AND CITY GAZETTE, SC WEEKLY GAZETTE (1783-1827), SC Historical Magazine, many articles in Volumes 16-67.
__L. K. Wells, MARRIAGE AND OBITUARY NOTICES FROM THE YORKVILLE COMPILER, SC Historical Magazine, Volume 72, 179-83, 234-5.
__T. C. Wilkinson, EARLY ANDERSON COUNTY NEWSPAPERS, MARRIAGES, AND OBITUARIES, 1841-82, Southern Historical Press, Easley, SC, 1978.
__T. E. Wilson and J. L. Grimes, MARRIAGE AND DEATH NOTICES FROM THE SOUTHERN PATRIOT, Southern Historical Press, Easley, SC, 1982, Volume 1 (1815-30).

31. Published genealogies for the US

There are many published indexes, microfilm indexes, and card indexes which list large numbers of published genealogies at the national level. The most important indexes dealing exclusively with SC were listed in section 17. These listings included the card catalogs in SCL, SCHS, GSU, and BLGSU. This paragraph sets out further indexes to genealogies all over the US. These indexes contain many references to South Carolinians and therefore you must not fail to look into them. Among the larger ones are:
__F. Rider, AMERICAN GENEALOGICAL INDEX, Godfrey Memorial Library, Middletown, CT, 1942-52, 48 volumes. [Millions of references]
__F. Rider, AMERICAN GENEALOGICAL & BIOGRAPHICAL INDEX, Godfrey Memorial Library, Middletown, CT, 1952-83, over 120 volumes. [Millions of references]
__The Newberry Library, THE GENEALOGICAL INDEX OF THE NEWBERRY LIBRARY, G. K. Hall, Boston, MA, 1960, 4 volumes. [500,000 names]
__The NY Public Library, DICTIONARY CATALOG OF THE LOCAL HISTORY & GENEALOGY DIVISION OF THE NEW YORK PUBLIC LIBRARY, G. K. Hall, Boston, MA, 1974, 20 volumes. [318,000 entries]
__J. Munsell's Sons, INDEX TO AMERICAN GENEALOGIES, 1711-1908, reprint, Genealogical Publishing Co., Baltimore, MD, 1967. [60,000 references]
__M. J. Kaminkow, GENEALOGIES IN THE LIBRARY OF CONGRESS, Magna Carta, Baltimore, MD, 1972, 4 volumes, with

COMPLEMENT, 1981. [over 25,000 genealogies]
These volumes are available in SCL, SCHS, GSU (BLGSU), LGL, some RL, and some LL.

Also available at SCL, SCHS, GSU (BLGSU), LGL, and in some RL and LL are several regional volumes which can lead you to genealogical information on SC families:
__Z. Armstrong, NOTABLE SOUTHERN FAMILIES, Lookout Publishing Co., Chattanooga, TN, 1918-33, 6 volumes.
__J. B. Boddie, HISTORICAL SOUTHERN FAMILIES, Pacific Coast Publishers, Redwood City, CA, 1957-80, 23 volumes.
__M. W. Collier, BIOGRAPHIES OF REPRESENTATIVE WOMEN IN THE SOUTH, 1861-1920, The Author, Atlanta, GA, 1920-9, 5 volumes.
__W. A. Crozier, A KEY TO SOUTHERN PEDIGREES, Southern Book Co., Baltimore, MD, 1953.
__E. K. Kirkham, INDEX TO SOME OF THE FAMILY RECORDS OF THE SOUTHERN STATES, Everton, Publishers, LOGAN, UT, 1979.

32. Regional records

In addition to state and local publications, there are some valuable regional publications which should not be overlooked by any SC researcher. These publications apply to specific regions which are made up of a few or many SC counties. Among them are some of the newspaper volumes which were mentioned in the latter portion of section 30. Other books which are to be recognized and used include:
__V. Alexander, C. Elliott, and B. Willie, PENDLETON DISTRICT AND ANDERSON COUNTY WILLS, 1793-1857, PROBATE RECORDS, AND TAX RETURNS, Southern Historical Press, Easley, SC, 1980.
__M. B. Bethea, ANCESTRAL KEY TO THE PEE DEE, Manning and Shine, Latta, SC, 1979.
__A. Gregg, HISTORY OF OLD CHERAWS, 1730-1810, Genealogical Publishing Co., Baltimore, MD, 1975.
__G. L. C. Hendrix, SC SOURCE BOOK OF INHABITANTS THROUGH 1800 SOUTH SIDE OF SALUDA RIVER, The Author, Greenville, SC, 1980.
__B. H. Holcomb, A GUIDE AND INDEX TO RECORDS OF WASHINGTON EQUITY DISTRICT, A Press, Greenville, SC, 1982.
__B. H. Holcomb, NINETY-SIX DISTRICT, SC, JOURNAL OF THE

COURT AND ORDINARY INVENTORY BOOK WILL BOOK, 1781-6, Southern Historical Press, Easley, SC, 1978.
_B. H. Holcomb and E. O. Parker, OLD CAMDEN DISTRICT WILLS AND ADMINISTRATIONS, 1781-7, Southern Historical Press, Easley, SC, 1978.
_B. H. Holcomb and M. Clark, NINETY-SIX DISTRICT JOURNAL OF THE COURT OF ORDINARY, INVENTORY BOOK, WILL BOOK, 1781-6, Southern Historical Press, Easley, SC, 1978.
_B. H. Holcomb and S. E. Lucas, Jr., SOME SC COUNTY RECORDS, Southern Historical Press, Easley, SC, 1976-81, 2 volumes.
_B. H. Holcomb and E. O. Parker, OLD CAMDEN DISTRICT WILLS AND ADMINISTRATIONS, 1781-7, Southern Historical Press, Easley, SC, 1981.
_J. B. Landrum, COLONIAL AND REVOLUTIONARY HISTORY OF UPPER SC, Reprint Co., Spartanburg, SC, 1897 (1959).
_J. S. Owen and A. S. Smith, PATENT LAND SURVEY, A Press, Greenville, SC, 1979. [5 counties in Old Ninety-Six District]
_L. Pursley, 7500 MARRIAGES FROM NINETY-SIX AND ABBEVILLE DISTRICTS, 1774-1890, Southern Historical Press, Easley, SC, 1980.
_R. W. Simpson, HISTORY OF THE OLD PENDLETON DISTRICT AND GENEALOGY OF LEADING FAMILIES, Southern Historical Press, Easley, SC, 1978 (1981). [Over 40,000 names]
_B. Willie, PENDLETON DISTRICT DEEDS, 1790-1806, Southern Historical Press, Easley, SC, 1982.
_J. E. Wooley, A COLLECTION OF UPPER SC GENEALOGICAL AND FAMILY RECORDS, Southern Historical Press, Easley, SC, 1979-81, 3 volumes. [Over 120,000 names]
_P. Young, ABSTRACTS OF OLD NINETY-SIX AND ABBEVILLE DISTRICT: WILLS, BONDS, ADMINISTRATIONS, 1774-1860, Southern Historical Press, Easley, SC, 1950 (1972). [About 30,000 names]

33. **Tax, voter, & jury lists**

There are available a number of listings of people in various parishes, counties, and districts of SC. The most important of these lists are those of tax payers, voters, and persons serving on juries. There were sizable numbers of these lists compiled, but unfortunately, only a small fraction survive. A number of early **tax lists** (1783-99) are available for some parishes and a few districts. These include the following, some being quite incomplete:

__SC TAX RETURNS, 1783-99, listed in GUIDE TO
MISCELLANEOUS SC RECORDS, SCDA, Columbia, SC: St.
Bartholomew's Parish (1783-7, 1798), St. Paul's Parish
(1783, 1785-96, 1798-9), Christ Church Parish (1784,
1786, 1788, 1793-9), Prince Frederick's Parish (1784,
1786), St. Andrews Parish (1784-5, 1787, 1789, 1791,
1795), Prince George's Parish (1786-7), Orangeburg
District (1787), Ninety-Six District (1787), Lexington
County (1788), St. John's Berkeley (1793), St. James
Goose Creek (1796), Lancaster County (1797), St.
Helena's Parish (1798), Prince William's Parish (1798),
St. Luke's Parish (1798-9).

A series of tax returns, almost exclusively for the low country, still exists for the year 1824. These have been indexed in the following large index compilation:

__COMBINED ALPHABETICAL INDEX, 21 microfilm rolls, SCDA, Columbia, SC, includes Comptroller General Tax Returns from 1824.

A number of tax lists exist for the various districts/counties after 1800. These have been indicated under the county listings in Chapter 4. The records themselves are in SCDA. Their content varies considerably, but all those listed give the names and the locations, with more detail sometimes being added. Other tax returns of less importance or less availability are listed in:

__M. C. Chandler and E. W. Wade, THE SC ARCHIVES, A SUMMARY GUIDE, Third Edition, SCDA, Columbia, SC, 1985/6.

In addition to the tax lists, there are also some <u>voter lists</u>. These are available for practically every county which was in existence when they were compiled. The records are in SCDA:

__VOTER REGISTRATIONS: 1867-8 (12 cartons), 1868 (8 volumes), 1898 (35 volumes), SCDA, Columbia, SC.

Indicators of these records are provided in the individual county listings in Chapter 4. Finally, there are some <u>jury lists</u> which can also be of value. Two published works bring together many of these data in very useful forms:

__G. L. C. Hendrix and M. M. Lindsay, THE JURY LISTS OF SC, 1778-9, Genealogical Publishing Co., Baltimore, MD, 1980. [9000 names.]

__M. B. Warren, SC JURY LISTS, 1718-83, Heritage Papers, Danielsville, GA, 1977.

34. Will and probate records

When a person died leaving any property (an estate), it was necessary for the governmental authorities to see that the property was properly distributed according to the law. If a will had been written, it was usually presented for authentication to a court or other authority (Court of Ordinary or Court of Probate, Ordinary or Probate Judge, or early in the colony the Gorvernor or his Council or the Secretary of the Colony). The authority then approved or appointed an executor (or administrator, the terms sometimes being used interchangeably) who did the actual work of distributing the estate in accordance with the will. The will itself was then copied into the records, and the original was filed. If no will had been written (called an intestate situation), the ordinary or probate authority appointed an administrator who did the work of distributing the estate in accordance with the requirements of the law. In the various actions by which executors and adminstrators (under the probate supervision) distributed the property of the deceased, many records were generated because accounting to the probate or ordinary authorities was required. These records may include appointments of executors and administrators, bonds, papers, accounts, inventories, appraisals, sales, newspaper ads informing people of the sales, settlements, guardian records, annual returns accounting for safe keeping of inheritances of minor children, petitions, land divisions, and others. The records may be found loose, in files, in bound volumes under various titles, but you should take special care to attempt to find the package (which will contain all existing records of the proceedings related to the estate gathered together in one place). The more recent the death, the greater the probability that the package survives. In the early years, some of the records may be intermingled with conveyance records or they may appear in court minutes. The records of Courts of Equity must always be looked into. Many of these records have been transcribed and/or microfilmed.

Up until 1781, all will and probate records for SC are in the Charleston records. The easiest access to these materials is through a number of published indexes and abstracts. These volumes should be examined before

you venture into the original records because they will
save you much time by leading directly to the originals.
They are:
__C. T. Moore, ABSTRACTS OF THE WILLS OF SC, 1670-1800,
  Bryan Co., Columbia, SC, 1960-74, 4 volumes.
__B. H. Holcomb, PROBATE RECORDS OF SC: INVENTORIES,
  1746-84, JOURNAL OF THE COURT OF ORDINARY, 1771-5,
  LETTERS OF ADMINISTRATION, 1775-1821, JOURNAL OF THE
  ORDINARY, 1764-71, Southern Historical Press, Easley,
  SC, 1977-9, 3 volumes.
__Charleston Free Library, INDEX TO WILLS OF CHARLESTON
  COUNTY, SC, 1671-1868, Genealogical Publishing Co.,
  Baltimore, MD, 1974. (Contains will references for all
  SC during 1671-1782.)
__INDEX TO WILLS, INVENTORIES, AND MISCELLANEOUS RECORDS,
  1687-1746, typescript, SCDA, Columbia, SC. Cross index
  to names mentioned in wills, inventories, and other
  documents.
__C. T. Moore, ABSTRACTS OF RECORDS OF THE SECRETARY OF
  THE PROVINCE OF SC, 1692-1721, Bryan Co., Columbia, SC,
  1978. [Wills, administrations, bonds, bills of sale,
  powers of attorney.]
__A. S. Salley, Jr., ABSTRACTS FROM THE RECORDS, COURT OF
  ORDINARY (PROBATE), 1692-1700, SC Historical and
  Genealogical Magazine, 1907-12, volumes 8-13, see SC
  Historical Society, INDEXES TO SC HISTORICAL AND
  GENEALOGICAL MAGAZINE, The Society, Charleston, SC,
  1960, index to volumes 1-40.
The original records from which these abstracts were
taken or to which the indexes refer are in the SCDA and
copies are in the Probate Court Office of Charleston
County in Charleston, SC. The original records include:
__CHARLESTON COUNTY TRANSCRIPTS OF WILLS, 1671-1731, 2
  volumes on 1 reel, SCDA, Columbia, SC, leads to
  original clerk's entry books.
__Secretary of the Province, WILLS, 1732-76, 14 volumes,
  SCDA, Columbia, SC, indexed.
__Secretary of the Province, INVENTORIES OF ESTATES,
  1736-76, 17 volumes, SCDA, Columbia, SC, partially
  indexed.
__Court of Ordinary, JOURNAL OF THE COURT OF ORDINARY,
  1771-5, 1 volume, SCDA, Columbia, SC.
__Court of Ordinary, INVENTORIES OF ESTATES, 1776-82, 3
  volumes, SCDA, Columbia, SC.
__Court of Ordinary, WILLS, 1776-82, 3 volumes, SCDA,
  Columbia, SC.

In 1781, the Circuit Court Districts which had begun functioning in 1772 (see Chapter 2, section 11), were each given a Court of Ordinary (Probate). The districts (Charleston, Beaufort, Georgetown, Orangeburg, Camden, Cheraws, and Ninety-Six) functioned from 1781-7. However, the records for only three of them have survived: Charleston, Camden, and Ninety-Six.

__CHARLESTON DISTRICT ORDINARY/PROBATE RECORDS: WILLS (1783-), ADMINISTRATIONS (1783-), LETTERS (1778-), INVENTORIES (1783-), SCDA, Columbia.

__CHARLESTON COUNTY TRANSCRIPTS OF WILLS, 1776-1793, Volumes 18-22, on microfilm, SCDA, Columbia, SC.

__B. H. Holcomb and E. O. Parker, OLD CAMDEN DISTRICT WILLS AND ADMINISTRATIONS, 1781-7 (1770-96), Southern Historical Press, Easley, SC, 1981.

__B. H. Holcomb and M. Clark, NINETY-SIX DISTRICT JOURNAL OF THE COURT OF ORDINARY, INVENTORY BOOK, WILL BOOK, 1781-6, Southern Historical Press, Easley, SC, 1978.

__P. Young, ABSTRACTS OF OLD NINETY-SIX AND ABBEVILLE DISTRICT: WILLS, BONDS, ADMINISTRATIONS, 1774-1860, Southern Historical Press, Easley, SC, 1950 (1977).

As you will recall (Chapter 1, section 11), in 1785 the districts were each divided into counties. For the low-country districts (Charleston, Beaufort, Georgetown, Orangeburg), the counties refused to function or functioned only part of the time up until about 1800. In the up-country districts (Camden, Cheraws, Ninety-Six), the counties began functioning. In 1787, the counties in the up-country districts received courts of ordinary and began to record wills and estate actions, but the low-country districts continued to act and keep the records regarding probate matters as they had done before. That is, during 1787-1800, some districts (Charleston, Beaufort, Georgetown, Orangeburg) had the courts of ordinary (probate), but in other districts (Camden, Cheraws, Ninety-Six) each county had its own court of ordinary (probate). A degree of caution needs to be exercised, however, because in some areas the changeover was erratic. The simplest way to keep from missing material is to look for will and probate records in both your ancestor's district and county during these years (1787-1800).

In 1800, the old large districts were dissolved, 25 new small districts were formed, and each of them was given a court of ordinary (probate). Through the years 1800-68, these 25 new small districts expanded into 30. Then in 1868, all districts were designated counties, these counties then dividing into the 46 that SC now has. The original records for old districts (1787-1800), old counties (1787-1800), new districts (1800-68), and new counties (1868-present) are located at SCDA and/or in the offices of the probate judges in the counties. Those which are readily available in original, microfilmed, or transcribed form in SCDA and/or SCL are listed in Chapter 4 under the various existing counties. There are also some published and microfilmed materials which can be of considerable help, including:

__Charleston Free Library, INDEX TO WILLS OF CHARLESTON COUNTY, SC, 1671-1868, Genealogical Pubishing Co., Baltimore, MD, 1974.

__M. L. Houston, INDEXES TO THE COUNTY WILLS OF SC, 1766-1853, Genealogical Publishing Co., Baltimore, MD, 1946 (1970). (Charleston County not included; actual compiler is Mrs. J. D. Rogers.)

__Works Progress Administration, INDEXES TO THE COUNTY WILLS OF SC, University of SC Press, Columbia, SC, 1939.

__P. Young, A GENEALOGICAL COLLECTION OF SC WILLS AND RECORDS, Southern Historical Press, Easley, SC, 1955 (1981), 2 volumes.

__SC WILL TRANSCRIPTS, Microcopy No. 9, SCDA, Columbia, SC, 1980, 31 rolls, alphabetical index in the 1st roll. (Transcripts of pre-Civil War wills of 21 SC counties), explained in detail in J. M. Brimelow and W. A. Wates, SC WILL TRANSCRIPTS PAMPHLET, 1782-1868, SCDA, Columbia, SC, 1980.

The last material indicated above contains records for all SC districts as of 1853 except Beaufort, Chesterfield, Colleton, Georgetown, Lancaster, Lexington, Orangeburg (no pre-Civil War probate records survive for these districts), and Charleston.

35. *WPA* and *CWA* transcripts

Beginning in the middle 1930s and up through 1942, the Works Progress Administration (WPA) and its predecessor, the Civil Works Administration, employed many people who surveyed, inventoried, transcribed, typed, and indexed numerous state, county, municipal, church, cemetery, newspaper, vital statistics, and manuscript records of SC. Many of them are out of date and have been superseded, but others are still of great genealogical research value. Among the very useful items are over 870 volumes of typescript county records covering 28 SC counties. These are to be found in SCDA and are included in Chapter 4 in the listings of available records for each of the SC counties, although practically all of them duplicate original and/or microfilmed records.

Another set of useful WPA typescript volumes are over 120 books listing tombstone inscriptions taken from cemeteries in 33 SC counties. The volumes may be found in SCL. A listing of the cemeteries involved appears in:
__R. N. Cote, LOCAL AND FAMILY HISTORY IN SC, Southern Historical Press, Easley, SC, 1981, pp. 373-6.
The WPA also inventoried church records of many churches in SC. The original inventories are in SCL and copies are available in SCHS, Winthrop College Archives (Rock Hill), Francis Marion College Library (Florence), and Furman University Library (Greenville). Churches for which these inventories are extant are listed in:
__R. N. Cote, LOCAL AND FAMILY HISTORY IN SC, Southern Historical Press, Easley, SC, 1981, pp. 381-414.
Somewhat useful, but not as much as those above, are the WPA inventories of the records in the county archives at that time (1937-41) for 14 SC counties:
__Works Progress Administration, INVENTORY OF COUNTY ARCHIVES OF SC [ABBEVILLE, AIKEN, ALLENDALE, ANDERSON, CHEROKEE, DILLON, FLORENCE, JASPER, LEE, McCORMICK, OCONEE, PICKENS, RICHLAND, SALUDA], Historical Records Survey, WPA, Columbia, SC, 1937-41, 14 volumes.
The WPA materials mentioned above will be included in Chapter 4 in the listings of available records for each of the SC counties, although practically all of the county record transcripts duplicate original and/or microfilmed records.

LIST OF ABBREVIATIONS

A	=	Agricultural census
BLGSU	=	Branch Library(ies) of the Genealogical Society of UT (Utah)
C	=	Civil War Union veterans census
CH	=	Court house(s)
GSU	=	Genealogical Society of UT (Utah)
I	=	Industrial census records
LGL	=	Large genealogical library(ies)
LL	=	Local library(ies)
M	=	Mortality census records
NA	=	National Archives
P	=	Pensioner census, Revolutionary War
R	=	Regular census records
RBNA	=	Regional Branches of the National Archives
RL	=	Regional library(ies)
S	=	Slaveholder census records
SC	=	South Carolina
SCDA	=	SC Department of Archives
SCHS	=	SC Historical Society
SCL	=	South Caroliniana Library
X	=	State census records
*	=	When on libraries, indicates good genealogical collection
*	=	When on records, indicates index

Chapter 3

RECORD LOCATIONS

1. Court houses (CH)

As you will recall, there were no county (district) records in SC before 1785; records were kept only at the colony or state level. Most SC county (district) records of any genealogical importance for the years 1785-1865 are held by SCDA either as the originals, or as microfilm or as transcripts. In addition, they also hold a large number of original or microfilm copies of numerous county records during the period from 1865 toward, up to, and/or into the 20th century (1900s). SCDA continues its program of collecting original or microfilm copies of county records, and additions to its holdings increase from month to month. In short, only if you are interested in county records after 1900 should you consider starting your work at the local CH. Even in this case, you should take a look at what records are available at SCDA (see Chapter 4) before deciding to visit the county CH. Chapter 4 lists the county records available in SCDA and SCL for each county, and the following volume, which will be published shortly, will provide even more detail on them:
_ THE SC ARCHIVES: A SUMMARY GUIDE, SCDA, Columbia, SC, 3rd edition, to be published in 1985/6.

Thus, you can see that once you have located the county of your SC ancestor, it is usually not a good idea to go there first. It is best to first explore the originals, microfilm copies, and transcript copies of the records in SCDA, the transcribed and published copies in SCL and SCHS, and the manuscripts in SCL and SCHS. If you are not near SCDA, SCL, and SCHS, you could examine the copies of SC records held by GSU, which are listed in the microfilm indexes of the numerous BLGSU, and are available on interlibrary loan through these BLGSU. Their holdings, however, constitute only a fraction of what is available at SCDA, SCL, and SCHS. Only after you or your hired researcher have exhausted the resources of SCDA, SCL, and SCHS should you visit or send a hired researcher to look into the CH records. And this should only be done after letters of inquiry to county officials

(Clerk of Court, Probate Court, Register of Mesne Conveyance) and the local library (County and/or City Library) have been answered to the effect that they have the records you are seeking. Write <u>very</u> brief letters (less than half a page), give the dates you are interested in, ask about the types of records available, and enclose an SASE.

Briefly, you need to remember the SC <u>county/district records</u> (clerk of court, Confederate pension, conveyance, coroner, commissioner, court of common pleas, court of general sessions, court or master of equity, district court, estate, guardian, lien, magistrate, mortgage, plat, sheriff, tax, voter, will) before 1900 should be sought in SCDA, SCL, and SCHS. Supplementary research then may be needed in CH. For county records after 1900, it is still best to first inquire at SCDA, then if necessary, inquire at the CH. The major SC <u>state records</u> (court, land grant, conveyance, memorial, military, will, estate before 1785, and court, land grant, military after 1785) are to be found in SCDA. Many of the major SC <u>federal records</u> (bounty land, census, military, pension) are in SCDA, but more are available at the National Archives. The major SC <u>non-governmental records</u> (Bible, biography, cemetery, church, directory, DAR, genealogical compilations, genealogical periodicals, historical, manuscript, mortuary, newspaper) are located in SCL, SCHS, GSU (BLGSU), LGL, church archives, RL, and LL.

2. The <u>major facilities</u>

The best overall place in the world to do SC genealogical research is in Columbia, SC. This city contains the two most heavily stocked SC genealogical resource collections in existence: the SC State Department of Archives and History (SCDA) and the South Caroliniana Library of the University of SC (SCL). These two installations are within a couple of blocks of each other in downtown Columbia and not too far away is the SC Division of Vital Records. Just 113 miles away is Charleston, where the SC Historical Society Library (SCHL) is located, along with some other repositories which are especially valuable for colonial SC and Charleston County.

In Salt Lake City, UT, is the largest genealogical library in the world, the Library of the Genealogical Society of UT (GSU). This facility has microfilm copies of many of the records in SCDA and many of the books in SCL. The Library (GSU) has over 350 branch libraries (BLGSU) located all over the world. The vast microfilm holdings of GSU can be borrowed through its branches. Each branch has copies of three exceedingly large indexes to the holdings of GSU. Included among the BLGSU are three in SC, in Charleston, Columbia, and Greenville.

Another facility of importance is the National Archives (NA) in Washington, DC, along with the Regional Branches of the National Archives (RBNA) located in or near Atlanta, GA, Boston, MA, Chicago, IL, Denver, CO, Fort Worth, TX, Kansas City, MO, Los Angeles, CA, New York, NY, Philadelphia, PA, Seattle, WA, and San Francisco, CA. The National Archives (NA) houses many _federal records_ relating to SC including census, passenger arrival, military service, bounty land, pension, claim, land, and court records. Many of these, especially the census, military service, bounty land, and pension records are available in microfilm copy in the Regional Branches of the National Archives (RBNA). The Atlanta Branch (1557 St. Joseph Ave., East Point, GA 30344) serves SC (among other nearby states) and also serves as the record repository for records of federal field offices which operate in the area.

3. The SC Department of Archives (SCDA)

The SC Department of Archives and History, referred to in this volume as the SC Department of Archives (SCDA), is located at 1430 Senate St., Columbia, SC 29211. This location is at the intersection of Senate and Bull Sts., just two blocks from the State House. The mail address is SC Department of Archives and History, PO Box 11669, Columbia, SC 29211, and the telephone number is 1-803-758-5816. There is a parking lot provided for visitors with its entrance just south of SCDA on Bull Street. After parking in this lot, you must obtain a parking permit at the Main Desk in the Search Room of SCDA, then you must return the permit to your car where it is to be displayed through the windshield. Cars not displaying a permit are subject to parking tickets and/or towing. At this writing, the SCDA is open 9:00 am-9:00

pm Monday-Friday, 9:00 am-6:00 pm Saturday, and 1:00 pm-9:00 pm Sunday. Senior archivists are present only 9:00 am-5:00 pm Monday-Friday, so if you are making your first visit or otherwise need expert help, these are the times to come. It is closed 01 January, 04 July, Labor Day, Thanksgiving Day, and 24-25-26 December. But times change, so don't dare go without calling ahead to check. The nearest motels, which are within walking distance include the Carolina Inn, 937 Assembly St., Columbia, SC 29201 (1-803-799-8200), the Town House, 1615 Gervais St., Columbia, SC 29202 (1-803-771-8711), the Holiday Inn-City Center, 630 Assembly St., Columbia, SC 29201 (1-803-799-7800 or 1-800-465-4329), the Columbia Marriott, 1200 Hampton St., Columbia, SC 29201 (1-803-771-7000 or 1-800-228-2180), and the Governor's House, 1301 Main St., Columbia, SC 29201 (1-803-779-7790).

The Search Room of the SCDA, where genealogical research is carried out, occupies the east wing of the building. It is at street level and should be entered through the entrance on Bull Street. Upon entering, show the staff member at the Main Desk some identification, and then store all your materials except pencils, brief notes, and note-taking paper in the lockers at the Main Desk, and leave your wraps in the coat area near the Main Desk. Next, ask for and fill out a registration form, after which you should request copies of the pamphlet RESEARCH IN THE SC ARCHIVES and the regulation sheets. Find yourself a seat and read these materials. You will discover that they tell you much about the operation of the SCDA, chief among the items being: (1) all materials are to be handled with extreme care, (2) removal, mutilation, or writing on records or equipment are strictly forbidden, (3) no food, drink, or smoking are permitted, (4) the permission of the Divisional Director must be obtained for any use of typewriters or of electronic, duplicating, or photographic equipment of any sort, (5) excessive and loud talk are to be avoided, (6) records are to be requested by filling out a call slip and taking it to the Main Desk, (7) all such records are to be returned to the Main Desk, (8) some microfilms must be requested but some are available on open access shelves, (9) microfilms obtained from the Main Desk must be returned there, but microfilms taken off the open shelves are to be placed on a special credenza near the microfilm readers, (10) books and periodicals are not to be reshelved, they are to be left on the table, and (11) only one hour is permitted on a microfilm reader if others are waiting.

Upon completion of the above, ask for a brief interview with a staff member, <u>briefly</u> explain your needs, and request advice on sources to consult. Please remember that staff members cannot do research for you; they can only advise you on how to do your own research. Now glance around a bit, and you will discover that the Search Room is actually divided into three smaller areas. In the center are the Main Desk, a tall index table, and two card files. Here you will ask advice of those staffing the desk, search indexes, request records, receive records, and return records. To the right of the Main Desk (as you face it) is the Salley Room where books and manuscripts are to be used. The room seats 30 at comfortable tables, and its walls are lined with reference volumes, finding aids, indexes, and important published books and periodicals. To the left of the Main Desk (as you face it) is the Easterby Room which contains microform reading equipment, special cubicles for use of typewriters or tape recorders (permission required!), a special light for reading faded records, and restrooms (in the SW corner). There is a public telephone in the vestibule, and adjacent to the Search Room there is a small lounge area where researchers may relax and confer.

Now, let us describe what you will find in the Search Room. At the Main Desk there are a number of loose-leaf finding aids which will be of a great deal of use to you. They must be asked for at the Main Desk.

__SC COUNTY AND DISTRICT RECORD LISTINGS, includes Archives microfilms, LDS microfilms, original records, and WPA transcripts, listed by county or district; lead to microfilms, transcripts, or records which SCDA holds for the various counties.

__SC COLONIAL AND STATE GOVERNMENT RECORD LISTINGS, includes colonial and state government records on microfilm, transcribed, or original form; listed are records of Secretary of Colony and State, Governor, Military Department, Courts, Councils, Assembly, Attorney General, Treasurer, Auditor, Comptroller General, and others; lead to microfilms, transcripts, or records.

The SCDA intends to publish these two in combined form as:
__M. C. Chandler and E. W. Wade, THE SC ARCHIVES: A SUMMARY GUIDE, Third Edition, SCDA, Columbia, SC, 1985/6.
Other loose-leaf finding aids available by request at the Main Desk are:
__GUIDE TO SCDA MICROFILMS OF STATE AND COLONIAL LEGISLATIVE JOURNALS, leads to microfilms.
__GUIDE TO NATIONAL ARCHIVES MICROFILMS HELD BY SCDA, leads to microfilms.
__SCDA LOOSELEAF GAZETTEER, lists creeks, streams, rivers, places.
__GUIDE TO MISCELLANEOUS SC RECORDS, includes state tax returns 1783-99, writs of partition 1749-74, Winton County tax list 1800, tax return books by district 1800-67, jury lists 1731-83.
__GUIDE TO SC COLONIAL AND REVOLUTIONARY MICROFILM, includes court records, British army papers, manuscripts, early state records, Loyalist transcripts, Revolutionary pension and bounty land applications, Revolutionary accounts audited, Continental regiments, bounty land grants, leads to microfilms.
__GUIDE TO POST-REVOLUTIONARY SC MICROFILM, includes US courts, Official Records of the War of the Rebellion, Freedmans Bureau, agricultural, industrial, and mortality censuses 1850-80, several manuscripts, leads to the microfilms.
There are some card file indexes which are kept back in the storage areas which must be asked for at the Main Desk. Among them are:
__CARD FILE INDEX OF 1919-26 SC CONFEDERATE PENSION APPLICATIONS, leads to applications.
__CARD FILE INDEX TO SPANISH-AMERICAN WAR PERSONNEL RECORDS, leads to records.

Just across from the Main Desk sits a tall table with numerous indexes on shelves beneath it:
__1790, 1800, 1810, 1820, 1830, 1840, 1850, 1850 Mortality, 1860, 1860 Mortality FEDERAL CENSUS INDEXES.
__COMBINED ALPHABETICAL INDEX, 21 microfilm rolls, a consolidated index to many early and important SC records.
__COLONIAL LAND RECORD MICROFILM INDEXES, Charleston deeds 1719-85 (1 roll), Unrecorded plats 1730-1853 (1 roll), bills of sale (3 rolls), miscellaneous maps,

plats and deeds (1 roll), colonial plats (4 rolls), royal grants (2 rolls), memorials (5 rolls).
__INDEXES TO MISCELLANEOUS RECORDS: One-letter series 1776-1846 (2 volumes), Records since 1846 (1 volume), Three and four-letter series (1 volume), Five letter series (1 volume).
__GREEN'S INDEX TO LAND RECORDS (GRANTS, WARRANTS, CONVEYANCES), 1675-1739, 1 volume.
__GENERAL INDEX TO MISCELLANEOUS RECORDS AND BILLS OF SALE, 1729-1825, 7 volumes.
__INDEX TO MARRIAGE SETTLEMENTS, 1785-1887, 1 volume.
__INDEXES TO STATE PLATS: Series 1, 1784-1840 (4 volumes), Series 2, 1784-1840 (2 volumes), Series 3, 1840-82 (1 volume).
__INDEXES TO STATE GRANTS, 1784-1821 (4 volumes), 1822-45 (1 volume), 1843-70 (1 volume).
Behind the tall table on the East wall on either side of a window are two card file cabinets containing the following card file indexes:
__MILITIA PAY ROLLS, 1759-60, leads to records.
__AUDITOR GENERAL'S ACCOUNTS, 1778-80, leads to records.
__MISCELLANEOUS RECORDS, FIVE LETTER SERIES, leads to records.
__PUBLISHED VOLUMES ON SEARCH ROOM SHELVES, leads to volumes.
__WAR OF 1812 PAYROLL LISTS, leads to further records.
__CROSS INDEX OF NAMES IN COLONIAL PLATS, leads to plats.
__SEARCH ROOM NON-COUNTY MICROFILM, leads to microfilms.
__MAPS, leads to maps.
__CITIZENSHIP (NATURALIZATION) INDEX, leads to records.
__MEXICAN WAR PALMETTO REGIMENT MEMBERS, brief data, leads to further data.
__LOYALISTS, brief data, leads to other records.
__REVOLUTIONARY WAR STUB INDENTS AND ACCOUNTS AUDITED, leads to records.
__CONFEDERATE WAR PARTICIPANTS, gives brief data, leads to further records.

Now turning to the Salley Room (to the right of the Main Desk), you will find that its walls are filled with shelves containing books and microfilms. Beginning at the corner nearest the Main Desk and moving around the room clockwise, you will see general literary works, library and archives reference volumes, genealogical research books, and manuscript guides. Then beginning at the third set of shelves along the West wall you will see many microfilm boxes: census and census index microfilms, early state record microfilms, microfilmed SC will transcripts and indexes to them, Revolutionary War indexes and rolls, and War of 1812 indexes. The microfilm boxes continue with indexes for some of the major records (conveyance, court, plat, estate, will) for most of the counties. Then there appear microfilms for Charleston (colony) wills, inventories, and miscellaneous records, followed by microfilms from the British Public Record Office of materials relating to SC. After this there are the microfilm indexes to the service records of SC Confederate participants, and just after them, the microfilms of the service records themselves. Finally, the microfilm boxes end up with the microfilms of the British Manuscript Project which carry SC information. Completing the contents of the West wall are published church histories and records. Turning the NW corner of the room, there will be found along the North wall the WPA county archive inventories, national biographical works, SC Indian volumes, SC black publications, Revolutionary War books, War of 1812 books, and SC Confederate histories. This will bring you to the NE corner, which will start the East wall on which will be found these materials in this order: Civil War books, SC genealogical periodicals, SC genealogical publications, SC state, regional, district, county, city, and town histories, materials on other states, atlases and map compilations, colonial and state records of SC, and finally, legislative records and statutes of SC. You need to remember that the published works in this room are meant to be only a supplement to the original records (and copies of original records). There is a sizably larger collection of published works just a couple of blocks away at SCL (see next section).

You are free to use all the materials in front of the Main Desk at the tall table and the card file cabinets and everything on the shelves in the Salley Room. You should not reshelve books from the Salley Room, but leave them out on the tables. You may take the various microfilms to the readers in the Easterby Room where you may use them. However, if you are not completely familiar with the use of the readers, please ask for help so as not to risk damaging the microfilms. Upon finishing with the microfilms do not return them to the shelves, but leave them on the credenza near the readers. In using the finding aids, indexes, books, and microfilms, when you run across records you wish to examine, fill out a request form (obtainable at the Main Desk), carefully answering all questions, and submit it to an attendant at the Main Desk. Your materials will be brought out from the storage area to the Main Desk where you may obtain them. After use, return the materials to the Main Desk.

The staff of SCDA cannot do genealogical research for you by mail. They are kept busy serving the State and the patrons who come to them in person. They will provide you with a list of researchers if you cannot make a personal visit. Dispatch them a request and an SASE. They will provide for you the answer to one or two <u>very specific</u> questions which can be answered by taking a brief look at an index. You must include the following in your request: (1) full name of person, (2) name of county, (3) specific document desired, and (4) approximate date.

4. The <u>South Caroliniana Library</u> (<u>SCL</u>)

The South Caroliniana Library (SCL), a component library of the several libraries located on the campus of the University of SC, is just a few blocks from the SCDA near the corner of Pendleton and Sumter Sts. in downtown Columbia. The building which houses the SCL is the historic Old South Carolina College Library built in 1840. The telephone number of the Book Division is 1-803-777-3131 and that of the Manuscript Division is 1-803-777-5173. <u>During the Fall and Spring Semesters</u>, the Book Division is open Monday through Saturday from 8:30 am to 5:00 pm with hours extended to 8:00 pm on Tuesday and Thursday. The Manuscript Division is open 8:30 am to 5:00 pm Monday through Friday, and 8:30 am to 1:00 pm on Saturday. <u>During the summer</u>, the hours of both Divisions are 8:00 am to 5:00 pm Monday through Friday, and 8:30 am to 1:00 pm Saturday. <u>Between sessions</u>, the hours tend to be those observed during the summer. However, because of this variety in hours, please call ahead before going to the library in order to make sure you don't find them closed. Motels and hotels listed in the previous section are ones which are in walking distance of SCL. Parking for SCL is available at several parking lots within a few blocks. However, it is important to remember that SCL is both on a university campus and in a downtown area, so parking can be a problem, especially during the regular school year. That is precisely why we have given you motels within walking distance (see previous section).

As indicated above, the SCL is composed of two main divisions, the Book Division on the second floor and the Manuscript Division on the first floor. The Book Division has well over 60,000 volumes, rolls of microfilm, and original and microfilmed newspapers. Essentially every book relating to SC mentioned in Chapter 2 will be found here. There are biographical reference works, books listing vital records (birth, death, divorce, marriage), published cemetery records, census indexes, volumes of church records, city directories, histories (towns, city, county, district, state, church, ethnic, military), published colonial records, newspaper abstracts, will and probate compilations, military lists and histories, pension indexes, atlases, gazetteers, maps, and pictures. The Manuscript Division is equally rich since its holdings include over 1,300,000 manuscripts, pamphlets, original records, transcripts, tombstone inscription collections, unpublished genealogical records, Bible records, military papers, church records, letters, merchants' records, documents, records of professional men, and school records.

When you enter the SCL, you will find yourself in a long hall. On your left will be the door into the Manuscript Division, on your right will be a small hall leading to the rest rooms, and straight ahead will be the circular stairs leading to the second floor where the Book Division is located. Go up these stairs, then enter the door into the Book Division. Straight ahead will be the Service Desk which is located in the center of the South Wall. To the right of the Service Desk there are three book alcoves, and to the left there are three book alcoves. As you continue to stand just inside the door (on the North Wall), you will also observe three more book alcoves on the North Wall to your right, and three book alcoves to your left. There are therefore 12 book alcoves, three over in the NW corner, three in the NE corner, three in the SE corner, and three in the SW corner. At the East end of the room (to your left) you will see microfilm readers and a large map case, and at the West end of the room (to your right), you will observe two doors entering into a small museum, the Kendall Memorial Room. Now, go to the Service Desk, fill out a registration card, and ask for a copy of the rules. Find yourself a seat at one of the tables and carefully read the rules, especially noting that (1) only pencils are to be used, (2) all materials are to be handled very carefully, (3) there is to be no eating, drinking, smoking, or loud conversation, (4) all materials are subject to search by the staff at any time, (5) it is unlawful to mark, deface, or mutilate any of the materials in any way, (6) permission to use certain volumes on certain shelves (which are marked) must be obtained from the staff, and (7) no volumes are to be reshelved by you, they are to be left on the tables after you finish using them.

Now you need to take a general look around the room to see what materials are on the shelves. To assist you in doing this, we will number the 12 book alcoves starting with number 1 in the NW corner and moving clockwise around the room. Numbers 1, 2, and 3 contain general genealogical reference works, indexes, and periodicals (mostly national and for states other than SC) plus family genealogical works. Number 4 contains Charleston and Columbia City Directories and some major historical and genealogical periodicals of SC. Number 5 contains a very old library collection (of W. G. Simms) and Charleston City Yearbooks. Number 6 (in the NE corner) has in it the many volumes of the Official Records of the Union and Confederate Forces in the Civil War. Number 7 (over in the SE corner) contains F. Rider's AMERICAN GENEALOGICAL-BIOGRAPHICAL INDEX, several series of WHO'S WHO volumes, several series of National Biographical works, and numerous maps in a special map display. Numbers 8, 9, and 11 contain SC Legislative Records, with number 11 also having volumes of the Laws of SC. Number 10 alcove has shelved in it major reference volumes and finding aids for SC genealogy and also contains a small reference desk usually served by a staff member. Please note that the majority of SC volumes are not out on the shelves in these alcoves; they are stored in the stacks. In order to locate the SC materials, you must use the main catalog which occupies alcove number 3 and the positions just to the right and left of the door. In addition, there is a large biographical reference card index in alcove number 2, and a large file card cabinet which occupies alcove number 4 contains indexes of SC publications (by name), newspapers (by place, by date, by title), maps (by place, by date), and periodicals (by name). Behind the Service Desk are card file indexes to pictures and to vertical files which contain miscellaneous items. Let us remind you again that the tremendous volume of SC works which SCL holds are largely in the stack area. They are referenced in the main card catalog and may be obtained from the personnel at the Service Desk.

Begin your work by proceeding to the main card catalog, and start to look for materials of interest to your research by remembering the word SLANT. S stands for subject, so look under various subject headings. The titles of the sections in Chapter 2 will give you a good idea of the sort of things you need to search, but you will not find them all. Other subject headings that you must not overlook are: Registers of births, etc. (vital records may be found here), Church denominations, Church names, Epitaphs, Genealogy, Newspapers, Obituaries, and Probate Records. L stands for locality, therefore examine all cards under the heading South Carolina, then all under the name of the county and district, then all under the names of cities and/or towns in the county and district which might be pertinent. A stands for author, thus examine the author listings for any books mentioned in Chapters 2 and 4 which you might want to find. N stands for name, which reminds you to look under all the surnames which you are searching for to see if there are books which might be relevant. T stands for title, and hence your final step is to look under the titles of books, periodicals, and agencies (such as Daughters of the American Revolution, United Daughters of the Confederacy, Works Progress Administration, US National Archives) which sponsored publications. The word SLANT is simply a memory device, and does not indicate the best order to look for things in. To shorten your research time, it is recommended that you do L (locality) first [county and district first, then state], then N (name), then S (subject), then A (author), and finally T (title). This procedure will give you good coverage of the library holdings which are indexed in the card catalog. Among them you will find almost all of the published materials mentioned in Chapters 2 and 4.

When you run across pertinent materials, write the call numbers down (upper left corner of the card) on a request form, then finish filling it out. Take the completed request form to the Service Desk and give it to a staff member. The staff member will obtain the book for you from the stacks. When you finish with the volume, return it to the Service Desk. Please do not forget to make good use of the materials in the alcoves, especially the SC reference and finding aids (alcove number 10), the biographical card index (alcove number 2), and the newspaper, map, and periodical indexes (alcove number 4). Also do not fail to ask a staff member to look into the picture and vertical file indexes (behind the Service Desk). Finally, be sure and consult the library staff about your search and make it a point to ask about any other special indexes or finding aids which might help you.

Now return to the hall on the first floor, and go back through the door on the West into the Manuscript Division. In preparation for your visit here, it will have served you very well if you have used the indexes of the following two volumes, since they will have alerted you to materials in this repository which might be pertinent to your searches.
__A. H. Stokes, Jr., A GUIDE TO THE MANUSCRIPT COLLECTION OF THE SOUTH CAROLINIANA LIBRARY, University of SC, Columbia, SC, 1982.
__R. N. Cote, LOCAL AND FAMILY HISTORY IN SC, Southern Historical Press, Easley, SC, 1981.
As you enter, stop at the register immediately in front of you, sign in, then read the rules posted above the register. Also recall the rules which were summarized above in the discussion of the Book Division. Now, glance around the room and famiiliarize yourself with its layout and the locations of its equipment. The main card catalog is located in the far left-hand corner (SW corner). In it the various manuscripts are listed under name (personal, institutional, corporate), location, and some subject headings. This catalog must be used to obtain the call numbers of the materials in the volumes mentioned above and the call numbers of other manuscripts which may not be in them. In a partially partitioned area to your left along the South Wall you will find a

microfiche reader, a list of the WPA county record transcripts held by the Archives, the National Union Catalog of Manuscripts, several other catalogs of manuscripts in large US manuscript repositories, finding aids and calendars to some of the larger manuscripts in SCL, and a list of dissertations and theses on SC subjects which have been written at universities all over the US.

Just to your right will be found the Service Desk which is staffed by an archivist. She or he will obtain materials for you when you present a properly filled-out request slip showing the call numbers obtained from the main card catalog. Behind the desk and along the North Wall is a work area for the staff. A door in the far right-hand corner (NW corner) of the room leads to a small nook which contains a microfilm reader, a card index of various WPA materials (narratives, county tour guides, miscellaneous materials), and a chronological card file of manuscript holdings. As you seek manuscript materials on your ancestors, please be certain to look into a series of publications which list the yearly additions to the collection. Here you will find materials not shown in the books by Stokes and Cote.
__Reports of the Annual Meetings of the University South Caroliniana Society, The Society, Columbia, SC, 1981-.
You will find them behind the partial partition on the South Wall.

The staff of librarians and archivists at SCL cannot do genealogical research for you by mail. They are kept busy serving the State and the patrons who come to them in person. They will provide you with a list of researchers if you cannot make a personal visit. Dispatch them a request and an SASE. They will provide for you the answer to one or two <u>very specific</u> questions which can be answered by taking a brief look at an index. You must include the following in your request: (1) full name of person, (2) name of county/district, (3) specific document desired, and (4) approximate date. For example, a specific question might be: Is a Thomas McCRARY[1] mentioned in the Laurens District[2] census index[3] for 1800[4]? Questions less specific than this will require a personal visit or a hired genealogical researcher.

5. The <u>South Carolina Historical Society</u> (SCHS)

The South Carolina Historical Society (SCHS) maintains an excellent library at 100 Meeting St., Charleston, SC 29401. This is in the heart of the historic downtown district. The telephone number is 1-803-723-3225. There is a public parking facility just one block north and one block west at the corner of King and Queen Sts. and an entrance to another large parking building just across Meeting St. from the SCHS. Motels, hotels, and inns within walking distance of the SCHS include the Charleston Mills House, 115 Meeting St., Charleston, SC 29401 (1-800-465-4329 or 1-803-577-2400), Elliott House Inn, 78 Queen St., Charleston, SC 29401 (1-803-723-1855), Days Inn, Charleston, Historic District, 155 Meeting St., Charleston, SC 29401 (1-800-325-2525 or 1-803-722-8411), Meeting Street Inn, 173 Meeting St., Charleston, SC 19401 (1-803-723-1882), Battery Carriage House, 20 South Battery, Charleston, SC 29401 (1-803-723-9881), Indigo Inn, One Maiden Lane, Charleston, SC 29401 (1-800-845-7639 or 1-577-5900 in SC), Heart of Charleston Motor Inn, 200 Meeting St., Charleston, SC 29401 (1-803-723-3451), and Best Western King Charles Inn, 237 Meeting St., Charleston, SC 29401 (1-803-723-7451).

When you arrive at the SCHS building, go up the outside stairs to the entrance, and ring the bell. The librarian or an assistant will answer and admit you. You will be asked to show identification, to register, and to pay a small daily research fee, and to read and adhere to the regulations. The three major research rooms rest along the west side of the second floor of the building (the floor on which you entered). In the <u>first</u> of these rooms are the information and registration desk. The walls are lined with bookshelves containing state, regional, district, county, city, and town histories, volumes for Indian research, and numerous genealogical books. These latter include guide books, finding aids, compendia, census indexes, SC record indexes, abstracts, rosters, and many published records. There are also microform copies of many records, some Charleston city directories, and a great deal of other Charleston material. In the <u>second</u> room are a large worktable and bookshelves with family histories and genealogies, national, state, and regional biographies, church histories, black history publications, and SC genealogical periodicals. In the _third_ room are historical biographical material and historical books largely of a non-genealogical character. In the rooms on the east side of the second floor and on the third floor are offices and storage areas for the very large manuscript collection of the SCHS. On the first floor are rest rooms and a photocopying machine.

The key to practically all of the holdings of the SCHS is a set of card catalogs located in the hall just outside the third room referred to above. In this set, there are _three_ catalogs into which you should look: (1) the publications card catalog which lists all published books and pamphlets [use SLANT as described in the previous section], (2) the manuscript card catalog which refers you to the manuscript materials, and (3) the WPA tombstone index which is an alphabetically-arranged file of a very large number of gravestone readings made by the WPA. In the southeast corner of the third room there are also a few special card indexes which you should not overlook. One of these is an alphabetical file of family researchers. There are also some calendars and indexes to various manuscript collections, and an index to numerous account books. In addition, there is a card index to tombstone inscriptions from many Charleston church cemeteries with the volume containing the records themselves sitting on top of the file. Before visiting the SCHS, it will be of great help to you if you have carefully gone through the following volume and its supplements:
__D. Moltke-Hansen and S. Dosser, SCHS MANUSCRIPT GUIDE, SCHS, Charleston, SC, 1979. Supplements published in SC HISTORICAL MAGAZINE, SCHS, Charleston, SC, 1979-.
It could also be of assistance to you to glance at the indicated pages in:
__R. N. Cote, LOCAL AND FAMILY HISTORY IN SC, Southern Historical Press, Easley, SC, 1981, pp. 281-5.

6. _Genealogical Society of UT (GSU) & Its Branches (BLGSU)_

The largest genealogical library in the world is the Library of the Genealogical Society of UT (GSU). This library, which holds well over a million rolls of microfilm plus a vast number of books, is located at 50

East North Temple St., Salt Lake City, UT 84150. The basic key to the library is composed of three indexes: the international genealogical index, the surname index, and the locality index. In addition to the main library, the Society maintains a large number of Branches (BLGSU) all over the US. Each of these branches has a microfiche copy of the international genealogical index, a microfilm copy of the surname index, and a microfilm copy of the locality index. In addition each Branch has a supply of forms for borrowing microfilm copies of the records at the main library. This means that the astonishingly large holdings of the GSU are available through each of its numerous BLGSU.

The BLGSU in SC are as follows:
__Charleston Stake, BLGSU, PO Box 9434, Hanahan, SC 29410.
__Columbia Stake, BLGSU, 115 Saddlemount Dr., Hopkins, SC 29061.
__Greenville Stake, BLGSU, PO Box 129, Greenville, SC 29678,
Other BLGSU are to be found in the cities listed below. They may be located by looking in the local telephone directory under the listing CHURCH OF JESUS CHRIST OF LATTER-DAY SAINTS-GENEALOGY LIBRARY or in the Yellow Pages under CHURCHES-LATTER-DAY SAINTS.
__In AL: Birmingham, Huntsville, in AK: Anchorage, Fairbanks, in AZ: Cottonwood, Flagstaff, Globe, Holbrook, Mesa, Page, Phoenix, Prescott, Safford, St. David, St. Johns, Show Low, Snowflake, Tucson, Winslow, Yuma, in AR: Little Rock,
__In CA: Anaheim, Bakersfield, Barstow, Blythe, Camarillo, Carlsbad, Cerritos, Chico, Covina, El Centro, Escondido, Eureka, Fairfield, Fresno, Garden Grove, Glendale, Gridley, Hacienda Heights, Hemet, La Crescenta, Lancaster, Long Beach, Los Angeles, Menlo Park, Modesto, Monterey, Napa, Newbury Park, Oakland, Orange, Palmdale, Palm Springs, Pasadena, Redding, Ridgecrest, Riverside, Sacramento, San Bernardino, San Diego, San Jose, San Luis Obispo, Santa Barbara, Santa Clara, Santa Maria, Santa Rosa, Simi Valley, Stockton, Upland, Ventura, Whittier,
__In CO: Arvada, Boulder, Colorado Springs, Cortez, Denver, Durango, Fort Collins, Glenwood Springs, Grand Junction, La Jara, Littleton, Montrose, Pueblo, in CT: Hartford, in DE: Newark, in FL: Boca Raton, Cocoa,

Gainesville, Hialeah, Jacksonville, Lakeland, Marianna, Miami, Orlando, Pensacola, St. Petersburg, Tallahassee, Tampa, in **GA**: Dunwoody, Macon, Marietta, in **HI**: Hilo, Honolulu, Kaneohe, Kona, Laie,

__In **ID**: Blackfoot, Boise, Burley, Caldwell, Driggs, Firth, Idaho Falls, Iona, Lewiston, Malad, Montpelier, Moore, Nampa, Pocatello, Post Falls, Rexburg, Salmon, Shelley, Twin Falls, in **IL**: Champaign, Chicago Heights, Naperville, Rockford, Wilmette, in **IN**: Fort Wayne, Indianapolis, in **IA**: Cedar Rapids, Davenport, Des Moines, in **KS**: Topeka, Wichita, in **KY**: Hopkinsville, Lexington, Louisville, in **LA**: Baton Rouge, Shreveport,

__In **ME**: Augusta, in **MD**: Silver Spring, in **MA**: Boston, in **MI**: Bloomfield Hills, Grand Blanc, Grand Rapids, Lansing, Midland, Westland, in **MN**: Minneapolis, St. Paul, in **MS**: Hattiesburg, in **MO**: Columbia, Kansas City, Liberty, Springfield, St. Louis, in **MT**: Billings, Bozeman, Butte, Great Falls, Helena, Kalispell, Missoula, in **NE**: Omaha,

__In **NV**: Elko, Ely, Fallon, Las Vegas, Logandale, Reno, Sparks, in **NH**: Nashua, in **NJ**: East Brunswick, Morristown, in **NM**: Albuquerque, Farmington, Gallup, Grants, Las Cruces, Roswell, Santa Fe, in **NY**: Albany, Buffalo, Ithaca, New York, Plainview, Rochester, Syracuse, in **NC**: Asheville, Charlotte, Fayetteville, Hickory, Kinston, Raleigh, Wilmington, in **OH**: Cincinnati, Cleveland, Columbus, Dayton, Kirtland, Toledo,

__In **OK**: Norman, Oklahoma City, Tulsa, in **OR**: Beaverton, Bend, Coos Bay, Corvallis, Eugene, Fairview, Grants Pass, Gresham, Klamath Falls, LaGrande, Lake Oswego, Medford, Nyssa, Oregon City, Portland, Prineville, Roseburg, Salem, The Dallas, in **PA**: Philadelphia, Pittsburgh, Reading, State College, York, in **SC**: Charleston, Columbia, Greenville, in **TN**: Chattanooga, Kingsport, Knoxville, Memphis, Nashville, in **TX**: Austin, Beaumont, Corpus Christi, Dallas, El Paso, Friendswood, Houston, Hurst, Longview, Lubbock, Odessa, Richardson, San Antonio,

__In **UT**: Beaver, Blanding, Bountiful, Brigham City, Cedar City, Delta, Duchesne, Fillmore, Heber City, Hurricane, Kanab, Lehi, Logan, Moroni, Mt. Pleasant, Nephi, Ogden, Parowan, Price, Provo, Richfield, Riverton, Roosevelt, St. George, Sandy, Santaquin, Springville, Trementon, Vernal, in **VA**: Annandale, Charlottesville, Fairfax, Norfolk, Oakton, Richmond, Roanoke,

__In WA: Bellevue, Bellingham, Bremerton, Everett, Longview, Moses Lake, Mt. Vernon, Olympia, Pasco, Pullman, Quincy, Richland, Seattle, Spokane, Sumner, Tacoma, Vancouver, Walla Walla, Wenatchee, Yakima, in WI: Appleton, Beloit, Milwaukee, in WY: Afton, Casper, Cheyenne, Cody, Evanston, Gillette, Green River, Kemmerer, Lovell, Rock Springs, Worland.
The GSU is constantly adding new branches so this list will probably be out-of-date by the time you read it. An SASE and a $2 fee to GSU (address in first paragraph above) will bring you an up-to-date listing of BLGSU.

When you go to GSU or BLGSU, first ask for the SC international genealogical index microfiche and examine it for the name of your ancestor, then if you are at GSU, request the records. If you are at BLGSU, ask them to borrow the microfilm containing the record from GSU. The cost is only a few dollars, and when your microfilm arrives (usually 4-6 weeks), you will be notified so that you can return and examine it. Second, ask for the surname catalog at GSU or the microfilm copy of it at BLGSU. Examine it for all listings of the surname of your ancestor. If you think any of the references relate to your ancestral line, and if you are at GSU, request the records. If you are at BLGSU, ask them to borrow the record for you. Third, ask for the SC locality catalog. It will be a card catalog at GSU and a microfilm copy of the card catalog at BLGSU. Examine all listings under the main heading of SOUTH CAROLINA. Then examine all listings under the subheading of the county/district you are interested in. These listings follow those for the state of SC. Toward the end of each of the county/district listings, there are listed materials relating to cities and towns in the county/district. Be sure not to overlook them. If you are at GSU, you can request the materials which are of interest to you. If you are at BLGSU, you may have the branch librarian borrow them for you. A large number of the books and records referred to in Chapter 2 and those listed under the counties in Chapter 4 will be found in the SC locality catalog.

If you happen to be at GSU, there are several other important indexes that you should examine thoroughly. Included among them are the Pedigree Index File, Temple Index Bureau, and the Family Group Records Archive (if

the Temple Index Bureau indicates). Further details concerning the records in GSU and BLGSU along with instructions for finding and using them will be found in:
__R. Cunningham and E. Evans, A HANDY GUIDE TO THE GENEALOGICAL LIBRARY AND CHURCH HISTORICAL DEPARTMENT, Everton Publishers, Logan, UT, 1980.

7. **National Archives (NA) and its Branches (RBNA)**

The National Archives and Records Service (NA), located at Pennsylvania Ave. and 8th St., Washington, DC 20408, is the national repository for federal records, many being of importance to genealogical research. The NA does not concern itself with colonial records (pre-1776) or with state records or with records of smaller local regions, such as counties. Among the most important records which pertain to SC are the following ones (with the section in Chapter 2 where they were discussed): census 1790-1910 (section 6), emigration and immigration (section 14), military (sections 25-27), and naturalization (section 29). Please recall that there are many types of records under the military category (military service, bounty land, pension, claims, civilian). Extensive detail on these records is provided in:
__NA Staff, GENEALOGICAL RESEARCH IN THE NATIONAL ARCHIVES, National Archives and Records Service, Washington, DC, 1982.

The many records of the NA may be examined in Washington in person or by a hired researcher. Microfilm copies of many of the major records and/or their indexes may also be seen in the Regional Branches of the National Archives (RBNA) which are located in or near Atlanta, Boston, Chicago, Denver, Fort Worth, Kansas City, Los Angeles, New York, Philadelphia, San Francisco, and Seattle. They may be located by looking in the telephone directories of these cities under FEDERAL ARCHIVES AND RECORDS CENTER. Many of the more important SC records available in the NA are also available as microfilm copies in SCDA, especially the census and military records.

8. **Regional Libraries (RL)**

In the state of SC there are a number of regional

libraries (RL) which have genealogical collections. Their holdings are larger than those of most local libraries, but are smaller than the holdings of SCL and SCHS. As might be expected, the materials in each RL are best for the immediate and surrounding counties. Among the best of these RL are:

__(Aiken) Aiken- Bamberg- Barnwell- Edgefield Regional Library, 224 Laurens St., Aiken, SC 29801.
__(Beaufort) Beaufort County Library, 710 Craven St., Beaufort, SC 29902.
__(Bennettsville) Marlboro County Library, Market St., Bennettsville, SC 29512.
__(Charleston) Charleston Library Society, 164 King St., Charleston, SC 29401.
__(Charleston) College of Charleston Library, 66 George St., Charleston, SC 29401.
__(Charleston) Charleston County Library, 404 King St., Charleston, SC 29403.
__(Chester) Chester County Free Public Library, Main and Wylie Sts., Chester, SC 29706.
__(Clemson) Clemson University Library, Clemson, SC 29631.
__(Georgetown) Georgetown County Memorial Library, Highmarket and Screven Sts., Georgetown, SC 29440.
__(Greenville) Greenville County Library, 300 College St., Greenville, SC 29601.
__(Greenwood) Abbeville-Greenwood Regional Librry, North Main St., Greenwood, SC 29646.
__(Lancaster) Lancaster County Library, 313 S. White St., Lancaster, SC 29720.
__(Laurens) Laurens County Library, 321 S. Harper St., Laurens, SC 29360.
__(Marion) Marion Public Library, 101 E. Court St., Marion, SC 29751.
__(Newberry) Newberry-Saluda Regional Library, 1300 Friend St., Newberry, SC 29108.
__(Orangeburg) SC State College Library, College Ave., Orangeburg, SC 29117.
__(Rock Hill) York County Library, 138 E. Black St., Rock Hill, SC 29731.
__(Rock Hill) Winthrop College Library, 810 Oakland Ave., Rock Hill, SC 29733.
__(St. Matthews) Calhoun County Library, 208 N. Raysor Dr., St. Matthews, SC 29135.
__(Spartanburg) Spartanburg County Library, 333 S. Pine St., Spartanburg, SC 29304.

__(Sumter) Sumter County Public Library, 111 N. Harvin Street, Sumter, SC 29150.

When a visit is made to any of these libraries, your _first_ endeavor is to search the card catalog. You can remember what to look for with the acronym SLANT, the use of which was described in section 4 of this chapter. This procedure should give you very good coverage of the library holdings which are indexed in the card catalog.

The _second_ endeavor at any of these libraries is to ask about any special archives, indexes, catalogs, collections, manuscripts, or materials which might be pertinent to your search. You should make it your aim particularly to inquire about Bible, cemetery, church, map, manuscript, military, mortuary, and newspaper materials. In some cases, microform (microfilm, microfiche, microcard) records are not included in the regular card catalog but are separately indexed. It is important that you be alert to this possibility.

In addition to the RL mentioned above, there are several libraries in SC which have highly-specialized collections which are pertinent to facets of SC genealogy. Many of these have been listed in section 7 of chapter 2 which names church record centers. Other specialized collections are mentioned in:

__J. B. Howell, SPECIAL COLLECTIONS IN LIBRARIES OF THE SOUTHEAST, Southeastern Library Association, Jackson, MS, 1978.
__AMERICAN LIBRARY DIRECTORY, Bowker, New York, NY, latest edition.

9. Local libraries (LL)

Listed under the SC counties in Chapter 4 are most of the important local libraries (county, city, consolidated, college, university) in the state. These libraries are of a very wide variety, some having sizable holdings of genealogical materials, some having practically none. However, you must never overlook a LL in a county or city of your interest since quite often they have local records or collections available nowhere else. In addition, local librarians are frequently very knowledgeable concerning genealogical sources in their areas. Further, they are also usually acquainted with people in the county who are experts in the county's history and genealogy. Thus, both local libraries and local librarians can be of exceptional value to you.

When you visit a LL, the general procedure described previously should be followed: <u>First</u>, search the card catalog. Look under the headings summarized by SLANT: subject, location, author, name, title, doing them in the order L-N-S-A-T. Then, <u>second</u>, inquire about special indexes, catalogs, collections, materials, and microforms. Also ask about any other local sources of data such as cemetery records, church records, maps and atlases, genealogical and historical societies, mortuary records, and old newspaper records and indexes.

If you choose to write a LL, please remember that the librarians are very busy people. Always send them an SASE and confine your questions to one straight-forward item. Librarians are usually glad to help you if they can employ indexes to answer your question, but you must not expect them to do research for you. In case research is required, they will usually be able to supply you with a list of researchers which you may hire.

10. <u>Large genealogical libraries</u>

Spread around the US there are a number of large genealogical libraries (LGL) which have at least some SC genealogical source materials. In general, those libraries nearest SC (GA, KY, NC, TN, VA) are the ones that have the larger SC collections, but there are exceptions. Among these LGL are:
__In <u>AL</u>: Birmingham Public Library, Library at Samford University in Birmingham, AL Archives and History Department in Birmingham, in <u>AZ</u>: Southern AZ Genealogical Society in Tucson, in <u>AR</u>: AR Genealogical Society in Little Rock, AR History Commission in Little Rock, Little Rock Public Library, in <u>CA</u>: CA Genealogical Society in San Francisco, Los Angeles Public Library, San Diego Public Library, San Francisco Public Library, Sutro Library in San Francisco,
__In <u>CO</u>: Denver Public Library, in <u>CT</u>: CT State Library in Hartford, Godfrey Memorial Library in Middletown, in <u>FL</u>: FL State Library in Tallahassee, Miami-Dade Public Library, Tampa Public Library, in <u>GA</u>: Atlanta Public Library, in <u>ID</u>: ID Genealogical Society, in <u>IL</u>: Newberry Library in Chicago, in <u>IN</u>: IN State Library in

Indianapolis, Public Library of Fort Wayne, in __IA__: IA State Department of History and Archives in Des Moines, in __KY__: KY Historical Society Library in Frankfort,

In __LA__: LA State Library in Baton Rouge, in __ME__: ME State Library in Augusta, in __MD__: MD State Library in Annapolis, MD Historical Society in Baltimore, in __MA__: Boston Public Library, New England Historic Genealogical Society in Boston, in __MI__: Detroit Public Library, in __MN__: Minneapolis Public Library, in __MS__: MS Department of Archives and History in Jackson, in __MO__: Kansas City Public Library, St. Louis Public Library,

In __NE__: NE State Historical Society in Lincoln, Omaha Public Library, in __NV__: Washoe County Library in Reno, in __NY__: NY City Public Library, NY Genealogical and Biographical Society in NY City, in __NC__: NC State Library in Raleigh, in __OH__: Cincinnati Public Library, OH State Library in Columbus, Western Reserve Historical Society in Cleveland, in __OK__: OK State Historical Society in Oklahoma City, in __OR__: Genealogical Forum of Portland, Portland Library Association, in __PA__: Historical Society of PA in Philadelphia, Carnegie Library of Pittsburgh,

In __SD__: State Historical Society in Pierre, in __TN__: TN State Library and Archives in Nashville, in __TX__: Dallas Public Library, Fort Worth Public Library, in __UT__: Brigham Young University Library in Provo, in __VA__: VA State Library and VA Historical Society Library in Richmond, in __WA__: Seattle Public Library, in __WV__: WV Department of Archives and History in Charleston, in __WI__: Milwaukee Public Library, State Historical Society in Madison.

Chapter 4

RESEARCH PROCEDURE & COUNTY LISTINGS

1. Finding the county/district

Now that you have read Chapters 1-3, you should have a good idea of SC history, its genealogical records, and the locations and availability of these records. Your situation is that now you can begin to use these resources. The single most important thing to discover about a SC ancestor is the parish, district, or county in which he or she lived. This is especially important after 1785, because after this date the basis of most SC genealogical records is in the district or county. If your ancestor lived in SC in or after 1900, this information is probably available to you from older members of your family. There are also completely indexed 1900 and 1910 censuses (section 6, Chapter 2), and the state-wide birth and death records for the period after 1915 (sections 4 and 13, Chapter 2). However, it is often the case that for a SC ancestor during 1785-1900 all you know is that he or she lived somewhere in the state. If the case relates to the time before 1785, it is not too serious since most genealogical records for this period were kept at the state or colony level. If you happen to know the parish, district, or county, you are fortunate because this permits you to proceed without working through the problem of locating it. You may skip directly to section 2 of this chapter. If you don't know the parish, district, or county, discovery of it is your first priority.

Should your ancestor's period be 1785-1900, the federal census records for 1790, 1800, 1810, 1820, 1830, 1840, 1850, 1860, 1870, 1880, and 1900 will be of a great deal of help (section 6, Chapter 2). Indexes are available for all of these except 1870, but the 1880 index is only partial. If these fail to locate your forebear, then you need to look into a number of other state-wide indexes which could list her or him. Among the most useful of these for the period 1785-1900 are:
__Biographies (section 3, Chapter 2).
__Surname search of book, manuscript, and tombstone card catalogs in SCHS.

__Surname search of book and manuscript card catalogs in SCL.
__Surname search of index in R. N. Cote, LOCAL AND FAMILY HISTORY IN SC, Southern Historical Press, Easley, SC, 1981.
__Genealogical indexes for SC for this period (section 17, Chapter 2).
__Land grant and plat indexes for this period (section 21, Chapter 2).
__Manuscript guide indexes and manuscript indexes (section 22, Chapter 2).
__Military record indexes (sections 25-27, Chapter 2).
__Newspaper marriage and death notices from state-wide newspapers for this period (section 30, Chapter 2).

If your ancestor's period falls in the 1670-1785 era, the extremely useful combined Alphabetical Index of the SCDA is the first item to be consulted. It is a consolidation of indexes of plats (1680-1855), land grants (1694-1776), memorials (1731-75), conveyances (1719-85), renunciations of dower (1726-1887), court records (1703-1867), tax returns (1824), property bills of sale (1773-1872), and Revolutionary War claim accounts audited (1778-1804). This index is being added to continually, and when you read this, there may be other pre-1785 records in it.
__COMBINED ALPHABETICAL INDEX, SCDA, Columbia, SC.
Should you not succeed in finding your ancestor in this index, then the following sources should be looked into. They are the most likely ones for obtaining references to the location of your forebear. Please recall that almost all governmental records before 1785 were at the state or colony level, but location information is usually to be found in them. This information will permit you to locate your ancestor when SC began to establish district and county sub-divisions.
__Biographies (section 3, Chapter 2).
__Surname search of book, mansucript, and tombstone card indexes in SCHS.
__Surname search of book and manuscript indexes in SCL.
__Surname search of index in R. N. Cote, LOCAL AND FAMILY HISTORY IN SC, Southern Historical Press, Easley, SC, 1981.
__Colonial record compilations for SC (section 10, Chapter 2).
__Genealogical indexes for SC for this period (section

17, Chapter 2).
_Land grant, plat, and memorial indexes for this period (section 21, Chapter 2).
_Manuscript guide indexes and manuscript indexes (section 22, Chapter 2).
_Military record indexes (sections 24 and 25, Chapter 2).
_Newspaper marriage and death notices from colony-wide and state-wide newspapers for this period (section 30, Chapter 2).
_Early SC court records (section 11, Chapter 2).
_Early SC will and estate records (section 34, Chapter 2).

As you can see from the above considerations, the key items for the period <u>after 1900</u> are the 1900 and 1910 censuses and their indexes. These are to be found in SCDA, the NA, the RBNA, the GSU, many LGL, and some RL. They may also be borrowed on interlibrary loan through your LL. The key items for the period <u>1785-1900</u> are again the censuses (every 10 years 1790-1880) and their indexes (all available except 1870). Again these are available in the SCDA, the NA, the RBNA, GSU, many LGL, and some RL. Microfilms of the census records (1790-1880) and the 1790 index may be borrowed on interlibrary loan through your LL. The key item for the period <u>1670-1785</u> is The Combined Alphabetical Index which is located at the SCDA. Once you locate in the many indexes and records mentioned above a person you think to be your ancestor, you may then dig into the details of the records of the colony or state (before 1785) or the district and/or county (after 1785). For the period 1775-90, it is advisable to look in all possible places (state, district, county).

2. Recommended approaches

Having identified the county/district of your ancestor's residence, you are in position to begin to ferret out the details. Remember that before 1785, practically all governmental records were kept in Charleston on a state-wide level. These records and state-wide records after that date have been discussed in sections 4, 6, 11, 12, 13, 21, 23-27, 29, 33, and 34 of Chapter 2. Later on in this chapter you will find summaries of the most important county/district records which are readily available for seeking data on your progenitor. The listings are meant to give you a good idea of what is available in SCDA and what you should look for. They include original records, microfilm copies of original records, transcripts of original records, and indexes to the original records. Details on most of these records have been given in Chapter 2. You should make a thorough examination of <u>all</u> the records which apply to your ancestor's dates in the colony/state and county/district, since this will give you the best chance of finding the maximum amount of information.

The <u>best</u> <u>approach</u> is one in which (1) you examine all the holdings of LL, LGL, and any RL near you, then (2) you go to Columbia to use the materials in SCDA and SCL and to Charleston to employ the collection at SCHS, and then (3) you go to the county seat and look into the CH and LL, if you deem that necessary. This third step will be important when SCDA's holdings for your ancestor's time period and county/district are incomplete. This will be the case when the county has retained the original records and the SCDA does not have copies. You <u>must</u> not fail to investigate this by asking by mail (with an SASE) both the SCDA and the pertinent county/district. A modification of this approach would be to hire researchers to do the work for you at some or all of SCDA, SCL, SCHS, and perhaps the LL and CH.

The <u>second</u> <u>best</u> approach is one in which (1) you examine all the holdings of LL, LGL, and any RL near you, then (2) you go to Salt Lake City and use the materials in GSU, then (3) you hire a researcher to examine the items in SCDA, SCL, and SCHS which you have not seen at GSU, and then (4) you hire a researcher to look into the records at the LL and the CH, if called for. When you hire a researcher, be careful to explain exactly which records you have already seen. This will avoid needless duplication of effort and extra expense on your part.

<u>Another</u> <u>approach</u> is one in which (1) you examine all the holdings of LL, LGL, and perhaps RL, near you, then (2) you go to the nearest BLGSU, order the microfilms you need, wait for them to come, return to BLGSU to read them, then (3) you hire a researcher to examine the materials in SCDA, SCL, and SCHS which you have not seen in BLGSU, then (4) you hire a researcher to look into the

records at the LL and CH, if called for. When you hire a researcher, carefully explain exactly which records you have already examined, so as to avoid unnecessary duplication and expense.

In selecting an approach, whether it be one of the above or one at which you arrive by consideration of Chapter 3, you need to think about three items carefully. The *first* is expense. In visiting SCDA, SCL, and SCHS *or* GSU 3 or 4 full working days should be planned for, usually more. This means you will have travel costs plus at least 3 nights' lodging. To visit a county seat (LL and CH) requires at least a portion of a day. So travel costs and 1 night's lodging will be involved, although this could be combined with the trip to SCDA, SCL, and SCHS, which might cut the expense somewhat. In visiting a BLGSU, your initial visit for index checking and microfilm-ordering will require about half a day, but your return visits will take more time depending on how many microfilms you order or whether they come together or piecemeal. Thus travel and perhaps lodging costs for several trips could be involved, plus the cost of borrowing the films. This will run several dollars per film, and in many cases, between 25 and 45 films might be needed for full coverage. This means that the film cost alone could run well over $100. All of this travel, lodging, and film rental must be weighed over against the cost of hiring a researcher to go to SCDA-SCL-SCHS or making the trip yourself. Of course, your desire to look at the records for yourself may be an important consideration.

The *second* *item* is a reminder about interlibrary loans. With the exception of the microfilms of BLGSU and the census and military National Archives microfilms available through your LL, very few libraries and even fewer archives will lend out their genealogical holdings on interlibrary loan. This is almost always the case for original records and manuscripts. This means that the amount of information you may obtain through interlibrary loan is ordinarily quite limited.

The *third* *item* is also a reminder, this being a restatement of what was said in Chapter 3. You will have noticed that correspondence with librarians and archivists of SCDA, SCL, SCHS, GSU, BLGSU, LGL, RL, and county employees has not been mentioned in the above paragraphs. This is because these helpful and hard-working state, local, and private employees seldom have time to do detailed work for you because of the demanding duties of their offices. In many cases, these people are willing to look up one specific item for you (a land grant date, a conveyance record, a will, an entry in a plat book, a military pension) if an overall index is available. But please don't ask them for detailed data. If you do write them, enclose a long SASE, a check for $4 with the payee line left blank, a brief (no more than one-third page) request for a specific item, and a request that if they do not have the time, that they hand your letter and check to a researcher who can do the work.

3. State-wide records

In this section, a summary of the most-important readily-available state-wide records of genealogical significance for SC is given. This listing is to remind you of the sorts of things you should look for at the state level. These state-wide records have been discussed in some detail in Chapter 2, and practically all of them are available in Columbia at SCDA and SCL and some in Charleston at SCHS. Those which are indexed, or partially indexed, or arranged alphabetically, or partially arranged alphabetically are indicated by an asterisk *.

First, we will list important original or microfilm governmental records in SCDA. These records are especially important for the years before 1785, during which no local governmental records were kept. Secretary of Colony and Secretary of State records: miscellaneous (1671-1973), land grants* (1731-1936), wills* (1732-76), ships registers (1734-80), mortgages* (1736-1873), estate inventories* (1736-76), marriage settlements* (1785-1902), court of ordinary (1771-5), memorials of conveyances* (1785-1824), Palmetto regiment documents (1846-9), voter registrations (1867-8, 1898), direct tax (1862-6), colonial plats* (1731-75), state plats (1784-1932). Governor's records: taxes paid (1862-6). Military Department records: Seminole War troops (1836), draft substitutes (1862), militia enrollments (1869), order books (1860-1914), draft-exempted overseers (1862),

Spanish-American War personnel (1898), Confederate rolls and histories (1861-1910). Register of the Province records: conveyances (1694-1712). Court records: SC Grand Council (1671-92), SC Court of Ordinary (1776-82), SC Court of Common Pleas (1703-90), SC Court of General Sessions (1758, 1769-76), SC Court of Vice Admiralty (1716-63), SC Court of Chancery (1715-91), SC Court of Appeals in Equity (1809-24, 1836-59), SC Court of Appeals (1824-36, 1859-68), SC Court of Errors (1840-67), SC Court of Appeals in Law (1836-59), SC Supreme Court (1868-1919), Court of Claims (1878).

General Assembly records: petitions (1776-1862), reports & resolutions* (1795-1974), claims (1870-7), Cherokee expedition pay lists (1759-60). Receiver General records: quit rents (1733-74). His Majesty's Council records: council papers & journals (1706-74). State Treasurer records: tax (1787), stub indents* (1779-91), tax returns (1800-65), vouchers (1791-1810), Revolutionary War annuities (1799-1857). Auditor General records: memorial books* (1731-75). Comptroller General records: Revolutionary War accounts audited*, Confederate pension applications (1919-25), Confederate pension board papers (1888-90, 1903-26). Department of Agriculture records: agriculture and population census (1868-75). Confederate Home Commission records: inmates (1909-57), admission applications (1909-55). These SCDA records are further described and others are given in:
__THE SC ARCHIVES, A SUMMARY GUIDE, Third Edition, SCDA, Columbia, SC, 1985/6.

Second, we will list important types of records which often have state-wide applicability. Details were given in Chapter 2, so this is simply a summarized reminder. Other records: Baptist,* Bible, biography,* birth,* business, cemetery,* census,* Christian,* colonial compilations,* death,* Episcopal,* family,* Friends,* genealogical indexes,* genealogical periodicals,* immigrants,* Jewish,* Lutheran,* manuscript,* Methodist,* military,* naturalization, newspaper,* Presbyterian,* published genealogies,* Roman Catholic.*

4. The format of the listings

In the numerous sections to follow summaries of the

most important readily available records of the SC
counties/districts are given. These records are for the
most part those available in SCDA and SCL. In general
there are six major sources of original SC
county/district records: (1) original records which have
been transferred to SCDA, (2) original records which
remain in the counties, (3) microfilm copies of the
original records made by the SCDA, (4) microfilm copies
of the original records made by the GSU, (5) transcripts
of the original records made by the WPA, and (6)
published transcripts of the original records made by
various individuals and organizations. All except those
of item (2) are in SCDA or SCL. The holdings in SCDA
have been listed in:

__THE SC ARCHIVES, A SUMMARY GUIDE, Third Edition, SCDA,
  Columbia, SC, 1985/6.

Take a look at the Abbeville County materials (the
next section) which we will use to illustrate the format
for the county/district record summaries. First, the
name of the county is given, then the county seat with
its zip code in parentheses. Next comes the date of
formation and the district, county, or territory out of
which it was formed. Along with this is a brief history
of name changes it has undergone. This information
should alert you to track your ancestor back through the
parent counties and/or districts if he or she was living
there at the time of formation. Following this, if
appropriate, data are given regarding disastrous events
in which records were destroyed.

The next section under each county lists various
govenmental <u>county/district</u> records which started before
1900, except in the cases of counties which were created
after 1900 (Allendale, Calhoun, Dillon, Jasper, Lee, and
McCormick). Listed along with the names of the records
are the years of availability. The record designations
in general refer to labels on various items (books,
boxes, files, folders, microfilms) and to the major
contents of these items. The dates given in parentheses
indicate the span of years in which you may expect to
find sizable records, although every year may not
necessarily be represented. Two very important notes
regarding these governmental county records need to be
recognized. <u>First</u>, you must bear in mind that the
general record categories often represent a wide variety

of separate record types. The most important categories in these county listings are as follows (with the various types included being given in parentheses): Clerk of Court (voter, naturalization, county official registers, apprentice, juror, justice of peace oath, estray, local census, alien registration, physician, Confederate veteran enrollment), Confederate pension (lists, applications, letters), conveyance (deed, plat, mortgage, lien, homestead), coroner (inquest, reports), county commissioner, court of common pleas (judgments, pleadings, journals, dockets, calendars, rolls, petitions, orders, decrees, guardian), court of general sessions (journals, dockets, indictments), court or master of equity (judgments, bills, petitions, sales, returns, summaries, decrees, minutes, guardian, reports, files, journals, accounts, bonds, receipts, returns, papers), district court, estate (administration, papers, sales, inventories, probate, returns, letters, bonds, appraisements, guardian), guardian (in records of common pleas, court or master of equity, and estate records), lien, magistrate (free holder, justice of peace, constable), mortgage (also in conveyance records), plat (location), sheriff (writ, execution, sales, jail), tax (duplicates, assessments, registers, receipts, returns, notices, delinquent), voter, and will. The references to these record types have largely been compiled from the GSU microfilm catalog, the SCDA microfilm catalog, listings of SCDA original records, listings of WPA county record transcripts, and the SCL card catalog for published works. Those records which have an asterisk * attached are indexed or partially indexed.

Following the county/district court house records, there appears a section listing other records which are valuable for the county/district and can be sought in SCDA, SCL, SCHS, GSU, BLGSU, RL, LGL, and LL. The listings largely represent the sorts of records available before 1900, except for the counties created after 1900 (Allendale, Calhoun, Dillon, Jasper, Lee, and McCormick). The major record categories that you will find under this heading are Baptist, Bible, biography, cemetery, census, Christian, city history, Episcopal, family, genealogical society, historical society, LDS, Lutheran, manuscript, map, Methodist, newspaper, Presbyterian, Roman Catholic, town history, and WPA inventory. Special designations accompany the census records: R stands for the regular census schedules, A for the agricultural schedules, I for the industrial schedules, M for the mortality schedules, S for the slaveholder schedules, P for the special 1840 Revolutionary War pension schedules, C for the special 1890 Civil War Union veteran schedules, and X for SC state censuses.

After the listing of other records, there is a section which gives the local <u>libary</u> or libraries in the county. Those libraries which are marked with an asterisk * are the ones which have notable genealogical collections for their regions. Finally, there are listed one or more <u>county histories</u> which often contain sizable genealogical information.

5. <u>ABBEVILLE COUNTY</u>, County seat: Abbeville (29620), before 1868 known as Abbeville District, which in 1785 was formed from Ninety-Six District, which in 1769 was established as an original district. Probate records include Ninety-Six District probates. Conveyance records were burned in 1873.

<u>County records</u>: Confederate pension (1916-32), conveyance* (1872-1925), county commissioner (1840-68), court of common pleas* (1791-1906), court or master of equity* (1791-1906), estate* (1782-1958), guardian (1840-68), land grant, plat (1916-25), tax (1856, 1865-7, 1877), voter (1867-8, 1898), will* (1772-1868).

<u>Other records</u>: Baptist, biography, cemetery, census (1790R in Ninety-Six District, 1800R, 1810R, 1820RI, 1830R, 1840RP, 1850RAIMS, 1860RAIMS, 1869X, 1870RAIM, 1880RAIM, 1890C, 1900R, 1910R, 1920R), Christian, Episcopal, family, historical society, manuscript, maps, marriage (1777-1852), newspaper, Presbyterian, town history, WPA inventory.

<u>Libraries</u>: Abbeville-Greenwood Regional Library,* 106 N. Main St., Greenwood, SC 29646; Erskine College Library,* Due West, SC 29639. <u>Histories</u>: Abbeville Historical Society, ABBEVILLE COUNTY BICENTENNIAL, 1758-1958, The Society, Abbeville, SC, 1958; J. G. Carroll, ABBEVILLE COUNTY FAMILY HISTORY, Intercollegiate Press, Clinton, SC, 1979.

6. <u>AIKEN COUNTY</u>, County seat: Aiken (29801), formed in 1871 from Edgefield, Orangeburg, Barnwell, and Lexington Counties.

<u>County records</u>: Clerk of Court (1896-1957), city

(1839-1959), Confederate pension (1888-1937), conveyance* (1872-1967), coroner (1901-33), county commissioner (1895-1925), court of common pleas (1871-1939), court of general sessions (1871-1943), court or master of equity (1884-1916), estate* (1873-1975), guardian (1872-1954), lien (1883-1901), magistrate (1871-1927), plat (1872-1920), sheriff (1872-1909), tax (180-1920), voter (1896-1957), will* (1873-1904).
Other records: Baptist, biography, cemetery, census (1880RAIM, 1890C, 1900R, 1910R, 1920R), Episcopal, family, historical society, Lutheran, manuscript, Methodist, town history, WPA inventory.
Library: Aiken-Bamberg-Barnwell-Edgefield Regional Library,* 224 Laurens St., Aiken, SC 29801. Histories: P. F. Henderson, A SHORT HISTORY OF AIKEN AND AIKEN COUNTY, Bryan, Columbia, SC, 1951; Highway Guides of America, ONE HUNDRED YEARS IN AIKEN COUNTY, The Guides, Aiken, SC, 1971; C. L. Toole, NINETY YEARS IN AIKEN COUNTY, Walker, Evans, & Cogswell, Charleston, SC, 1957; D. K. MacDowell, AN AIKEN SCRAPBOOK, The Author, Aiken, SC, 1982.

7. ALLENDALE COUNTY, County seat: Allendale (29810), formed 1919 from parts of Barnwell and Hampton Counties. The county records listed below will be found in the county, not at SCDA.
County records: Confederate pension* (1920-), conveyance* (1919-), coroner* (1921-), county board (1920-), court of common pleas* (1919-), court of general sessions* (1919-), estate* (1919-), magistrate (1933-), mortgage* (1919-), plat* (1919-), sheriff* (1919-), tax* (1919-), voter* (1920-), will* (1919-).
Other records: Baptist, biography, cemetery, census (1920R), Episcopal, family, historical society, manuscript, map, Methodist, newspaper, Presbyterian, Roman Catholic, town history, WPA inventory.
Library: Allendale-Jasper Regional Library, War Memorial Bldg., Allendale, SC 29810. History: A. E. Lawton and M. R. Wilson, ALLENDALE ON THE SAVANNAH, Bamberg Herald Printers, Bamberg, SC, 1970.

8. ANDERSON COUNTY, County seat: Anderson (29620), before 1868 known as Anderson District, which in 1826 was formed from Pendleton District, Pendleton District being abolished. Records of Pendleton County (1790-9) and Pendleton District (1800-28) are in with Anderson County

records.

County records: Clerk of Court (1790-1920), Confederate pension (1892-1962), conveyance* (1790-1948), coroner (1901-20), county commissioner (1851-1929), court of common pleas* (1790-1904), court of general sessions (1790-1917), court or master of equity* (1819-1907), estate* (1790-1972), guardian (1843-69), lien (1872-1907), magistrate (1792-1863), mortgage (1872-1907), plat* (1802-1904), sheriff (1820-30, 1877-1913), tax (1835-1914), voter (1867-8, 1882-90), will* (1791-1907).

Other records: Baptist, biography, cemetery, census (1790R listed under Pendleton County in Ninety-Six District, 1800R, and 1810R and 1820RI listed under Pendleton District, 1830R, 1840RP, 1850RAIMS, 1860RAIMS, 1869X, 1870RAIM, 1880RAIM, 1890C, 1900R, 1910R, 1920R), city history, Episcopal, family, historical society, Lutheran, manuscript, map, marriage, newspaper, Presbyterian, Roman Catholic, town history, WPA inventory.

Library: Anderson County Library, 316 Boulevard St., Anderson, SC 29621. Histories: L. A. Vandiver, TRADITIONS AND HISTORY OF ANDERSON COUNTY, R. M. Smith, Anderson, SC, 1970; E. B. Fuller, ANDERSON COUNTY SKETCHES, Anderson County Tricentennial Commission, Anderson, SC, 1969; F. A. Dickson, JOURNEYS INTO THE PAST: THE ANDERSON REGION'S HERITAGE, The Author, Anderson, SC, 1975.

9. BAMBERG COUNTY, County seat: Bamberg (29003), formed in 1897 from Barnwell County. All county records are in the county, not at SCDA.

County records: Confederate pension (1916-), conveyance* (1897-), coroner (1897-), county commissioner (1897-), court of common pleas* (1787-), court of general sessions* (1897-), court or master of equity* (1897-), estate* (1897-), mortgage* (1897-), sheriff* (1897-), tax* (1897-), will* (1897-).

Other records: Baptist, biography, census (1900R, 1910R, 1920R), Christian, Lutheran, manuscript, map, Methodist, newspaper, Presbyterian, town history.

Library: Aiken-Bamberg-Barnwell-Edgefield Regional Library, 224 Laurens St., Aiken, SC 29801. History: D. G. Copeland, MANY YEARS AFTER, A BIT OF HISTORY AND RECOLLECTIONS OF BAMBERG COUNTY, typescript, SCL, Columbia, SC, no date.

10. BARNWELL COUNTY, County seat: Barnwell (29812), before 1868 known as Barnwell District, which in 1800 was renamed Barnwell District instead of Winton County, which in 1785 came from Orangeburg District, which in 1769 was established as an original district. Records include those of Winton County (1786-1800). Records for 1791-1800 were lost in a fire.

County records: conveyance* (1786-1884), county & intermediate court (1786-92), court of common pleas (1800-32), court of general sessions (1800-80), court or master of equity (1818-68), district court (1866-8), estate* (1787-1958), magistrate (1853-4), plat* (1784-1949), tax (1800, 1865-7, 1877), voter (1867-8, 1898), Winton County (1785-91), will* (1787-1958).

Other records: Baptist, biography, cemetery, census (1790R listed in South Division of Orangeburg District, 1800R, 1810R, 1820RI, 1830R, 1840RP, 1850RAIMS, 1860RAIMS, 1869X, 1870RAIM, 1880RAIM, 1890C, 1900R, 1910R, 1920R), Episcopal, family, historical society, manuscript, map, marriage, Methodist, newspaper, Presbyterian, Roman Catholic, town history.

Library: Aiken-Bamberg-Barnwell-Edgefield Regional Library,* 224 Laurens St., Aiken, SC 29646. History: HISTORICAL CHRONICLES OF THE SOUTH: BARNWELL COUNTY, Volume 1, Number 5, The Green River Sprite, Columbia, KY; 1975.

11. BARTHOLOMEW COUNTY, designated as a subdivision of Charleston District in 1785, abolished 1800 when it was taken into Colleton District. Never did keep records.

12. BEAUFORT COUNTY, County seat: Beaufort (29902), before 1868 known as Beaufort District, which in 1769 was established as an original district. Most records burned in 1865.

County records: city tax (1867-83), conveyance* (1863-1980), plat* (1865-1980), tax (1871, 1877), voter (1867-8, 1898). Records which should be sought in the county include Confederate pension, coroner, county commissioner, court of common pleas, court of general sessions, court or master of equity, estate, guardian, mortgage, sheriff, and will.

Other records: Baptist, biography, cemetery, census (1790R, 1800R, 1810R, 1820RI, 1830R, 1840RP, 1850RAIMS, 1860RAIMS, 1869X, 1870RAIM, 1875X, 1880RAIM, 1890C, 1900R, 1910R, 1920R), Christian, Episcopal, family, historical society, Jewish, LDS, manuscript, map, Methodist, newspaper, Presbyterian, Roman Catholic, town history.

Library: Beaufort County Library,* 710 Craven St., Beaufort, SC 29902. **Histories**: N. L. Willet, BEAUFORT COUNTY, THE SHRINES, EARLY HISTORY, & TOPOGRAPHY, Chamber of Commerce, Beaufort, SC, 1940; J. E. McTeer, BEAUFORT, NOW AND THEN, Beaufort Book Co., Beaufort, SC, 1971.

13. BERKELEY COUNTY, County seat: Moncks Corner (29461), formed in 1882 from Charleston County.

County records: Clerk of Court (1883-1956), Confederate pension (1916-9), conveyance* (1884-1927), coroner (1883-1927), county commissioner (1882-1920), court of common pleas (1881-1963), court of general sessions* (1882-1954), court or master of equity (1883-91), estate* (1883-1947), lien (1886-1909), magistrate (1893-6, 1923-60), plat* (1898-1937), tax (1882-3), voter (1883-91, 1918), will* (1883-1933).

Other records: Baptist, biography, cemetery, census (1890C, 1900R, 1910R, 1920R), Episcopal, family, historical society, LDS, manuscript, map, Methodist, town history.

Library: Berkeley County Library, 100 Library St., Moncks Corner, SC 29461. **History**: HISTORIC BERKELEY COUNTY, 1671-1900, Comprint, Charleston, SC, 1973.

14. CALHOUN COUNTY, County seat: St. Matthews (29135), formed in 1908 from Lexington and Orangeburg Counties. All county records are in the county, not at SCDA.

County records: Confederate pension* (1919-), conveyance* (1908-), coroner* (1908-), county board (1908-), court of common pleas* (1908-), court of general sessions* (1908-), estate* (1908-), mortgage* (1908-), plat* (1908-), sheriff* (1908-), tax (1908-), voter* (1908-), will* (1908-).

Other records: Baptist, biography, cemetery, census (1910R, 1920R), Episcopal, family, historical society, Lutheran, manuscript, map, Methodist, Presbyterian.

Library: Calhoun County Public Library,* 208 N. Rayson Dr., St. Matthews, SC 29135. **History**: CALHOUN COUNTY JUBILEE, 1958, Calhoun County, Moncks Corner, SC, 1958.

15. CAMDEN DISTRICT, formed in 1769 as an original district, during 1785-91 subdivided into 7 counties and one other district, partially abolished in 1800 as a local record-keeping entity. Records are among those of Kershaw County. Records: census (1790R), Clerk of Court (1790-8), court of common pleas (1782-1805), court of general sessions (1786-99), court or master of equity (1792-1823), estate (1782-7), plat* (1784-1841), will* (1781-1823).

16. CHARLESTON COUNTY, County seat: Charleston (29401), before 1868 known as Charleston District, which in 1769 was formed as an original district. From the beginning of the SC colony until 1785, Charleston was the center of practically all record keeping. In Charleston a researcher should not fail to go to SCHS, Charleston Library Society, Charleston County Library, Charleston City Archives, Charleston County Probate Court, Charleston County Clerk of Court, Charleston County Register of Mesne Conveyances and Charleston County Auditor. See R. N. Cote, GENEALOGIST'S GUIDE TO CHARLESTON COUNTY, Cote Publications, Ladson, SC, 1978.

County records: citizenship (1796-1905), city birth (1871-1926), city burial (1899-1927), city death* (1821-1926), city court (1774-1906), city lot survey (1858-9), city marriage (1871-87), city orphan (1790-1960), city tax (1858-9, 1964), city voter (1877, 1879), Clerk of Court (1700-1935), Confederate pension (1916-59), conveyance* (1671-1915), coroner (1878-1912), court of common pleas* (1733-1929), court of general sessions* (1733-1984), court or master of equity* (1790-1900), district court (1867-77), estate* (1671-1927), magistrate (1829-31, 1867-83), marriage (1879-1984), mortgage* (1719-1930), orphan* (1790-1960), plat* (1742-1965), tax (1855-67, 1871-), voter (1867-8, 1898), will* (1671-1927).

Other records: Baptist, biography, cemetery, census (1790R, 1800R, 1810R, 1820RI, 1830R, 1840RP, 1850RAIMS, 1860RAIMS, 1869X, 1870RAIM, 1880RAIM, 1890C, 1900R, 1910R, 1920R), Christian, city directory (1782-), city yearbook (1881-1951), Congregational, directories (1867-), Episcopal, family, genealogical society, historical society, Hugenot, Jewish, Lutheran, manuscript, map, Methodist, newspaper, Presbyterian, Roman Catholic, town history.

Libraries: Charleston County Library,* 404 King St.,

Charleston, SC 29403; Charleston Library Society,* 164 King St., Charleston, SC 29401; College of Charleston Library,* 66 George St., Charleston, SC 29401; SC Historical Society Library,* 100 Meeting St., Charleston, SC 29401; BLGSU,* Charleston Stake, Hanahan, SC 29410; SC Genealogical Library,* 315 King St., Charleston, SC 29401. History: T. P. Lesesne, HISTORY OF CHARLESTON COUNTY, Cawston, Charleston, SC, 1931.

17. CHERAWS DISTRICT, formed as an original SC district in 1769, subdivided into three counties and abolished as a local record-keeping organization in 1785, but kept regional records after that.

18. CHEROKEE COUNTY, County seat: Gaffney (29340), formed in 1897 from Union, York, and Spartanburg Counties. Some records are in SCDA, but most important ones are only in the county.
County records: Clerk of Court (1897-1929), Confederate pension (1897-1915), conveyance* (1897-), coroner* (1897-1949), county commissioner (1897-9, 1913-69), court of common pleas* (1897-1926), court of general sessions (1897-1962), court or master of equity* (1897-), estate* (1897-), lien (1897-1909), magistrate (1906-25), mortgage* (1897-), sheriff (1897-1957), tax (1897-1940), voter (1897-1940), will* (1897-9).
Other records: Baptist, biography, cemetery, census (1900R, 1910R, 1920R), Episcopal, family, historical society, manuscript, map, newspaper, Presbyterian, WPA inventory.
Library: Cherokee County Public Library, 300 E. Rutledge Ave., Gaffney, SC 29340. History: B. G. Moss, THE OLD IRON DISTRICT: A STUDY OF THE DEVELOPMENT OF CHEROKEE COUNTY, 1750-1897, Jacobs Press, Clinton, SC, 1972.

19. CHESTER COUNTY, County seat: Chester (29706), before 1868 known as Chester District, which before 1800 was known as Chester County, which was formed in 1785 from Camden District, which was established in 1769 as an original district.
County records: citizenship (1785-1901), Confederate pension (1902), conveyance* (1785-1867), county commissioner (1868-72), county & intermediate court (1785-99), court of common pleas* (1785-1828), court of general sessions (1800-85), court or master of equity

(1820-74), estate* (1787-1874), guardian* (1841-68), naturalization (1802-65), plat (1846-75), tax (1863-7, 1877), voter (1867-8, 1898), will* (1787-1908).

Other records: Baptist, biography, cemetery, census (1790R listed under Camden District, 1800R, 1810R, 1820RI, 1830R, 1840RP, 1850RAIMS, 1860RAIMS, 1869X, 1870RAIM, 1880RAIM, 1890C, 1900R, 1910R, 1920R), family, genealogical society, historical society, manuscript, map, Methodist, newspaper, Presbyterian, town history, WPA inventory.

Library: Chester County Free Public Library,* Main and Wylie Sts., Chester, SC 29706. History: Chester News, THE SPIRIT OF CHESTER, The Chester News, Chester, SC, 1932.

20. CHESTERFIELD COUNTY, County seat: Chesterfield (29709), before 1868 known as Chesterfield District, which before 1800 was known as Chesterfield County, which was formed in 1785 from Cheraws District, which in 1769 was established as an original district. Most records were burned in 1865.

County records: Clerk of Court (1834-74, 1894-1947), Confederate pension (1887-90), conveyance* (1861-1936), coroner (1890-1906), county commissioner (1895-1924), court of common pleas (1859-1959), court of general sessions (1866-1968), court or master of equity (1823, 1842-68), district court (1868-71), estate* (1865-1978), guardian (1866-1937), lien (1885-1907), magistrate (1869-70, 1878-1911), plat*, sheriff (1847-1934), tax (1865-7, 1872-1966), voter (1867-8, 1898), will* (1865-1878).

Other records: Baptist, biography, cemetery, census (1790R listed under Cheraws District, 1800R, 1810R, 1820RI, 1830R, 1839X, 1840RP, 1850RAIMS, 1860RAIMS, 1869X, 1870RAIM, 1880RAIM, 1890C, 1900R, 1910R, 1920R), Episcopal, family, historical society, manuscript, map, Methodist, newspaper, Presbyterian, Roman Catholic, town history.

Library: Chesterfield County Public Library, 130 Main St., Chesterfield, SC 29709. History: HISTORICAL CHRONICLES OF THE SOUTH, Volume 1, Number 8, The Green River Sprite, Columbia, KY, 1975.

21. CLAREMONT COUNTY, formed from Camden District in 1785, abolished in 1800 when it was absorbed into Sumter District. All records burned in Sumter CH fire in 1801.

22. CLARENDON COUNTY, formed in 1855 from Sumter District. Had been defunct since 1800, but previous to that was Old Clarendon County, which had been formed in 1785 from Camden District, which was established in 1769 as an original district. Records of Old Clarendon lost in fire in 1801. Some records burned in 1911.

County records: Confederate pension (1916-37), conveyance* (1857-1980), coroner (1877-1941), county commissioner (1874-5, 1907-52), court of common pleas (1857-1958), court of general sessions (1859-1947), court or master of equity (1858-70), district court (1867-8), estate* (1874-1903), lien (1878-1909), magistrate (1877-1950), plat (1867, 1878-9), sheriff (1870-1937), tax (1866-7, 1877-1967), voter (1867-8, 1882-1958), will* (1871-96).

Other records: Baptist, biography, cemetery, census (1790R listed under Camden District, 1860RAIMS, 1870RAIM, 1875X, 1880RAIM, 1890C, 1900R, 1910R, 1920R), Christian, Episcopal, family, historical society, manuscript, map, Methodist, newspaper, Presbyterian, Roman Catholic, town history.

Library: Sumter County Library (also serves Clarendon County), 111 N. Harvin St., Sumter, SC 29510.

Histories: V. K. Orvin, HISTORY OF CLARENDON COUNTY, The Author, Manning, SC, 1961; Clarendon County Historical Society, CLARENDON CAMEOS, R. L. Bryan Co., Columbia, SC, 1976.

23. COLLETON COUNTY, County seat: Walterboro (29488), before 1868 known as Colleton District, which between 1785-1800 was a non-functioning county of Charleston District, which in 1769 was established as an original district. Records burned in 1805 and 1865. Not all records are in SCDA, some need to be sought in county.

County records in SCDA: conveyance* (1866-1980), estate* (1866-), list of persons (1880), plat (1802-21, 1827-34, 1897-1922), sheriff (1807-1931), tax (1867-1932), voter (1882), will* (1866-). Look for other records in the county.

Other records: Baptist, biography, cemetery, census (1790R listed under Charleston District, 1800R, 1810R, 1820RI, 1830R, 1840RP, 1850RAIMS, 1860RAIMS, 1869X, 1870RAIM, 1880RAIM, 1890C, 1900R, 1910R, 1920R), Episcopal, family, historical society, Jewish, manuscript, map, Methodist, newspaper, Presbyterian, Roman Catholic.

Library: Colleton County Memorial Library, 600 Hampton St., Walterboro, SC 29488. History: B. Glover, NARRATIVES OF COLLETON COUNTY, The Author, Walterboro, SC, 1962.

24. DARLINGTON COUNTY, County seat: Darlington (29532), before 1868 known as Darlington District, which before 1800 was known as Darlington County, which in 1785 was formed from Cheraws District, which in 1769 was established as an original district. Many records lost about 1806 in a fire.
County records: Clerk of Court (1876), Confederate pension (1863-4), conveyance* (1806-1980), court of common pleas (1806-20), court of general sessions (1806-26, 1840-55, 1869-76), court or master of equity* (1801-74), district court (1867), estate* (1783-1905), magistrate (1870-9), plat* (1803-1980), tax (1823, 1861, 1865-7, 1877), voter (1867-8, 1876, 1898), will* (1785-1905).
Other records: Baptist, biography, cemetery, census (1790R listed under Cheraws District, 1800R, 1810R, 1820RI, 1830R, 1840RP, 1850RAIMS, 1860RAIMS, 1869X, 1870RAIM, 1880RAIM, 1890C, 1900R, 1910R, 1920R), Episcopal, family, historical society, Jewish, LDS, manuscript, map, Methodist, newspaper, Presbyterian, town history.
Library: Darlington County Library, 127 N. Main St., Darlington, SC 29532. Histories: Darlington County Historical Society, RECORDS AND PAPERS, The Society, Darlington, SC, 1944; E. C. Ervin and H. F. Rudisill, DARLINGTONIANA: A HISTORY OF PEOPLE, PLACES, & EVENTS, R. L. Bryan, Columbia, SC, 1964.

25. DILLON COUNTY, County seat: Dillon (29536), formed in 1910 from Marion County. County records are in the county, not in SCDA.
County records: Confederate pension (1916-), conveyance* (1910-), county commissioner (1910-), court of common pleas* (1910-), court of general sessions* (1910-), estate* (1910-), guardian* (1910-), magistrate (1910-), mortgage (1910-), plat* (1910-), sheriff (1910-), tax (1910-), voter (1928-), will* (1910-).
Other records: Baptist, biography, cemetery, census (1920R), family, historical society, manuscript, map, Methodist, Presbyterian, WPA inventory.
Library: Dillon County Library, 101 N. Main St.,

Latta, SC 29565. History: D. T. Stokes, THE HISTORY OF DILLON COUNTY, University of SC Press, Columbia, SC, 1978.

26. DORCHESTER COUNTY, County seat: St. George (29477), formed in 1897 from Berkeley and Colleton Counties. Some county records in SCDA, but most need to be sought in the county.
County records: Confederate pension (1919-), conveyance* (1897-), coroner* (1897), court of common pleas (1897-), court of general sessions (1897-), court or master of equity (1897-), estate* (1897-), lien* (1897, 1908), mortgage* (1897-), sheriff (1897-), tax (1897-), voter (1898), will* (1897-).
Other records: Baptist, biography, cemetery, census (1900R, 1910R, 1920R), Christian, Episcopal, family, historical society, manuscript, map, Methodist, Presbyterian, Roman Catholic, town history.
Library: Dorchester County Library, 506 N. Parler Ave., St. George, SC 29477. History: L. Walker, DORCHESTER COUNTY, A HISTORY, Walker, Charleston, SC, 1979.

27. EDGEFIELD COUNTY, County seat: Edgefield (29824), before 1868 known as Edgefield District, which before 1800 was known as Edgefield County, which in 1785 was formed from Ninety-Six District, which in 1769 was established as an original district.
County records: Confederate pension (1916-33), conveyance* (1786-1923), coroner (1844-1902), county commissioner* (1841-68), court of common pleas* (1785-1959), court of general sessions* (1785-1868), court or master of equity* (1800-70, 1890-6), estate* (1785-1975), guardian* (1800-1903), lien (1878-1907), magistrate (1865), mortgage* (1868-1923), plat (1802-1976), sheriff (1800-1961), tax (1863-71, 1877, 1889-90,. 1894-1931), voter (1867-8, 1898), will* (1785-1975).
Other records: Baptist, biography, cemetery, census (1790R listed under Ninety-Six District, 1800R, 1810R, 1820RI, 1830R, 1840RP, 1850RAIMS, 1860RAIMS, 1869X, 1870RAIM, 1880RAIM, 1890C, 1900R, 1910R, 1920R), family, historical society, manuscript, map, marriage, Methodist, newspaper, Roman Catholic, town history, WPA inventory.
Library: Aiken-Bamberg-Barnwell-Edgefield Regional Library,* 224 Laurens St., Aiken, SC 29801. Histories:

J. A. Chapman, HISTORY OF EDGEFIELD COUNTY TO 1897, Southern Historical Press, Easley, SC, 1897 (1976); O. K. Walker, HISTORIC EDGEFIELD COUNTY, 1787-1970, Commercial Printing Co., Augusta, GA, 1960.

28. FAIRFIELD COUNTY, County seat: Winnsboro (29180), before 1868 known as Fairfield District, which before 1800 was known as Fairfield County, which in 1785 was formed from Camden District, which in 1769 was established as an original district.

County records: Clerk of Court (1789-99, 1820-40, 1882-1970), Confederate pension (1889-91, 1902, 1909-43), conveyance* (1785-1902), county commissioner (1876-1901), county & intermediate court (1785-99), court of common pleas* (1785-1930), court of general sessions* (1791-1908), court or master of equity* (1807-1904), district court (1866-8), estate* (1787-1947), guardian (1822-69, 1881-1908), magistrate (1839-65, 1871-82), mortgage* (1872-1904), plat* (1784-1841), sheriff (1807-1913), tax (1792, 1822, 1843, 1863-7, 1877, 1882-1907), voter (1867-8, 1898), will* (1787-1904).

Other records: Baptist, biography, cemetery, census (1790R listed under Camden District, 1800R, 1810R, 1820RI, 1830R, 1840RP, 1850RAIMS, 1860RAIMS, 1869X, 1870RAIM, 1875X partial, 1880RAIM, 1890C, 1900R, 1910R, 1920R), Episcopal, family, historical society, manuscript, map, Methodist, newspaper, Presbyterian.

Library: Fairfield County Library, Garden and Washington Sts., Winnsboro, SC 29180. History: F. H. McMaster, HISTORY OF FAIRFIELD COUNTY TO 1942, State Co., Columbia, SC, 1946.

29. FLORENCE COUNTY, County seat: Florence (29501), formed 1888 from Marion, Darlington, Clarendon, and Williamsburg Counties. Very few county records in SCDA, most should be sought in county.

County records: Confederate pension (1916-37), conveyance* (1889-), coroner (1889-), county commissioner (1889-), court of common pleas* (1889-), court of general sessions (1890-), estate* (1889-), magistrate (1897-), mortgage* (1889-), plat* (18895), sheriff (1889-), tax (1889-), voter (1888-), will* (1889-).

Other records: Baptist, biography, cemetery, census (1890C, 1900R, 1910R, 1920R), city history, Episcopal, family, historical society, LDS, Lutheran, manuscript, map, Methodist, newspaper, Presbyterian, town history,

WPA inventory.
Library: Florence County Library, 319 S. Irby St., Florence, SC 29501. **History**: G. W. King, RISE UP SO EARLY: A HISTORY OF FLORENCE COUNTY, Reprint Co., Spartanburg, SC, 1981.

30. **GEORGETOWN COUNTY**, County seat: Georgetown (29440), before 1868 known as Georgetown District, which in 1769 was established as an original district. Most records burned in 1865. Records listed here are in SCDA, but further records need to be sought in the county.
County records: conveyance* (1862-1923), court of common pleas* (1819-26), magistrate (1783), plat* (1866-1936), sheriff (1789-23), tax (1870-1963), voter (1867-8, 1898), will* (1862-1912).
Other records: Baptist, biography, cemetery, census (1790R, 1800R, 1810R, 1820RI, 1830R, 1840RP, 1850RAIMS, 1860RAIMS, 1869X, 1870RAIM, 1880RAIM, 1890C, 1900R, 1910R, 1920R), city history, Episcopal, family, historical society, Jewish, manuscript, map, Methodist, newspaper, Presbyterian, town history.
Library: Georgetown County Memorial Library,* Highmarket and Screven Strs., Georgetown, SC 29440. **History**: G. C. Rogers, THE HISTORY OF GEORGETOWN COUNTY, University of SC Press, Columbia, SC, 1970.

31. **GRANVILLE COUNTY**, designated as a subdivision of Beaufort District in 1785, abolished in 1800. Never did keep records.

32. **GREENVILLE COUNTY**, County seat: Greenville (29601), before 1868 known as Greenville District, which before 1800 was known as Greenville County, which in 1786 was formed from Ninety-Six District, which in 1769 was established as an original district.
County records: Clerk of Court (1852-83, 1881-1958), Confederate pension (1891, 1901, 1905-6, 1910-1), conveyance* (1785-1913), county commissioner (1873-1912), county & intermediate court (1786-1800), court of common pleas* (1800-1956), court of general sessions* (1800-1949), court or master of equity* (1822-69), estate* (1787-1967), guardian (1837-1905), magistrate (1847-61, 1873-85, 1891-1900, 1905-9), mortgage* (1788-1928), plat* (1784-1975), sheriff (1848-56, 1866-1923), tax (1865-7, 1869-70, 1877), voter (1867-8, 1898, 1925-56), will* (1787-1907).

Other records: Baptist, biography, cemetery, census (1790R listed under Ninety-Six District, 1800R, 1810R, 1820RI, 1830R, 1840RP, 1850RAIMS, 1860RAIMS, 1869X, 1870RAIM, 1880RAIM, 1890C, 1900R, 1910R, 1920R), Christian, city history, death, Episcopal, family, genealogical society, historical society, Jewish, LDS, Lutheran, manuscript, map, marriage, newspaper, Presbyterian, Roman Catholic.
Libraries: Furman University Library,* Greenville, SC 29613; Greenville County Library,* 300 College St., Greenville, SC 29601; BLGSU,* Greenville Stake, Greenville, SC 29678.. Histories: J. M. Richardson, HISTORY OF GREENVILLE COUNTY, Cawston, Atlanta, GA, 1930; S. S. Crittenden, THE GREENVILLE CENTURY BOOK, Greenville News, Greenville, SC, 1903.

33. GREENWOOD COUNTY, County seat: Greenwood (29646), formed 1897 from Edgefield and Abbeville Counties. Most county records are in the county, not in SCDA.
County records: Confederate pension (1897-), conveyance* (1897-), county commissioner (1897-), court of common pleas* (1897-), court of general sessions* (1897-), court or master of equity* (1897-), estate* (1897-), mortgage* (1897-), sheriff* (1897-), tax (1897-), voter (1898), will* (1897-).
Other records: Baptist, biography, cemetery, census (1900R, 1910R, 1920R), Christian, Episcopal, family, genealogical society, historical society, Lutheran, manuscript, map, Methodist, newspaper, Presbyterian, town history.
Library: Abbeville-Greenwood Regional Library,* 106 N. Main St., Greenwood, SC 29646. Histories: C. M. Calhoun, LIBERTY DETHRONED (GREENWOOD COUNTY), The Author, Greenwood, SC, 1903; M. J. Watson, GREENWOOD COUNTY SKETCHES, Attic Press, Greenwood, SC, 1970.

34. HAMPTON COUNTY, County seat: Hampton (29924), formed 1878 from Beaufort County. Very few county records in SCDA, most need to be sought in the county.
County records: Confederate pension (1919-), conveyance* (1879-1928), coroner (1879-), court of common pleas* (1878-), court of general sessions (1878-), court or master of equity* (1878-), estate* (1878-), mortgage* (1878-), sheriff (1878-), tax* (1878-), voter (1898), will* (1878-).
Other records: Baptist, biography, cemetery, census

(1880RAIM, 1890C, 1900R, 1910R, 1920R), Christian, Episcopal, historical society, Lutheran, manuscript, map, Methodist, newspaper, Presbyterian, town history.

Library: Allendale-Hampton-Jasper Regional Library, War Memorial Bldg., Allendale, SC 29810. History: Hampton County Tricentennial Commission, BOTH SIDES OF THE SWAMP: HAMPTON COUNTY, Bryan, Columbia, SC, 1970.

35. HILTON COUNTY, designated in 1785 as a subdivision of Beaufort District,zabolished 1800. Never did keep records.

36. HORRY COUNTY, County seat: Conway (29526), before 1868 known as Horry District, which in 1801 was formed out of territory that had 1785-1800 been called Kingston County (non-functioning) in Georgetown District, which in 1769 was established as an original district.

County records: Clerk of Court (1843-1915), Confederate pension (1889-1919), conveyance* (1803-1942), coroner (1849-74), court of common pleas* (1803-1944), court of general sessions (1804-74, 1885-1932), court or master of equity (1841-69), district court (1866-9), estate* (1803-1959), lien (1878-1909), magistrate (1881-1908), plat (1913-50), sheriff (1868-73, 1920-42), tax (1845-9, 1851, 1860, 1865-7, 1876-7, 1895, 1905-20), voter (1867-8, 1898), will* (1799-1907).

Other records: Baptist, biography, cemetery, census (1810R, 1820RI, 1830R, 1840RP, 1850RAIMS, 1860RAIMS, 1869X, 1870RAIM, 1880RAIM, 1890C, 1900R, 1910R, 1920R), Christian, family, historical society, manuscript, map, Methodist, newspaper, Presbyterian, town history.

Library: Horry County Memorial Library, 1008 Fifth Ave., Conway, SC 29526. Histories: J. A. Norton, THE NARRATIVE OF HORRY COUNTY HISTORY, typescript, Conway, SC, no date; The Independent Republic Quarterly, THE INDEPENDENT REPUBLIC OF HORRY, Horry Printers, Conway, SC, 1970; J. S. Rogers, III, THE HISTORY OF HORRY COUNTY, MA Thesis, University of SC, Columbia, SC, 1972.

37. JASPER COUNTY, County seat: Ridgeland (29936), formed 1912 from Beaufort and Hampton Counties. No county records in SCDA, all must be sought in the county.

County records: Confederate pension (1913-9), conveyance* (1912-), coroner* (1912-), court of common pleas* (1912-), court of general sessions* (1912-), estate* (1912-), guardian* (1912-), magistrate (1916-),

mortgage* (1912-), plat* (1912-), sheriff* (1912-), tax* (1912-), voter (1912-), will* (1912-).
Other records: Baptist, biography, cemetery, census (1920R), historical society, LDS, WPA inventory.
Library: Allendale-Hampton-Jasper Regional Library, War Memorial Bldg., Allendale, SC 29810. History: G. F. Perry, MOVING FINGER OF JASPER COUNTY, Jasper County Conference Centennial Commission, Jasper, SC, 1948.

38. KERSHAW COUNTY, County seat: Camden (29020), before 1868 known as Kershaw District, which before 1800 was known as Kershaw County, which in 1791 was formed from Fairfield, Lancaster, and Richland Counties. Records include some of Camden District and of Camden Equity District.
County records: Clerk of Court (1841-88, 1893-9), conveyance* (1791-1844), coroner (1811-23), county & intermediate court (1791-9), court of common pleas (1783-1908), court of general sessions (1786-1870), court or master of equity* (1786-18926), district court (1868), estate* (1782-1973), magistrate (1837-48), plat* (1787-1980), sheriff (1794-1858), tax (1784, 1815-6, 1832, 1865-7, 1877), voter (1867-8, 1898), will* (1782-1892).
Other records: Baptist, biography, cemetery, census (1790R listed under Camden District, 1800R, 1810R, 1820RI, 1830R, 1838X, 1840RP, 1850RAIMS, 1860RAIMS, 1869X, 1870RAIM, 1880RAIM, 1890C, 1900R, 1910R, 1920R), city history, Episcopal, family, historical society, manuscript, map, Methodist, newspaper, Presbyterian, Roman Catholic, town history.
Library: Kershaw County Library, 1304 Broad St., Camden, SC 29020. History: L. G. Inabinet, KERSHAW COUNTY LEGACY, Kershaw County Bicentennial Commission, Camden, SC, 1976.

39. KINGSTON COUNTY, designated as a subdivision of Georgetown District in 1785, abolished in 1800. Never did keep records.

40. LANCASTER COUNTY, County seat: Lancaster (29720), before 1868 known as Lancaster District, which before 1800 was known as Lancaster County, which in 1785 was formed from Camden District, which in 1769 was established as an original district. Some records burned in 1865.

County records: Confederate pension (1902), conveyance* (1762-1937), county commissioner (1873-1916, 1929-43), court of common pleas (1800-14, 1869-74), court of general sessions (1826-40), court or master of equity* (1822-7), estate* (1865-92), guardian (1820-70), magistrate (1896-1938), naturalization (1800-25), plat (1829-82), sheriff (1866-1973), tax (1860-1, 1865-1960), voter (1867-8, 1898), will* (1865-92).

Other records: Baptist, biography, cemetery, census (1790R listed under Camden District, 1800R, 1810R, 1820RI, 1830R, 1840RP, 1850RAIMS, 1860RAIMS, 1869X, 1870RAIM, 1875X partial, 1880RAIM, 1890C, 1900R, 1910R, 1920R), Episcopal, family, historical society, manuscript, map, Methodist, newspaper, Presbyterian.

Library: Lancaster County Library,* 313 S. White St., Lancaster, SC 29720. Histories: V. C. Floyd, HISTORICAL NOTES FROM LANCASTER COUNTY, Lancaster County Historical Commission, Lancaster, SC, 1977; V. C. Floyd, LANCASTER COUNTY TOURS, Lancaster County Historical Commission, Lancaster, SC, 1967.

41. LAURENS COUNTY, County seat: Laurens (29360), before 1868 known as Laurens District, which before 1800 was known as Laurens County, which in 1785 was formed from Ninety-Six District, which in 1769 was established as an original district.

County records: Clerk of Court (1789-1803, 1841-1969), Confederate pension (1896-1968), conveyance* (1774-1906), coroner (1872-1901), county census (1829), county commissioner (1895-1969), court of common pleas* (1796-1934), court of general sessions* (1800-1927), court or master of equity* (1795-1869), district court (1867-9), estate* (1788-1934), guardian (1836-9, 1859, 1869-1911), list of persons (1880), magistrate (1800-1959), mortgage* (1871-1905), plat (1784-1803, 1806-73), sheriff (1809-1942), tax (1865-1924), voter (1867-8, 1882-1940), will* (1766-1912).

Other records: Baptist, biography, cemetery, census (1790R listed under Ninety-Six District, 1800R, 1810R, 1820RI, 1830R, 1840RP, 1850RAIMS, 1860RAIMS, 1869X, 1870RAIM, 1880RAIM, 1890C, 1900R, 1910R, 1920R), Episcopal, family, Friends, historical society, Lutheran, manuscript, map, Methodist, newspaper, Presbyterian, town history.

Libraries: Laurens County Library,* 321 S. Harper St., Laurens, SC 29360; Presbyterian College Library,*

Clinton, SC 29325. Histories: J. S. Bolick, A LAURENS COUNTY SKETCHBOOK, Jacobs Press, Clinton, SC, 1973; W. P. Jacobs, THE SCRAPBOOK: A COMPILATION OF LAURENS COUNTY, Laurens County Historical Society, Laurens, SC, 1982.

42. LEE COUNTY, County seat: Bishopville (29010), formed 1902 from Darlington, Sumter, and Kershaw Counties. Most county records are in the county; very few are in SCDA.

County records: Confederate pension (1902, 1909-), conveyance* (1902-), coroner (1903-), county commissioner (1902-), court of common pleas* (1903-), court of general sessions (1903-), estate* (1903-), guardian (1903-), magistrate (1903-), mortgage* (1902-), sheriff (1902-), tax (1902-), voter (1904, 1908, 1914, 1916, 1918), will* (1903-).

Other records: Baptist, biography, cemetery, census (1910R, 1920R), Episcopal, family, historical society, Jewish, manuscript, map, Methodist, Presbyterian, Roman Catholic, town history, WPA inventory.

Library: Lee County Public Library, 102 N. Main St., Bishopville, SC 29010. Histories: A. W. Dick, LEE COUNTY, Bulletin of the University of SC, Columbia, SC, 1925; Lee County Bicentennial Commission, LEE COUNTY, The Commission, Bishopville, SC, 1976.

43. LEWISBURG COUNTY, formed from Orangeburg District in 1785, abolished in 1800. Kept records 1785-92, but they all were lost in Orangeburg Court House fire in 1865.

44. LEXINGTON COUNTY, County seat: Lexington (29072), before 1868 known as Lexington District, which in 1804 was formed from Orangeburg District out of territory which had been called Lexington County during 1785-1800, which in 1785 was formed from Orangeburg District, which in 1769 was established as an original district. Conveyances before 1839 and probate records before 1865 lost in fires.

County records: Clerk of Court (1840-1908), citizenship* (1840-60), Confederate pension (1888-1932), conveyance* (1839-1916), coroner (1890-1910), county commissioner (1849-1950), court of common pleas (1840-1916), court of general sessions (1840-1946), court or master of equity (1800-75), district court (1866-8), estate* (1865-1940), guardian* (1809-68), lien (1880-1905), magistrate (1873-1945), mortgage* (1872-1948), plat (1840-71), sheriff (1806-1931), tax

(1864-1964), voter (1867-8, 1896-1958), will* (1865-1908).
Other records: Baptist, biography, cemetery, census (1790R listed in Northern Division of Orangeburg District, 1800R, 1810R, 1820RI, 1830R, 1840RP, 1850RAIMS, 1860RAIMS, 1869X, 1870RAIM, 1880RAIM, 1890C, 1900R, 1910R, 1920R), Christian, Episcopal, family, historical society, Lutheran, manuscript, map, Methodist, newspaper, Presbyterian, town history.
Library: Lexington County Circulating Library, Armory & Mitchell Sts., Batesburg, SC 29006. Histories: L. G. Hall, THINGS AND INCIDENTS OF LONG AGO, State Co., Columbia, SC, 1970; H. F. Thogerson, THE LOG CABIN ERA OF LEXINGTON COUNTY, MA Thesis, University of SC, Columbia, SC, 1980.

45. LIBERTY COUNTY, designated in 1785 as a subdivision of Georgetown District, name changed in 1800 to Marion District. No records were kept 1785-1800.

46. LINCOLN COUNTY, designated in 1785 as a subdivision of Beaufort District, abolished in 1800. No records were ever kept.

47. MARION COUNTY, county seat: Marion (19571), before 1868 known as Marion District, which before 1800 was known as Liberty County, which in 1785 was formed from Georgetown District, which in 1769 was established as an original district.
County records: Clerk of Court (1844-7, 1878), conveyance* (1800-1920), court of common pleas* (1800-70), court or master of equity* (1800-70), estate* (1790-1925), marriage (1800-59), plat* (1800-1955), tax (1809, 1860, 1865-7), voter (1867-8), will* (1796-1888).
Other records: Baptist, biography, cemetery, census (1790R listed under Prince Fredericks and Prince Georges Parishes in Georgetown District, 1800R, 1810R, 1820RI, 1830R, 1840RP, 1850RAIMS, 1860RAIMS, 1869X, 1870RAIM, 1880RAIM, 1890C, 1900R, 1910R, 1920R), Episcopal, genealogical society, historical society, manuscript, map, Methodist, newspaper, Presbyterian, town history.
Library: Marion Public Library,* 101 E. Court St., Marion, SC 29571. History: W. W. Sellers, HISTORY OF MARION COUNTY, Marion Public Library, Marion, SC, 1902 (1977).

48. MARLBORO COUNTY, County seat: Bennettsville (29512), before 1868 known as Marlboro District, which before 1800 was known as Marlboro County, which in 1785 was formed from Cheraws District, which in 1769 was established as an original district.

County records: citizenship* (1805-82), Confederate pension (1889, 1898-1902, 1916-20), conveyance* (1786-1955), coroner (1870-1913), county commissioner (1785-1835), court of common pleas (1785-1902), court of general sessions* (1785-1958), court or master of equity* (1805-77), district court (1866-9), estate* (1787-1973), guardian (1817-68), magistrate (1840-1939), marriage (1788-1819), mortgage* (1869-1972), plat* (1786-1973), sheriff (1823-1900), tax (1810, 1813, 1816, 1819, 1865-7, 1877), voter (1867-8, 1898), will* (1787-1905).

Other records: Baptist, biography, cemetery, census (1790R listed under Cheraws District, 1800R, 1810R, 1820RI, 1830R, 1840RP, 1850RAIMS, 1860RAIMS, 1869X, 1870RAIM, 1875X, 1880RAIM, 1890C, 1900R, 1910R, 1920R), Episcopal, family, historical society, manuscript, map, Methodist, newspaper, physician, Presbyterian, town history.

Library: Marlboro County Library,* Market St., Bennettsville, SC 29512. Histories: J. H. Hudson, SKETCHES & REMINISCENCES, State Co., Columbia, SC, 1903; M. M. Kelly, A SHORT HISTORY OF MARLBORO COUNTY, Gateway Press, Baltimore, MD, 1979; J. A. W. Thomas, A HISTORY OF MARLBORO COUNTY, Regional Publishing Co., Baltimore, MD, 1897 (1971); D. D. McColl, SKETCHES OF OLD MARLBORO, State Co., Columbia, SC, 1916.

49. McCORMICK COUNTY, County seat: McCormick (29835), formed 1916 from Greenwood and Abbeville Counties. County records not in SCDA, must be sought in county.

County records: Confederate pension* (1917-), conveyance* (1916-), coroner (1917-), county commissioner (1916-), court of common pleas* (1917-), court of general sessions* (1916-), estate* (1917-), guardian* (1917-), lien* (1917-), mortgage* (1916-), plat* (1916-), sheriff* (1916-), tax* (1916-), voter* (1916-), will* (1917-).

Other records: Baptist, biography, cemetery, census (1920R), Episcopal, family, historical society, manuscript, map, Methodist, Presbyterian, WPA inventory.

Library: McCormick County Library, Pine St., McCormick, SC 29835. History: HISTORICAL CHRONICLES OF THE SOUTH, issue of 04 August 1975, The Green River

Sprite, Columbia, KY, 1975.

50. **NEWBERRY COUNTY**, County seat: Newberry (29108), before 1868 known as Newberry District, which before 1800 was known as Newberry County, which in 1785 was formed from Ninety-Six District, which in 1769 was established as an original district.

County records: Clerk of Court* (1787-1919), Confederate pension (1902-4, 1916-8), conveyance* (1776-1925), coroner (1879-1933), county & intermediate court (1785-98), county commissioner (1868-75), court of common pleas* (1839-1956), court of general sessions (1822-1949), court or master of equity* (1818-1920), district court* (1866-8), estate* (1785-1949), lien (1872-1920), magistrate (1870-1946), mortgage (1872-88), naturalization (1808-61), plat* (1800-1925), sheriff (1832-40, 1898-1964), tax (1840-55, 1865-7, 1877), voter (1867-8, 1882-1900), will* (1776-1885).

Other records: Baptist, biography, cemetery, census (1790R listed under Ninety-Six District, 1800R, 1810R, 1820RI, 1830R, 1840RP, 1850RAIMS, 1860RAIMS, 1869X, 1870RAIM, 1875X, 1880RAIM, 1890C, 1900R, 1910R, 1920R), Episcopal, family, Friends, historical society, Lutheran, manuscript, map, Methodist, newspaper, physician, Presbyterian, town history.

Libraries: Newberry-Saluda Regional Library,* 1300 Friend St., Newberry, SC 29108; Newberry College Library,* Newberry, SC 29108. Histories: T. H. Pope, HISTORY OF NEWBERRY COUNTY, University of SC Press, Columbia, SC, 1973; G. L. Sumner, NEWBERRY COUNTY, Genealogical Pubishing Co., Baltimore, MD, 1950 (1980); J. B. O´Neall and J. A. Chapman, THE ANNALS OF NEWBERRY, Genealogical Publishing Co., Baltimore, MD, 1892 (1974).

51. **NINETY-SIX DISTRICT**, made an original district in 1769, divided into counties in 1785, most local records were kept by these counties, but Ninety-Six District kept some regional records: court or master of equity (1791-1824), estate (1782-7), jurors (1777), plat (1784-1803), tax (1787).

52. **OCONEE COUNTY**, County seat: Walhalla (29691), formed 1868 from Pickens County. Most county records are not in SCDA, they need to be sought in the county.

County records: Confederate pension (1909-32), conveyance* (1868-), coroner (1869-1935), county

commissioner (1919-35), court of common pleas* (1868-), court of general sessions* (1869-), estate* (1868-), guardian* (1869-), magistrate* (1868-), mortgage* (1872-), plat* (1868-), sheriff* (1868-), tax* (1867-1959), voter (1896-), will* (1869-).
Other records: Baptist, biography, cemetery, census (1870RAIM, 1880RAIM, 1890C, 1900R, 1910R, 1920R), Christian, Episcopal, family, historical society, Lutheran, manuscript, map, Methodist, newspaper, Presbyterian, town history, WPA inventory.
Library: Oconee County Library, 501 W. South Broad St., Walhalla, SC 29691. Histories: N. D. Field, SENECA ECHOES, OCONEE COUNTY, Journal Co., Seneca, SC, 1954; Centennial Commission, OCONEE COUNTY CENTENNIAL, The Commission, Walhalla, SC, 1968.

53. OLD BERKELEY COUNTY, designated in 1785 as a subdivision of Charleston District, abolished 1800. Never did keep records.

54. OLD MARION COUNTY, designated in 1785 as a subdivision of Charleston District, abolished 1800. Never did keep records.

55. ORANGE COUNTY, formed in 1785 from Orangeburg District, abolished in 1800. Kept records 1785-91, but they perished in an Orangeburg Court House fire of 1865.

56. ORANGEBURG COUNTY, County seat: Orangeburg (29115), before 1868 known as Orangeburg District, which in 1769 was established as an original district. Most records burned in 1865.
County records: Clerk of Court (1833-1942), Confederate pension (1893-6, 1901-29), conveyance* (1865-1954), coroner (1885-1945), court of common pleas (1865-1975), court of general sessions (1866-1946), court or master of equity (1824-37. 1866-8), district court (1867-9), estate* (1865-1957), lien (1880-1950), magistrate (1877-1949), plat* (1824-37, 1866-1954), sheriff (1865-1934), tax (1851, 1868-1954), voter (1867-8, 1898), will* (1864-1957).
Other records: Baptist, biography, cemetery, census (1790R, 1800R, 1810R, 1820RI, 1830R, 1840RP, 1850RAIMS, 1860RAIMS, 1869X, 1870RAIM, 1880RAIM, 1890C, 1900R, 1910R, 1920R), Episcopal, historical society, Lutheran, manuscript, map, Methodist, newspaper, Presbyterian, town

history.

Libraries: Orangeburg County Library, 510 Louis St., Orangeburg, SC 29116; SC State College Library,* College Ave., Orangeburg, SC 29117. Histories: E. M. Bookhart, ORANGEBURG COUNTY, The Author, Orangeburg, SC, 2 volumes; FROM INDIANS TO INDUSTRY, Rogers, Orangeburg, SC, 1970; A. Kohn, A DESCRIPTIVE SKETCH OF ORANGEBURG, Berry, Orangeburg, SC, 1888; A. S. Salley, HISTORY OF ORANGEBURG COUNTY, Reprint Co., Spartanburg, SC, 1898 (1978).

57. PENDLETON COUNTY, formed 1789 from Indian territory in the NW section of SC, renamed Pendleton District in 1800, in 1826 split into Anderson and Pickens Districts and abolished. Records are among those of Anderson County.

58. PICKENS COUNTY, County seat: Pickens (29671), before 1868 known as Pickens District, which in 1826 was formed from Pendleton District, which was abolished.

County records: citizenship* (1823-71), Confederate pension (1922-56), conveyance* (1828-1967), county commissioner* (1841-68), court of common pleas* (1828-57), court of general sessions (1828-85), court or master of equity* (1823-70), estate* (1828-1959), guardian* (1835-84), magistrate (1840-6, 1859-67), plat* (1828-82 1917-52), tax (1865-7, 1877, 1899, 1915, 1917-35), voter (1867-8, 1898), will* (1828-62).

Other records: Baptist, biography, cemetery, census (1830R, 1840RP, 1850RAIMS, 1860RAIMS, 1869X, 1870RAIM, 1880RAIM, 1890C, 1900R, 1910R, 1920R), Episcopal, family, genealogical society, historical society, manuscript, map, Methodist, newspaper, Presbyterian, town history, WPA inventory.

Libraries: Pickens County Library, 110 W. First Ave., Easley, SC 29640; Clemson University Library,* Clemson, SC 29631; Central Wesleyan College Library,* Wesleyan Drive, Central, SC 29630.

59. RICHLAND COUNTY, County seat: Columbia (29202), before 1868 known as Richland District, which before 1800 was known as Richland County, which in 1785 was formed from Camden District, which in 1769 was established as an original district. Some records destroyed in fire of 1865. Columbia Equity District records included in Richland records.

County records: Confederate pension (1919-72),

conveyance* (1865-97), coroner (1848), county commissioner (1895-1951), court of common pleas* (1865-1923), court of general sessions (1866-1900), court or master of equity* (1793-1870), district court (1866-8), estate* (1787-1966), guardian* (1840-1966), magistrate (1847-52), tax (1863, 1865-7, 1876-1962), voter (1867-8, 1898), will* (1787-1966).

Other records: Baptist, biography, cemetery, census (1790R listed under Camden District, 1800R has been lost, 1810R, 1820RI, 1830R, 1840RP, 1850RAIMS, 1860RAIMS, 1869X, 1870RAIM, 1880RAIM, 1890C, 1900R, 1910R, 1920R), city history, Episcopal, family, historical society, LDS, Lutheran, manuscript, map, Methodist, Presbyterian, Roman Catholic, town history, WPA inventory.

Libraries: Richland County Library,* 1400 Sumter St., Columbia, SC 29201; South Caroliniana Library,* University of SC, Columbia, SC 29208; BLGSU,* Columbia Stake, Hopkins, SC 29601. Histories: E. L. Green, HISTORY OF RICHLAND COUNTY, Genealogical Publishing Co., Baltimore, MD, 1932 (1975); E. J. Scott, RANDOM COLLECTIONS [RICHLAND COUNTY], Bryan, Columbia, SC, 1884 (1969).

60. SALEM COUNTY, formed in 1792 from Clarendon and Claremont Counties, abolished and absorbed into Sumter District in 1800. All records burned in Sumter Court House fire in 1801.

61. SALUDA COUNTY, County seat: Saluda (29138), formed 1896 from Edgefield County. County records are in the county, not in SCDA, except for the conveyance, equity, estate, mortgage, plat, tax, and will records which are listed below.

County records: Confederate pension (1908-15), conveyance* (1896-1979), county commissioner (1897-), court of common pleas (1897-), court of general sessions (1897-), court or master of equity (1897-1929), estate* (1896-1959), guardian* (1887-), magistrate (1905-), mortgage* (1896-1960), plat (1912-28), sheriff (1897-), tax* (1895-1966), voter (1896-), will* (1897-1926).

Other records: Baptist, biography, census (1900R, 1910R, 1920R), Episcopal, family, historical society, Lutheran, manuscript, map, Methodist, newspaper, Presbyterian, Roman Catholic, WPA inventory.

Library: Newberry-Saluda Regional Library, 1300 Friend St., Newberry, SC 29108. Histories: Saluda County

Tricentennial Commission, SALUDA COUNTY IN SCENE AND STORY, Bryan, Columbia, SC, 1970; THE FAMILY HISTORY OF SALUDA COUNTY, Intercollegiate Press, Clinton, SC, 1980.

62. SPARTANBURG COUNTY, County seat: Spartanburg (29301), before 1868 known as Spartanburg District, which before 1800 was known as Spartanburg County, which in 1785 was formed from Ninety-Six District, which in 1769 was established as an original district.

County records: Clerk of Court (1836-1968), Confederate pension (1889-1935), conveyance* (1785-1900), county commissioner (1877-1950), county & intermediate court (1785-99), court of common pleas* (1800-1920), court of general sessions* (1800-1908), court or master of equity* (1816-72), district court (1865-8), estate* (1787-1917), guardian (1857-1912), magistrate (1824-1910), mortgage* (1872-1905), plat (1784-1870), sheriff (1807-1909), tax (1844-8, 1851-68, 1877), voter (1867-8, 1882-97), will* (1787-1903).

Other records: Baptist, biography, cemetery, census (1790R listed under Ninety-Six District, 1800R, 1810R, 1820RI, 1830R, 1840RP, 1850RAIMS, 1860RAIMS, 1870RAIM, 1890C, 1900R, 1910R, 1920R), city history, Episcopal, family, genealogical society, historical society, Jewish, LDS, Lutheran, manuscript, map, marriage, Methodist, newspaper, Presbyterian, town history.

Libraries: Spartanburg County Library,* 333 S. Pine St., Spartanburg, SC 29304; Wofford College Library,* N. Church St., Spartanburg, SC, 29301. Histories: J. B. Landrum, HISTORY OF SPARTANBURG, Reprint Publishing Co., Spartanburg, SC, 1900 (1960); SC Writers Program, A HISTORY OF SPARTANBURG COUNTY, Band and White, Spartanburg, SC, 1940.

63. SUMTER COUNTY, County seat: Sumter (29150), before 1868 known as Sumter District, which in 1800 was formed from Salem, Clarendon, and Claremont Counties, all three of which were formed out of Camden District (Salem in 1792, others in 1785), which in 1769 was established as an original district. Many records lost in an 1801 fire.

County records: Confederate pension (1901-19), conveyance* (1801-1949), county commissioner (1868-1903), court of common pleas* (1810-3, 1818-33, 1883-1908), court of general sessions (1827-57), court or master of equity* (1795-1870), estate* (1784-196), guardian* (1803-1915), magistrate (1852-68, 1884-5), plat*

(1802-1949), sheriff (1821-3), tax (1861, 1863-7, 1877), voter (1867-8, 1895,1898), will* (1774-1963).
Other records: Baptist, biography, cemetery, census (1790R listed under Camden District, 1800R, 1810R, 1820RI, 1830R, 1840RP, 1850RAIMS, 1860RAIMS, 1869X, 1870RAIM, 1875X partial, 1880RAIM, 1890C, 1900R, 1910R, 1920R), Christian, Episcopal, family, genealogical society, historical society, manuscript, map, Methodist, newspaper, Presbyterian, Roman Catholic, town history.
Library: Sumter County Library, 111 N. Harvin St., Sumter, SC 29150. Histories: A. K. Gregorie, HISTORY OF SUMTER COUNTY, Library Board, Sumter, SC, 1954; C. Nicholes, HISTORICAL SKETCHES OF SUMTER COUNTY, Historical Commission, Sumter, SC, 1975.

64. UNION COUNTY, County seat: Union (29379), before 1868 known as Union District, which before 1800 was known as Union County, which in 1785 was formed from Ninety-Six District, which in 1769 was established as an original district. Western Circuit and Pinckney Equity records in with Union County equity records.
County records: Clerk of Court (1840-1959), Confederate pension (1889-1963), conveyance* (1785-1921), coroner (1872-1945), county commissioner (1868-1962), county & intermediate court (1785-99), court of common pleas* (1800-1969), court of general sessions* (1800-1951), court or master of equity* (1796-1878), district court (1867-9), district records (1785-1800), estate* (1777-1963), guardian (1833-1913), lien (1870-1924), magistrate (1870-1929), mortgage* (1870-1909), plat* (1784-1956), sheriff (1802-1901), tax (1865-7, 1880-1920), voter (1867-8, 1898), will* (1777-1961).
Other records: Baptist, biography, cemetery, census (1790R listed under Ninety-Six District, 1800R, 1810R, 1820RI, 1830R, 1840RP, 1850RAIMS, 1860RAIMS, 1869X, 1870RAIM, 1880RAIM, 1890C, 1900R, 1910R, 1920R), Christian, Episcopal, family, historical society, Lutheran, manuscript, map, Methodist, newspaper, Presbyterian, town history, WPA inventory.
Library: Union Carnegie Library, 300 E. South St., Union, SC 29379. Histories: W. R. Feaster, A HISTORY OF UNION COUNTY, A Press, Greenville, SC, 1977; Union County Historical Foundation, A HISTORY OF UNION COUNTY, The Foundation, Union, SC, 1971; M. L. Mabry, UNION COUNTY HERITAGE, Union County Heritage Committee, Union, SC,

1981; L. G. Gibbs, LAKE'S UNION COUNTY, The Compiler, Union, SC, 1982.

65. WASHINGTON COUNTY, designated in 1785 as a subdivision of Charleston District, abolished in 1800. Records never were kept.

66. WILLIAMSBURG COUNTY, County seat: Kingstree (29556), before 1868 known as Williamsburg District, which in 1804 was formed out of part of Georgetown District, which 1785-1800 was known as Williamsburg County, which in 1785 was formed out of Georgetown District, which in 1769 was established as an original district.
County records: conveyance* (1806-1923), county commissioner (1871-7), court of common pleas (1814-70), court of general sessions (1814-21), court or master of equity* (1823-70), estate* (1806-1915), plat (1806-1981), sheriff (1845-9) tax* (1865-7), voter (1867-8, 1898), will* (1802-79).
Other records: Baptist, Bible, biography, census (1790R and 1800R listed under Georgetown District, 1810R, 1820RI, 1830R, 1840RP, 1850RAIMS, 1860RAIMS, 1869X, 1870RAIM, 1880RAIM, 1890C, 1900R, 1910R, 1920R), Civil War pension, Episcopal, family, historical society, Lutheran, manuscript, map, Methodist, mortuary, Presbyterian, Roman Catholic, town history.
Library: Williamsburg County Library, 135 Hampton Ave., Kingstree, SC 29556. Histories: S. D. McGill, REMINISCENCES IN WILLIAMSBURG COUNTY, Kingstree Lithographic Co., Kingstree, SC, 1952; W. W. Boddie, HISTORY OF WILLIAMSBURG, State Co., Columbia, SC, 1923.

67. WINTON COUNTY, formed in 1785 out of Orangeburg District, name changed in 1800 to Barnwell District, which in 1868 became Barnwell County. See Barnwell County for records.

68. WINYAH COUNTY, designated in 1785 as a subdivision of Georgetown District, abolished in 1800. Never did keep records.

69. YORK COUNTY, County seat: York (29745), before 1868 known as York District, which before 1800 was known as York County, which in 1785 was formed out of Camden District, which in 1769 was established as an original district. Pinckney District records included in York

County records.

County records: Clerk of Court (1840-1964), Confederate pension (1896-1964), conveyance* (1786-1950), coroner (1881-96), county commissioner (1863-4, 1869-1973), court & intermediate court* (1786-97), court of common pleas* (1792-1974), court of general sessions* (1792, 1800-1919), court or master of equity* (1812-85), district court (1866-8), estate* (1787-1969), guardian* (1812-63), lien* (1883-1908), magistrate (1840-1911), mortgage* (1872-1950), plat* (1786-1879), sheriff (1809-66), tax (1827, 1864-1964), voter (1867-8, 1884-95), will* (1786-1913).

Other records: Baptist, biography, cemetery, census (1790R listed under Camden District, 1800R, 1810R, 1820RI, 1830R, 1840RP, 1850RAIMS, 1860RAIMS, 1869X, 1870RAIM, 1880RAIM, 1890C, 1900R, 1910R, 1920R), city history, Episcopal, family, historical society, Lutheran, manuscript, map, marriage, Methodist, newspaper, Presbyterian, town history.

Libraries: York County Library,* 138 E. Black St., Rock Hill, SC 29731; Winthrop College Library,* 810 Oakland Ave., Rock Hill, SC 29733. Histories: G. B. Hartness, BY SHIP, WAGON, & FOOT TO YORK COUNTY, The Author, Columbia, SC, 1966; S. B. Mendenhall, THE HISTORY OF YORK COUNTY, typescript, York County Library, York, SC, no date; M. A. Moore, REMINISCENCES OF YORK, A Press, Greenville, SC, 1981.

LIST OF ABBREVIATIONS

A	=	Agricultural census
BLGSU	=	Branch Library(ies) of the Genealogical Society of UT (Utah)
C	=	Civil War Union veterans census
CH	=	Court house(s)
GSU	=	Genealogical Society of UT (Utah)
I	=	Industrial census records
LGL	=	Large genealogical library(ies)
LL	=	Local library(ies)
M	=	Mortality census records
NA	=	National Archives
P	=	Pensioner census, Revolutionary War
R	=	Regular census records
RBNA	=	Regional Branches of the National Archives
RL	=	Regional library(ies)
S	=	Slaveholder census records
SC	=	South Carolina
SCDA	=	SC Department of Archives
SCHS	=	SC Historical Society
SCL	=	South Caroliniana Library
X	=	State census records
*	=	When on libraries, indicates good genealogical collection
*	=	When on records, indicates index

Other books by George K. Schweitzer

CIVIL WAR GENEALOGY: A 72-paged book of 316 sources for tracing your Civil War ancestor. Chapters include I: The Civil War, II: The Archives, III: National Publications, IV: State Publications, V: Local Sources, VI: Military Unit Histories, VII: Civil War Events. $7 postpaid.

GENEALOGICAL SOURCE HANDBOOK: A 102-paged book describing all major and many minor sources of genealogical information with precise and detailed instructions for obtaining data from them. $8 postpaid.

KENTUCKY GENEALOGICAL RESEARCH: A 154-paged book containing 1191 sources for tracing your KY ancestor along with detailed instructions. Chapters include I: KY Background, II: Types of Records, III: Record Locations, IV: Research Procedure and County Listings (detailed listing of records available for each of the 120 KY counties). $8 postpaid.

NORTH CAROLINA GENEALOGICAL RESEARCH: A 192-paged book containing 1233 sources for tracing your NC ancestor along with detailed instructions. Chapters include I: NC Background, II: Types of Records, III: Record Locations, IV: Research Procedure and County Listings (detailed listing of records available for each of the 100 NC counties). $9 postpaid.

REVOLUTIONARY WAR GENEALOGY: A 106-paged book containing 407 sources for tracing your Revolutionary War ancestor. Chapters include I: History of the War, II: The Archives, III: National Publications, IV: State Publications, V: Local Sources, VI: Military Unit Histories, VII: Sites & Museums. $7 postpaid.

TENNESSEE GENEALOGICAL RESEARCH: A 138-paged book containing 1073 sources for tracing your TN ancestor along with detailed instructions. Chapters include I: TN Background, II: Types of Records, III: Record Locations, IV: Research Procedure and County Listings (detailed listing of records available for each of the 96 TN counties). $8 postpaid.

VIRGINIA GENEALOGICAL RESEARCH: A 188-paged book containing 1283 sources for tracing your VA ancestor along with detailed instructions. Chapters include I: VA Background, II: Types of Records, III: Record Locations, IV: Research Procedure and County Listings (detailed listing of records available for each of the 100 VA counties & 41 major cities). $9 postpaid.

WAR OF 1812 GENEALOGY: A 70-paged book of 289 sources for tracing your War of 1812 ancestor. Chapters include I: History of War, II: Service Records, III: Bounty Land & Pension Records, IV: National & State Publications, V: Local Sources, VI: Military Unit Histories, VII: War of 1812 Events. $7 postpaid.

All of the above may be ordered from Dr. Geo. K. Schweitzer, 7914 Gleason, C-1136, Knoxville, TN 37919. Or send an SASE for a FREE descriptive leaflet on any or all of the books.